# Rescue
# My Child

*THE STORY OF THE*
*EX-DELTA COMMANDOS*
*WHO BRING HOME CHILDREN*
*ABDUCTED OVERSEAS*

## NEIL C. LIVINGSTONE

SIMON & SCHUSTER
NEW YORK • LONDON • TORONTO
SYDNEY • TOKYO • SINGAPORE

*SIMON & SCHUSTER*
*Simon & Schuster Building*
*Rockefeller Center*
*1230 Avenue of the Americas*
*New York, New York 10020*
*Copyright © 1992 by Neil C. Livingstone*
*All rights reserved*
*including the right of reproduction*
*in whole or in part in any form.*
*SIMON & SCHUSTER and colophon are*
*registered trademarks*
*of Simon & Schuster Inc.*
*Designed by Edith Fowler*
*Manufactured in the United States of America*

10  9  8  7  6  5  4  3  2  1

*Library of Congress Cataloging-in-Publication Data*

*Livingstone, Neil C.*
  *Rescue my child : the story of the ex-Delta*
*commandos who bring home children abducted*
*overseas / Neil C. Livingstone.*
    *p.  cm.*
    *1. Kidnapping, Parental—United States—Case*
*studies. I. Title.*
*HV6598.L58  1992*
*362.82'9781'0973—dc20*                    92-22643  CIP
*ISBN 0-671-76934-0*

To my sister
ERIKA
and my brother
BILL

# Contents

# ONE
# Operation
# Laurie
# and
# Leila

# 1
# "Give Me
# My
# Daughter!"

HALLOWEEN NIGHT, 1988. Barbara Swint, a heavyset, middle-aged switchboard operator, mother of three children, from Lansing, Michigan, walked down the jetway at Dayton Airport and stared around apprehensively. She had $35,000 in twenties, fifties, and hundred-dollar bills taped inside a back brace around her midsection, and she was on her way to New York's LaGuardia Airport to give it to three people she had never before met. (It was more money than she'd ever seen at one time, and represented a good chunk of what she and her husband, Bill, had managed to save from a lifetime of work.)

In the past, when there was a family crisis, Barbara had often shut down emotionally and physically, looking to her husband, Bill, and her many siblings for help. But this time, there was no one else to turn to; Bill was abroad, and her son was recuperating from a near-fatal head-on collision. Now her daughter's life was at stake and everything depended on Barbara, and her ability to hold herself together long enough to do what had to be done. She had never been as frightened on any previous Halloween as she was this night.

As she looked up to find the number of the gate for her connecting flight to New York, she saw two dark, rough-looking young men standing nearby. One was wearing a black hat, the other sunglasses.

"She's arriving on this flight," she overheard one say to the other. "And she'll be on the next one." Was it just her imagination or were they talking about her?

Barbara didn't think anything more about them until she reached the gate and boarded the connecting flight. She took her seat by the window in the tourist cabin, next to another woman. Moments later, the two men she had overheard earlier walked down the aisle and sat down directly across from her.

"Oh, my God," she said to herself. "I'm being followed." The people she was on her way to meet had warned her to take care that she was not followed, and now her worst fears were coming true.

After they were airborne, the woman next to her struck up a conversation.

"Where are you going?" she wanted to know.

"New York," responded Barbara feebly.

"Oh, why?" The woman seemed genuinely interested. Maybe too interested.

"Ah, well, I'm just going shopping," Barbara stammered, realizing that the words sounded false, hollow, even as she said them. She had never shopped further from home than the local K-Mart, and now she was telling the woman next to her that she was flying to New York, like she was some kind of jet-setter instead of a switchboard operator who had once worked on an auto assembly line. Dressed as casually as she was in a comfortable pair of slacks and a red and black sweater, she knew that her wardrobe betrayed her statement, and that the woman next to her would know she wasn't telling the truth. "Think," she told herself. "Don't be so quick to answer." But lying didn't come naturally to her, not even little white lies.

She tried not to make eye contact and pretended to read, hoping the woman would stop pestering her with questions. In reality, she was so nervous at the thought of being followed that she couldn't concentrate, much less read. The minutes ticked by like an eternity as she flew through the dark sky toward New York.

When the plane landed and the passengers began to disembark, Barbara watched as one of the men across from her got up and made his way down the aisle. But his companion, the one with the black hat, stopped and motioned for the woman next to Barbara to leave. Then he waited for Barbara to step out into the aisle and followed right behind her.

"Oh, they're after me," she thought. "They know I've got this money." She hurried down the jetway, her legs turning to jelly as she went.

She was going to be met by a man wearing a leather jacket; that was all she knew, and as she disembarked, new doubts began to tug at her mind. What if there was more than one man in a leather jacket? Later, Bill would reflect that if she had just been told to look for the "Fonz" at the gate, she would have picked out Brooklyn-born Don Feeney with no trouble.

She stepped out into the reception area by the gate and was immediately approached by Feeney, who was not wearing his leather jacket but instead had it slung over his shoulder because the evening was so warm.

"Barbara?" he said, with a clipped Brooklyn accent.

"Y-yes," she responded, her voice almost failing her. Feeney was a wiry, muscular man, of average size, with an intense expression that conveyed both competence and a kind of don't-mess-with-me warning.

"Follow me."

"Get me out of here," she pleaded.

"Are you being followed?"

"Yes."

"Describe them."

"T-two men."

"Look around," he told her. "Do you see them?"

Barbara swung her head in a wide arc, but the two men had disappeared. She shook her head.

"Okay," he said. "Let's go."

Don was the president of Corporate Training Unlimited (CTU), a Fayetteville, North Carolina, firm made up largely of ex-Delta Force commandos and other former U.S. special operators. He recalled later that despite the fact that he lacked a picture of Barbara, or even a good verbal description, he had no trouble identifying her that evening. "While she was looking for me," he remembers, "I picked her out. I mean, she looked like someone one step short of panic . . . you could tell by the look on her face that she had a serious problem."

They walked rapidly, almost at a trot, down the long corridor and rode an escalator down to the baggage area in Terminal B. There they were joined by Judy, Don's 5 foot 5, 125-pound, taffy-blond wife, who was making her debut as an "operator" on this case, and by his partner, Dave Chatellier. Chatellier was meat all the way down to the shanks, with shoulders big enough to fill a doorway and a face as quiet as a mountain meadow on a summer afternoon. Where Don had the athletic, stiff-legged walk affected by so many ex-special operators, and reminded some of a terrier searching for someone to piss on, Dave had an easygoing, ambling gait that was just the opposite of menacing. Judy, by contrast, walked with a ramrod straight posture, attesting to the metal rods in her back from a rappelling accident two years earlier.

They stopped and looked around again for the two men, but they were nowhere to be seen. Don jerked his head in the direction of the exit and tried to make small talk with Barbara as they left the airport, in a vain attempt to put her at ease.

"I was thinking in my mind, what this woman must be thinking," says Feeney. "She's traveling with thirty-five thousand in cash to meet some stranger in the airport who's gonna take her to a hotel room." He also had some nagging doubts. Barbara looked like the real thing, but he couldn't be absolutely certain. He and Dave and Judy had talked of the possibility that it might be some kind of a federal "sting" operation, following the worldwide publicity they had received after their first rescue, that of little Lauren Bayan from Jordan. The State Department had officially apologized on behalf of the United States to the Jordanian government for CTU's actions, and word had been passed to Don and Dave through the network that the Feds weren't happy about the affair. Don also didn't like the fact that it was Halloween night; it would be just like the Feds to run some kind of scam against them on Halloween.

By contrast, Barbara felt totally safe, even more so because Judy was there. However, she was surprised when they informed her that they were going to spend the night in New York, at a hotel near the airport, instead of leaving immediately for Tunis, the capital of Tunisia, where her daughter Laurie was in hiding. They told her it was to ensure that she wasn't being followed, but in reality they needed time to size her up better and to hear her story. In addition, there was the question of logistics: they would have to transfer to New York's John F. Kennedy Airport, and it was nearly 11:00 P.M. Most, if not all, of the international flights had already departed.

They drove around for a while to shake any surveillance, then stopped at a Holiday Inn near the airport where Judy had booked several rooms. There they gathered together in one of the rooms to hear Barbara describe her daughter's desperate plight.

## LAURIE'S STORY

Barbara and her husband, Bill, were just ordinary working people who had managed to raise three children and buy a modest, but comfortable, ranch-style home in a Lansing suburb through hard work and determination. For many years, both Bill and Barbara had worked on the assembly line at the local General Motors plant, usually on opposite shifts so that one of them could always be home with the kids. Bill was a general foreman at the plant, in charge of keeping the assembly-line machinery running, with more than a hundred people working for him. The Swints were an extremely close-knit family. Barbara's eight brothers and sisters lived in the Lansing area, as did Bill's parents.

Their middle child, Laurie, had attended nearby Michigan State University. She lived in a one-bedroom apartment on campus with her younger sister, Valerie, better known as "Val," who also was enrolled at Michigan State. In March 1984, Laurie met a young engineering student with flashing dark eyes and black curly hair who told her his name was Fred, and that he was from Italy.

"Your name isn't Fred," she responded, after talking to him for a while.

He admitted that his real name was Foued Ghidaoui, and that he was from Tunisia. Soon they began to date. Laurie had always been attracted to foreign men, and had already gone out with young men from Spain, Ecuador, and Iran. Foreign men, she believed, were more romantic than Americans, and their lilting accents and strange customs awakened her imagination, conjuring up dreams of far-off places and an exotic life far from the grit and ordinariness of Lansing. Her sister, Val, says that Laurie always "had the illusion of foreign grandeur."

The relationship quickly went from casual to serious, and Foued moved in with Laurie, bringing the number of people residing in the cramped apartment to four, since Val was already living with her husband-to-be, Jerry. But Val soon married Jerry and they left to set up their own household. Foued sponged off Laurie, eating what he pleased and rarely contributing to the maintenance of the apartment. Bill Swint told his daughter, "You know, a person that will do that now, Laurie, he ain't gonna change if you're dumb enough to get serious about him." But Laurie refused to listen to criticism of Foued.

On August 29, 1984, Laurie and Foued became engaged. Barbara and Bill were deeply distressed about their daughter's decision. Barbara, in particular, had taken an instant dislike to Foued the first time they'd met, which had been over dinner at a local restaurant. Bill, by contrast, had been more sympathetic.

"Let's show him some American hospitality," he had told his wife, when Laurie first proposed the dinner. "Here he is, far away from home. I'd hate to think my kids would go to a foreign country and not have someone treat them decent."

On the way home following dinner, after dropping off Foued and Laurie, Bill had looked over at his wife and asked: "What do you think?"

"I think you're too damned liberal because you think we ought to treat these people nice," she told him, her normal mild manner giving way to a seething anger that surprised even herself. "I think he's a gold-digging no-good son-of-a-bitch."

As time passed, Barbara's opinion of Foued didn't improve; in fact, it only got worse. "All he could see in us was dollar signs," she reflects. "He was seeing a chance to come to the world of opportunity."

Val also had reservations about Foued, and their relationship, she says, rapidly went downhill after he moved into their apartment. The only member of the family that Foued seemed to get along with was Val's later husband, Jerry. Foued and Jerry would occasionally go out together, although even Jerry was disturbed by Foued's womanizing.

Against her parents' wishes, Laurie married Foued on March 29, 1986. The ceremony was performed by a justice of the peace at City Hall, since Barbara refused to throw her daughter a wedding.

Only at the last minute did Barbara and Bill even agree to attend the ceremony.

After Laurie graduated—the first and only college graduate in her entire family—she went to work, initially in a furniture store and later as a secretary, to support Foued. Foued's student visa prohibited him from working, but other foreign students held jobs and often were paid in cash. Foued, however, regarded himself as "above that." The couple moved out of the campus apartment and into an apartment in a rundown neighborhood, far from the Swint household. During this period, Foued tried to wean Laurie away from her family, prohibiting her from visiting home very often, or even calling. He knew Laurie's parents did not approve of him, and he complained to Jerry that the two of them would always be outsiders in the tightly knit Swint family.

Then Laurie became pregnant; as the date of delivery approached, she quit her job and, together with Foued, moved back into her parents' home. It was a tense period, aggravated by the young couple's money problems. Foued resented having to ask the Swints for money. According to Barbara, "Whenever he wanted money, he would say, 'Mr. Bill'—that's what he called Bill—'you and I have to talk business. We'll go outside.' " Such behavior enraged Barbara. "Mr. Bill and I both bring home a paycheck," she would explain to him. "Our finances are equal. If you want money from Mr. Bill, you have to ask me, too."

But money wasn't Foued's only source of friction with the Swints. Barbara, and to a lesser extent Val, bridled at his superior attitude toward women. He and Val had words after he told her that in his country, "women know their place." He repeated the same refrain to Barbara, adding that in Tunisia, "women walk behind their men." After observing him order Laurie around for some time, Barbara confronted her daughter, saying, "Laurie, he talks down to you. He doesn't treat you like an equal." But the more Barbara complained and pointed out Foued's shortcomings, the more adamantly Laurie defended him.

Their daughter, Leila, was born on January 30, 1987, and shortly thereafter Foued and Laurie announced that they were going to move to Tunisia, since Foued was required to return to his country for two years according to the terms of his U.S.-financed scholarship.

The Swints tried to persuade Laurie not to go, and when their words fell on deaf ears, pleaded with her to leave Leila behind until she and Foued were established. "Go over there," Barbara told her. "See what it's like. Then, if it's okay, we'll bring Leila." Laurie seemed to be wavering, but Foued protested that he "couldn't leave my baby" and that he'd "be so lost without my baby." Barbara was skeptical: "He didn't pay attention to the baby here, so why would he care if she's there?" she thought.

As a concession to her parents' concerns, Laurie called her congressman and spoke with a staff member, who assured her that she and her daughter were American citizens and could leave Tunisia at any time they wanted to. The staffer didn't know what she was talking about, but Laurie felt reassured, and her parents realized that nothing they said was going to keep their daughter from going and taking Leila with her.

It was an agonizing time for Barbara and Bill; they made no secret of their fears. "When I kissed her goodbye in Detroit," remembers Bill, "I really believed that I would never see Laurie back here again, except in a coffin."

## NIGHTMARE IN TUNISIA

After only a week in Tunisia, Laurie knew she had made a terrible mistake. Instead of the glamorous life she had expected, Tunisia turned out to be hot, dusty, and very poor. She and Foued arrived in Tunis on May 1, 1987, and then traveled to Sfax, a coastal city 187 miles south of the capital. Foued's father was a minor government functionary who worked in the post office, but there were dark rumors that he was involved in smuggling and selling black market goods, as well as other criminal activities. As Laurie would soon learn, he was feared by almost everyone in the town and frequently made sinister allusions to the violent fates that had befallen those who crossed him or his family.

Initially, the young couple and their infant daughter stayed in a farmhouse outside of town, which had been rented by Foued's family. It was filthy, and despite Laurie's best efforts to keep it clean, there was no way to keep the vermin out, including scorpions and a poisonous snake that slithered in one night. They had few furnishings and none of the conveniences that Laurie was used to in the States.

Foued spent little time at home, and would go off for days at a stretch, leaving his wife and daughter without any groceries or money. Often they were forced to subsist on bottled water and croissants, despite the fact that Laurie was still nursing Leila at the time. Laurie began to lose a great deal of weight, but Foued remained robust and well fed. It was only later that Laurie learned he was taking many of his meals at his parents' home.

After about three months, Foued, Laurie, and Leila moved in with his parents, who lived in an apartment building in town. Almost immediately there were problems between Laurie and her in-laws.

Like many Americans, Laurie was troubled by various cultural differences and had difficulty adjusting to the Tunisian way of doing things. Cleanliness had always been one of her fetishes, but Foued's family took a more relaxed attitude toward hygiene and sanitation. The family kitchen was grimy and rank. Laurie got up one night and found the kitchen crawling with large flying cockroaches, attracted by the crumbs and open storage of food. Instead of maintaining a cleaner kitchen, Foued's mother attempted to keep the cockroach population under control with regular sprayings of DDT, which horrified Laurie, since she had a baby crawling around on the floor. When she complained, Foued's mother accused her of being "a crazy American."

"There's nothing wrong with DDT," she cried in Arabic, unused to a daughter-in-law who had the audacity to openly challenge her mother-in-law. "It won't hurt you."

Laurie, in an effort to be a good sport and fit in, offered to do the dinner dishes, but was immediately reprimanded by her mother-in-law for heating water with which to wash them.

"Crazy American," she would scream. "You don't have to have hot water." Instead, she would simply give each dish a cursory dunk in a tub of tepid water and then wipe it off.

The bathroom also was a rude shock; the toilet was a hole in the floor which Laurie, like the other women in the household, was expected to squat over.

Laurie had anticipated that there would be adjustment problems, and felt that things would improve once she and Foued had a place of their own in town. But there were other, more disquieting, problems that she couldn't dismiss so easily. Foued seemed remote and distant, and failed to stand up for his wife when his mother berated her in a harsh and domineering manner. Laurie also bridled at the Tunisian custom of tying children to the furniture in the morning to keep them out from underfoot. Leila hated being restrained, and would tug on the rope and throw a tantrum whenever she was tied up. "That's the crazy American in her," Foued's mother would complain. "You've got to beat that American out of her. She has to learn to be tied like all good Arab children."

Laurie felt her in-laws displayed an underlying meanness of spirit that was difficult to accept. Nothing so symbolized that meanness to her as a game that Foued's father played with Leila. He would hold a stick in his hand and beckon her to come and get it. When she reached for it, he'd whack her on the hand.

"Don't do that to my baby," Laurie would plead, to no avail.

"Teach 'em when they're young to fear you," Foued's father would respond, "and they won't rebel against you when they get older."

Laurie was also shocked by the behavior of Foued's sisters and mother, who regarded anything she owned as community property. Her jewelry began to disappear, including a watch that she had been given by her parents. And she was deeply disturbed by his mother's refusal to permit her to phone her parents unless someone who spoke English was at home to monitor the conversation.

Things did not improve between Laurie and Foued when they moved into their own apartment, which was located in the same building where Foued's parents lived. The apartment was small, dingy, and hot, since there was no air conditioning in the building. But at least it was in town, and the high point of Laurie's week was the meeting of the expatriates' club, which included a number of Americans. Foued did not like her to attend the meetings of the "ex-pats" club, and often found reasons, or manufactured conflicts, to prevent her from going.

Before leaving the States, Foued had promised the Swints that Laurie and Leila could return to Lansing for Christmas. But as their first Christmas in Tunisia approached, Foued changed his mind. He had just gotten a new job with Shell Oil Company in Tunis, which would necessitate a move to the capital. Laurie, he said, had to set up the new household. He promised the Swints that he would let her visit at Easter.

The apartment in Tunis was much more spacious and comfortable than the one in Sfax. But the woman who lived upstairs was a prostitute, and employed a number of young girls from her home. Foued refused to put in a telephone, and Laurie had to go upstairs when she wanted to make a call. The prostitute, however, would listen to the conversation and report what was said to Foued. Laurie pleaded with her husband to get a telephone, but he complained that it was too expensive. When Barbara sent Laurie money to cover the cost of installing a phone, he still refused and, instead, kept the money. Still, despite such problems and inconveniences, Laurie was far happier in Tunis than she had been in Sfax. She made a few local friends and got to know a number of people at the American Embassy.

Barbara and Bill decided that if Laurie and Leila could not come back to the States, they would go to Tunisia for the holidays. They had never been further from home than California and had always dreamed of traveling to other countries, but Tunisia came as a rude shock. They were first struck by what Bill calls "the morons at the airport standing around with automatic weapons, with their fingers on the trigger, waving them at people." As for so many Americans visiting Third World countries for the first time, the grinding poverty and endemic chaos of Tunisia were profoundly upsetting. Bill had never felt rich or privileged until he saw the way most Tunisians lived.

They stayed with Foued and Laurie in Tunis. Laurie was thin, subdued, and not at all like her old self.

"Mom, why did you let me do this?" she cried, when she and her mother finally were alone together.

"I did everything I could to stop you," responded Barbara tearfully. "I cried. I fought you."

Foued, now back in his own country, was arrogant and condescending. One night, Barbara confronted him about his refusal to permit Laurie and Leila to return to Lansing for Christmas.

"You broke your promise," she told him.

"Laurie can go home anytime she wants," he responded. "But Leila isn't leaving Tunisia."

"That isn't fair," protested Barbara. "Leila's her whole life. Besides, what gives you the right to isolate them from their family?"

"Listen," he shot back, "they're in my country now. And they'll do as I say."

Barbara started up off the couch. "I was ready to hit him," she recalls. "I just wanted to go after him." As Foued shrank back in alarm, Barbara relented and sank back on the couch, glaring at him with contempt.

The following day, Bill went to the U.S. Embassy to see if there was any possibility of obtaining a visa for Foued, so that he could return to the States with Laurie and Leila. It seemed to Barbara that the visa was all he really wanted. It was apparent to everyone that he was using his control over her daughter and granddaughter to force the Swints to help him with the State Department.

A dinner with Foued and his parents was strained and full of veiled threats. Foued's father laughingly told them—in a story translated by Foued—about a young woman who had been found in a sack, "hacked up like beefsteak." Barbara expressed shock and asked why she had been murdered. Because her father and brother were in politics, came the response, and they had offended someone.

"My Lord," Barbara exclaimed. "Why would they want to kill her?"

"That's what's wrong with you stupid Americans," answered Foued. "You don't understand how things are. You don't kill the one that did you wrong. You kill the one they love most."

It was a chilling comment, and one that was to stay with Barbara for a long time. Throughout the Swints' eleven-day visit, Foued and his family continued to point out what they considered to be American inadequacies and flaws in the American character. Bill became particularly angry one day when Foued, translating for his father, observed that "you Americans are a very silly people. If we had your power, we would dominate the world. You are weak because you let your emotions rule what you do in life."

Despite the derogatory comments and obvious underlying tension, Foued was on relatively good behavior, and he and his family made a halfhearted attempt to be hospitable. On the surface, things between Laurie and Foued didn't appear to be perfect, but they also didn't seem to be at a crisis stage. What Bill didn't know was that Laurie was confiding to her mother the nightmare that her life had become. Most alarming of all, she told Barbara that Foued was physically abusing her.

Laurie couldn't bring herself, however, to tell her mother just how bad the abuse really was. Whenever she did something Foued didn't like, he would beat her, often leaving her covered with welts and bruises. If she left the house without telling him, she was liable to get a beating. If she got a phone call from her parents or one of the few friends she had made in Tunis, he might kick her or hit her. He threw an iron at her one night when he came home and discovered that his shirts hadn't yet been pressed.

According to Val, Foued "would come home and tell her, 'I never loved you. You're a fat, lazy American.' And here's Laurie who loves this man and worships him; it's her husband and the father of her child. She got to the point where she felt she was nothing, that she had no value and didn't even deserve the air she was breathing. That she deserved the beatings."

Barbara wanted Laurie to leave Foued immediately and return to the States with them, but Laurie told her that she had secretly gone to the American Embassy for help, and had been informed that while they would assist her in leaving the country, Leila could not accompany her without her father's permission. Moreover, under Tunisian law, "a non-Moslem mother cannot be granted custody of a child who is under five years of age."

"But we're both American citizens," she had pleaded.

"You're not in America now," they told her. Tunisia was a Moslem country, where women—especially non-Moslem women—had few rights.

Bill was never so happy to leave any place in his life. But his relief was mixed with sadness over the fact that his daughter and granddaughter were trapped in Tunisia and might not ever be able to leave. Before they departed, Bill told Laurie, "I wish we'd never come here because now we've got to go home and live knowing what you're going through."

"Just a minute, Dad," Laurie reassured her father. "You accomplished one thing: you gave me strength. Now I've got the strength to fight."

"We always wanted to travel abroad," Bill reflects. "But when we left Tunisia, I told Barb, as God is my witness, I'll never leave this country [the U.S.] again. They can have all that stuff. I've never seen such desolation or poverty or unfortunate people in my life."

Knowing that her husband might do something rash, Barbara waited until they were nearly home before telling Bill that Foued was abusing their daughter; even then, it was all he could do to contain his anger and not take the first flight back to Tunisia so that he could strangle his son-in-law with his bare hands. Val remembers that her parents returned from Tunis with long faces and red eyes, and that for the next two weeks, whenever she went over to their house, they were crying. For nearly a month they refused to tell her what the problem was, but it wasn't difficult to figure out that Laurie was in some kind of trouble.

It was evident to Barbara and Bill that they had to find some way to help Laurie; but after his emotions cooled down, it was also clear to Bill that any effort to confront Foued about his behavior, or to threaten him via long distance, was only likely to provoke him all the more. Laurie had told her mother that she never saw any of the money or gifts that her parents had sent her in the months since she had arrived in Tunisia. Foued, she explained, would pick up the mail at the post office and open anything that arrived from the Swints. If there was money inside, he and his father would pocket it. They would even sell clothing and food meant for Laurie and toys for Leila.

Barbara's subsequent efforts to hide money in ordinary items that she thought would be of little interest on the black market also proved fruitless. Foued and his father managed to discover the money she hid in a little Mickey Mouse coin purse she bought for Leila during a trip to Florida's Disney World. Foued also threw away a videotape of Disney World that the Swints gave Leila, which the little girl adored, accusing Laurie of trying to "brainwash" and "Americanize" his daughter.

Shortly after the Swints' visit, Foued lost his job in Tunis, and he and his family moved back to Sfax. He began increasingly to isolate Laurie, and prohibited her from attending meetings of the

local expatriates' club, claiming she didn't have appropriate transportation. When Barbara offered to pay for Laurie to take a taxi to
and from club meetings, Foued wouldn't permit it. He hired an old
man to follow her if she went out of the house. "I was in prison,"
observes Laurie. "Only it was a country."

"It was pure hell for her," Barbara contends. The punishment
Foued was inflicting on Laurie became so obvious that his father
advised him to hit her only in places where her clothes would cover
the evidence of abuse.

According to Laurie, "Foued started going out to bars and
leaving Leila and me at home until two and three in the morning."
He made little effort to conceal the fact that he was seeing other
women. "He came home one night," recalls Laurie, "and he had
mascara smeared across his forehead. I said, 'I'm not stupid,
Foued. I know what you're doing.' He started laughing, and said,
'There's nothing you can do about it, so just forget it.' Sadistically
laughing at me. One night, he had a big hickey on his neck and four
nail scratches across his back. I just sat and cried." He even expected her to wash his shirts with the collars covered with lipstick.
In addition to being sick at heart over Foued's obvious infidelities,
Laurie also was terrified that she might contract AIDS or a vene-
real disease from her husband.

For the Swints, it was a terrible period. "You're so helpless,"
observes Barbara. "What can you do? I think the thing that hurt me
the most was that there was nobody there that she could turn to.
No one to support her."

Laurie's situation was deteriorating rapidly. The beatings were
becoming more frequent and severe, and she suspected that Foued
might even be molesting little Leila. She found it impossible to
reason with Foued. Whenever she tried, "he told me he could take
her away from me, because in Tunisia, that's a man's right. Whenever we had problems, that was the threat he held over me." Even
more alarming, he threatened to send Leila off to live with his
father's relatives in Libya, where she would be raised as a Moslem
and undergo the painful and debilitating ritual of female circum-
cision (clitoridectomy), which involves the surgical removal of all
or part of the clitoris. Laurie knew that if Leila was sent to Libya,
which had no diplomatic relations with the United States, she
probably would never see her daughter again.

The turning point came when Laurie discovered that she was pregnant again. Because she was nursing Leila, she had stopped taking birth control pills. One night Foued came home and forced himself on her. She pleaded with him to let her get her diaphragm, but he refused, and the following month she missed her period. An abortion was out of the question. "It's not for me to say which of my children live or die," says Laurie. But then Foued told her, "Go ahead and have the baby. If it's a boy, I'll take it. You can take Leila and go. If it's a girl, you can take the baby and I'll take Leila."

There was no way Laurie would, or could, accept such an arrangement. In desperation, she consulted a local doctor about an abortion. She was three months' pregnant and he advised her that it was too dangerous to perform an abortion that late in Tunisia. She returned home resolving to have the baby, but vowing that it would be born into freedom. She would find some way out of Tunisia for herself and Leila.

On June 17, 1988, Laurie was able to get to a telephone and call her parents. Unbeknown to her, a few days earlier her brother, Jeff, had been involved in a head-on car collision and had nearly died. His face was badly cut and the doctors were worried that he might lose an eye; one of his ankles was crushed and there was no assurance he would ever walk again. Bill, Barbara, and most of her uncles, aunts, and cousins were at the hospital. Laurie's sister, Val, was at her parents' home and answered the phone.

"Mom?" crackled the voice on the other end of the line.

"No, it's Val." Pause. "Is that you, Laurie?"

"Y-yes. Val, I've got to talk to you. First of all, I can't talk long but I've got to get out of here. Foued's beating on me and I'm starving. He says he's going to divorce me and, if he does, the courts will give him Leila. I overheard him tell a friend he is going to take Leila to Libya. I've got to get out," she repeated. "And . . . I'm pregnant again and they won't let me leave with Leila."

"What can we do?" asked Val, shaken by her sister's near-frantic tone. "Where do we start?"

"Call our congressman. Call everybody you can."

Val assured Laurie that they would do everything in their power to help. Afterwards, she wrestled with whether or not to call her parents at the hospital. "They're already dealing with enough," she told herself. But her sister sounded desperate, and Val had promised that they would move heaven and earth if necessary to help Laurie and Leila escape Tunisia. Reluctantly, she picked up the phone, dialed the hospital, and spoke to her father. Already traumatized by Jeff's grave injuries, Bill nearly broke down on the other end of the line when Val relayed her sister's message to him.

"I told her not to go over there," he moaned. "Why didn't she listen to me?"

The Swints called various local politicians, their congressman, the State Department, the U.S. Embassy in Tunis, everyone they could think of—but to little avail. All were sympathetic, but no one had any real ideas how to help Laurie. As far as they were concerned, she was beyond the reach of U.S. authorities or American law.

During the following months, Foued stepped up his mental, as well as physical, abuse of Laurie. "At night," she says, "Foued would follow me into the kitchen and say, 'You might as well pack your bags. Leila is ours. There's nothing you can do. You're never going to have her. We're gonna drive you insane. My family is gonna make you miserable. You'll wish you would have left a long time ago.' "

Laurie would plead with him to leave her alone, but he persisted, and finally told her that he was going to file for divorce and that "he had it all fixed with the judge that he'd get custody of Leila."

In early October, Barbara and Bill received a letter from an American woman in Tunisia who had befriended their daughter. "Dear Mr. and Mrs. Swint," it began. "I feel an obligation to write you because I can imagine the anguish you have been going through over the past year and a half. As a concerned friend of your daughter, Laurie, I think you should be aware of exactly where things stand now, and what measures you must take." She went on to describe Laurie's deteriorating physical and mental condition, and Foued's abuse of her.

"As of the day before yesterday, Laurie is no longer 'allowed' to come over to my place. Her husband and his father came over and told me not to receive her. I agreed smilingly. My aim in cooperating is to throw her husband off the track because he suspects me of trying to arrange her escape."

According to the letter writer, it was imperative that Laurie get out of the country, implying that her very life was at stake. The letter described the efforts being made to assist her, noting that "When the big day comes, she must have the trust of her husband to at least get out of the house accompanied by the child."

"That letter just about broke us in half," Bill remembers. The Swints held a family council, but were at a loss as to what more they could do, other than go back to the U.S. government for help and provide Laurie the money to hire a local attorney. Laurie subsequently filed a petition requesting custody of Leila, in order to block Foued from taking Leila and shipping her off to Libya. But Foued and his family allegedly threatened the daughter of Laurie's attorney, and he withdrew from the case, forcing her to hire a second lawyer. The new attorney told Laurie that custody was probably out of the question, in view of her sex and religion, but that he might be able to persuade the court to allow her to live in Tunisia, apart from Foued, and raise Leila. It wasn't what she had hoped for, but if it meant that she could keep Leila, Laurie was willing to give it a try.

Outraged, Foued decided to go ahead and file for divorce; but in order to do so he needed a copy of their marriage certificate and other documents that Laurie had hidden. He ransacked the apartment, finally locating the marriage certificate, Leila's passport, and other papers, as well as some money that Barbara and Bill had sent to Laurie, which she had placed in a diaper and pinned to the bottom of Leila's mattress. "He was furious," Laurie contends, and although she was in the advanced stages of pregnancy, he began kicking her and slapping her across the face. Leila witnessed the scene and began screaming, "Mommy! Mommy!"

Laurie scooped up Leila and fled the house, not knowing where to go or what to do. She sought help from the American expatriate woman who had written the letter to her parents. "She bought us breakfast," remembers Laurie, "and then took us to the doctor, and he wrote a certificate that Foued had beaten me, that I had bruises on my arms, marks on my legs. Then she walked with me and Leila to the police station."

But instead of being concerned and solicitous, the police tried to talk Laurie out of filing a report. Only after she strenuously insisted did they reluctantly take a written report. In writing up the report, they quizzed her as to what she had done to provoke such treatment, asking her pointblank if she had been sleeping with other men. Once they finished the report, they advised her to return home.

Instead, Laurie—with Leila still in tow—met her attorney at a local hotel, where he was having coffee. Foued and his father arrived a short time later and began making a scene. They threatened the lawyer, accusing him of having an affair with Laurie and accepting sex as payment for his services. They tried to grab Laurie, and a shoving match ensued until the police arrived. The police took everyone's passports and identity papers, and ultimately convinced Laurie that she had to return home with Foued.

"He kept us up until two or three in the morning, telling me I was a worthless piece of trash, no good, a whore, that I'd never see Leila again as long as I live," Laurie says. "I went to the bathroom and threw up. Then, Leila and I slept on the sofa."

The following day, there was a raucous and contentious hearing before an administrative judge at the local police station. Foued accused her of lying about being physically abused and screamed that she was a "whore," contending that "it wasn't his baby she was carrying." She was having an affair with her attorney, he shouted. That's how she was paying him, and he had made her pregnant.

But Laurie showed the judge the bruises on her arms where Foued had grabbed her, and lifted her skirt enough so he could see the welts and bruises on her legs and thighs. The judge was shocked, and told Foued that he couldn't believe what he had done to his wife. He ordered that Leila should remain with her mother until the custody hearing.

A stranger in a foreign land, Laurie had neither friends nor money, and was forced to return to the home she shared with Foued, and even to rely on his mother to look after Leila while she met with her attorney to prepare her legal case.

On October 17, after attending a meeting with her attorney, Laurie came to pick up Leila from Foued's parents at their apartment. Foued was there and they began to argue. In the midst of the argument, Foued's mother tried to physically take Leila away from Laurie. She kicked Laurie, scratched her arm, pulled her hair, and grabbed the terrified child. A tug-of-war ensued, but not

wanting to see Leila hurt, Laurie let go of her and began screaming, in English: "Somebody help! Please call the police!" Then she
cried in Arabic, "Give me my daughter!"

Perhaps fearing that the neighbors would hear the commotion, Foued's mother pushed Leila back at Laurie, and then Foued,
in a rage, shoved both of them out the door. "Get the hell out and
don't ever come back!" he yelled.

Terrified and shaking, Laurie knew that she couldn't return
home this time. Foued was on a rampage and she was afraid of what
might happen if he found them at home that night. He had threatened before to kill them; this time he might just do it.

With no one else to turn to, Laurie ran to her attorney for
help. A short time later, Foued and his father appeared, but were
barred from entering. They waited outside, with two policemen in
tow, for Laurie and Leila to emerge, loudly declaring their intention to kill them both. Laurie called the U.S. Embassy in Tunis.
The consular official she spoke with told her that it was very unlikely she would get a fair custody hearing in Sfax, and asked her if
she wanted to try presenting her case to a judge in Tunis. She
readily agreed that it was the only option left to her.

Now there still remained the problem of how to get to Tunis
without encountering Foued and his father. The attorney called
one of his friends who operated a cab company and learned that
there was one driver who had not yet gone home for the evening
because he had had a flat tire. After nearly five hours barricaded in
the attorney's office, Laurie and Leila were hustled down the back
stairs and out to where the taxi was waiting in the alley. Laurie had
wrapped a scarf around her head to hide her identity, and had
taken off Leila's American-made Reeboks so as to appear more
Tunisian if they were stopped.

"Take us to Tunis, please!" she cried, as she and Leila tumbled
into the cab.

The driver sped away through the dark streets until he reached
the highway to Tunis, where he turned north. It was an old cab,
full of dents and rattles, but to Laurie and Leila it was the most
beautiful car they'd ever seen, for it was taking them to safety.
Hours later, they reached the Tunisian capital and drove directly to
the U.S. Embassy. Laurie only had 50 Tunisian dinars—about $40

in U.S. currency—to her name, which she had saved for just such an emergency. She had fled with nothing else; not even her glasses or a change of clothing. She gave the cabdriver the 50 dinars and her gratitude, and asked him to wait while she went inside and got the rest of his fare; but he begged off, saying it was enough just to help a mother and daughter in such grave trouble. With that, he turned around and began the long journey back to Sfax, knowing that he had made a dangerous enemy in the Ghidaoui family.

From the embassy, Laurie called her parents to report what had happened. She told them that under no circumstances would she return to Foued, and that she would kill both herself and Leila before she would let Foued take her daughter and bundle her off to Libya. She would need money, she said, to retain a lawyer in Tunis and fight for custody of Leila. She assumed that Foued had already filed for divorce, but knew that she had not been served any papers yet. If he hadn't filed, she wanted to preempt him and commence divorce proceedings immediately in Tunis. She repeated that the U.S. Embassy thought she was much more likely to get a sympathetic hearing in the capital city than in Sfax, where Foued's family could intimidate local attorneys and put the "fix" in the judicial system.

While shaken by the news, Bill and Barbara readily agreed to send money to the embassy and were provided with a point of contact. Officials at the embassy got Laurie and Leila a hotel room the first night. The following day, Foued and his father appeared at the embassy and had a heated confrontation with one of the consular officials, whom they accused of "plotting" against them. According to Barbara, Foued was so enraged that Laurie had run out on him that "if he had found her, he would have killed her, her and the baby."

Fearing for Laurie and Leila's safety, consular officials decided that it was too dangerous for them to remain at a hotel and moved them to a "safe house" the next day. They did so in the nick of time; Foued showed up at the hotel less than an hour after Laurie and Leila checked out. In the weeks that followed, they stayed with several different sympathetic families in Tunis so that Laurie didn't have to register at a hotel, where she might be discovered by Foued.

With the help of the embassy, she also hired a local attorney. She was crestfallen, however, when the attorney leveled with her, and explained to her, for the first time, that there was virtually no chance that she would get permanent custody of Leila. The best she could hope for, he told her, was temporary custody until Leila was five years old. She would not be permitted to leave the country with Leila, and Foued would most certainly be granted visiting rights. It wasn't what Laurie wanted to hear, but at least someone was finally telling her the truth. While far from ideal, temporary custody was better than nothing; it would buy time, and time was something she desperately needed. She told the attorney to proceed with the custody action. After that, they could attend to the divorce. In the meantime, a custody hearing had been set for November 15 in Sfax, and Laurie and her new attorney felt it imperative that they preempt that hearing with an earlier one in Tunis.

Laurie had begun to have second thoughts, though, even about the custody hearing in Tunis. The more she learned, the more it became clear that there was no assurance she would win the custody case. If she lost, Leila would be taken from her immediately and handed over to Foued. It was an unacceptable risk.

The stress, too, was beginning to take its toll. Laurie was beginning to come apart emotionally and physically. Each day brought a new set of frustrations and challenges, and with no one to lean on, her reserves of strength and perseverance were nearly depleted. In their telephone conversations, Barbara and Val could sense that she was close to a nervous breakdown.

### "SOMETHING HAS TO BE DONE. NOW!"

The crisis came to a head in late October, when the Swints received a desperate call from their daughter in Tunisia. Laurie said that she was phoning from a safe place, but couldn't talk openly because the Tunisian government monitored most international calls. "Something has to be done," she pleaded with her father. "Now! Before it's too late."

Bill then called an official at the U.S. Embassy who had befriended Laurie, and he confirmed that time was running out. In his judgment, he said, Laurie was in no condition to make decisions and a member of the family, preferably Bill, needed to come to Tunis at once.

Barbara confided to a co-worker just how bad things had become for Laurie in Tunisia and told her that Bill would probably be going back to see what he could do. The next day, the co-worker brought Barbara an old copy of *People* magazine with an article about the rescue, by American commandos, of Lauren Bayan from Jordan, saying, "Here, Barb, you've got to read this." The article stated that the firm that had been hired to rescue Lauren was called CTU, and that it was based in Fayetteville, North Carolina. But the article also reported, incorrectly, that CTU had charged Cathy Mahone, the mother, $200,000 for their services. "When I saw the two hundred thousand dollars, I said no way," recalls Barbara. "We just didn't have that kind of money."

That night the Swint family met to discuss what action to take. Initially, Barbara was going to accompany Bill to Tunis, but it was decided that it would be better for her to stay behind in case her help was needed stateside. Bill also thought that it just might be possible for him to pose as Laurie's husband and leave the country with her and Leila as a "family." To this end, Bill went out and bought some Grecian Formula in order to take the gray out of his hair and look less like Laurie's father, and more like her husband.

"This is the article one of the women at work showed me," said Barbara, passing it around the kitchen table, "about CTU, or whatever they are. It sounds good to me, but we can't afford them. Right?"

"Right," seconded Bill.

"Right," Val said.

But Jeff, who was still recuperating from his injuries, refused to make it unanimous. He expressed strong reservations about his father's trip, and worried that, if a crunch came, the State Department would renege on its commitment to help, especially if it meant challenging the Tunisian government or its laws. But even more to the point, he knew that his father had no experience when it came to dealing with the shadowy world of foreign intrigue and smuggling people across international borders. He was afraid Bill would get caught trying to pull something off, and then the family's problems would be compounded.

"Dad, why don't you hire someone who knows what they're doing?" he protested. "You're gonna go over there and I'm afraid you're not gonna be able to accomplish much."

He told them that he also had read about CTU in *Soldier of Fortune* magazine, and that they sounded like the right people for the job. Who knows, he told his parents, maybe they'll negotiate a better price. At the very least, he argued, let's talk to them as a back-up plan, in case something goes wrong.

"Jeff, life isn't some kinda *Rambo* world," Bill concluded. "And I'm not Chuck Norris."

Bill remained unconvinced that it would come to hiring ex-Delta Force commandos. It was too far out even to contemplate. Surely the State Department would do what was required to get Laurie and Leila home. Hadn't they said as much on the phone? "We really thought the State Department was going to help Bill and Laurie and the baby get out of there," says Barbara. "We honestly believed that."

"You'll learn, Dad," responded Jeff. "You'll learn."

Jeff was stung by his father's comparison of CTU to *Rambo*. He was well aware that *Rambo* was hardly a portrayal of real life, and regarded the CTU operators, by contrast, as highly trained professionals. But seeing that there was little enthusiasm for calling the commandos at the present time, he let the matter drop.

Because the Tunisian telephone lines were not secure, everyone agreed that some kind of code was needed to disguise their conversations and prevent the Tunisian authorities from learning what they were up to. Val came up with the idea of a code based on "Sesame Street," the popular children's program on public television. Bill's code name would be "Big Bird," Laurie's was "Oscar," and Leila's was "Cookie Monster." The "Sesame Street Gang" was the U.S. Embassy. If Bill told them that he "couldn't watch 'Sesame Street,'" it meant that he couldn't leave the country. If he said that Val's husband, Jerry, should bet a certain amount of money on the Lotto, on a particular date, it meant that he needed that amount wired to him in Tunis on that date. Should he refer to Val's son, Adam, by name in any conversation, it meant that things were getting bad and the family should call someone in Washington for help. What the Swint family code lacked in sophistication, it more than made up for in originality.

Bill left for Tunis on October 28 and arrived the following day. "It was the same desolate country I had left," he observes. Before he departed, he had sworn to his family that "I'm not coming back without her." But once in Tunisia, he rapidly began to have serious misgivings about his mission. He was met at the airport by a representative of the U.S. Embassy, but when Bill pressed him for details about what the embassy had in mind for getting Laurie and Leila out of the country, the man was noncommittal. It was easy to see that the embassy wasn't prepared to give them the kind of help they really needed. Embassy representatives even went so far as to warn Bill that if they learned he was contemplating an illegal act, they would have to inform the Tunisian government.

Even more discouraging, his own back-up plan—pretending to be Laurie's husband and slipping out of the country posing as a family—had little chance of success. "When I got there, I could see that it wouldn't work," says Bill. "The police were aware of Laurie and Foued and their situation, and there were probably a hundred and fifty armed policemen at the airport. The police followed me as soon as I got there, followed me everyplace."

Because of the Tunisian surveillance, Bill's embassy contact drove around for a while, doubling back on his route several times, to make sure they weren't being followed. Then he took Bill to the safe house where Laurie and Leila were staying. He dropped Bill off so that no one would spot his car near the house. Laurie and Leila, he said, were alone inside.

When Bill saw Laurie and his granddaughter, his eyes misted over with tears of joy. He gave Laurie a big hug but she didn't return it and, instead, stood like a statue in the middle of the room, with no hint of emotion.

"What's the plan?" she said curtly, staring at her father with vacant eyes.

"Can't you even give me a hug?" responded Bill. He had been closer to Laurie than either of his other children, and now she was treating him like a stranger.

"No," she snapped. "I haven't got time for that. My daughter's life, and mine, are at stake. I haven't got time to be emotional."

According to Bill, "that just about tore me apart, and I kinda let go." His tears of joy turned to tears of sadness and confusion. He had never felt so impotent in his life, but more than any other emotion, he felt anger toward Foued for intruding on his family and turning Laurie into someone he barely recognized.

"If that's all you're gonna do is cry," Laurie said in an absolutely flat voice, devoid of any emotion, "then get back on that damned plane and get outta here. I don't need someone standing in front of me crying."

Bill could see that the ordeal had drained virtually every last ounce of Laurie's strength. It was at this moment, recalls Bill, that he knew she was in real trouble. Her mental state was so fragile that he was afraid to say anything negative for fear she would shatter like a piece of fine crystal.

"Laurie," he said at last, "we didn't know what to prepare for. I couldn't talk to you on the phone. You know that. We can't even talk in this house. They might be listening."

They agreed, via sign language, not to speak aloud about their plans but rather to communicate by means of written notes, which they would then flush down the toilet. Upon reflection, they concluded that they had few real options, and so agreed that Bill would try a direct approach to Foued. Maybe he could reason with him.

Bill called Foued, but found him far from reasonable. Foued ranted and raved about the slights and injustices that Laurie and the Swint family had inflicted upon him, then said that he would go to any extreme to prevent Laurie and Leila from leaving the country, including killing them if he found them. He even threatened to sneak into the United States and kidnap Valerie's oldest boy, Jeremy, if Laurie and Leila eluded his grasp. He would hold Jeremy hostage until Leila was returned to him, he averred.

Throughout Foued's tirade, it took every ounce of self-control that Bill possessed to remain calm. "Don't be provoked," he told himself. "You're in his country, not the good old U.S. of A. He may be laying some kind of trap for you, to get you out of the way, so that you can't help Laurie." Inwardly, Bill wanted to kill Foued before he could harm his daughter and granddaughter; he would have gladly sacrificed his own life for Laurie's and Leila's. But Bill knew that that wouldn't be the end of it. If something happened to Foued, his father would get custody of Leila.

Foued finally agreed to meet Bill face to face in downtown Tunis, but he failed to appear for the appointment. After standing more than two hours in the hot sun, Bill gave up and returned to his hotel, wracked by conflicting emotions and uncertain what to do next.

Bill and Laurie were in constant touch with Barbara and Val back in Lansing. But they tried so hard to be elliptical in their communications, making up code words and vague references as they went, on top of the "Sesame Street" code, that Barbara and Val were often left shaking their heads after each call and wondering aloud what they had just been told. According to Val, she and her mother would sometimes sit for hours debating the meaning of various words and phrases.

As the stalemate in Tunis continued, Val could tell that time was rapidly running out. Bill hadn't given up, but he had run out of ideas and knew that Laurie was nearing the end of her rope. He was afraid she might do something precipitous.

On the phone, Laurie was confused and emotional, at times even irrational. After one particularly distressing call, Val walked outside to get a breath of fresh air. Her sister's predicament and deteriorating condition were tearing her up inside. Dusk was settling and the moon just coming up. Val stared up at the moon for a long time. She wondered if Laurie was, at that moment, gazing up at the same moon, the same starry sky. It gave her comfort to think so.

It was late at night in Tunis, in that void that precedes the dawn, when a person feels more alone than at any other time. Laurie was restless and couldn't sleep. She gazed over at Leila, who was slumbering softly, with that particular ability that only children have to sleep anywhere, unmindful of the storm outside or the cares and terrors of the day.

She got up and moved over to a chair by the window and peered out at the moon, so cold and silent, suspended against a curtain of twinkling stars, and wondered where Val was at that moment. Was she gazing upon the same moon, the same sky? Then something deep inside, something she couldn't explain, told her she was.

### "YOU DO WHATEVER YOU CAN"

The following afternoon, Val was at her mother's home when the phone rang. It was Bill. He sounded weary, frustrated, and there was an edge to his voice.

"I checked all the way over here and I couldn't get Oscar and Cookie Monster," he began, using the code they had devised earlier. "So go ahead and get them over there. Get 'em quick before they sell all of 'em." And he added for emphasis, "By quick, I mean right now, 'cause if you don't, they're all gonna be gone." Just so they didn't miss his meaning, he concluded by saying: "There's nothing I can do. You do whatever you can over there."

"Bill," said Barbara, being very direct, "it might take everything we've worked for all our lives."

"All that doesn't mean anything if it's at the expense of Laurie and Leila," he responded, without hesitation.

"That's the way I've felt all along," Barbara told him. "I'm just glad you feel that way, too."

After they hung up, Val ran to the kitchen and rummaged through a stack of bills and papers until she found the *People* magazine article about the CTU commandos. She dialed North Carolina information, but the operator couldn't locate a listing for CTU, since she didn't know what city it was in or what the initials stood for. Ever resourceful, Val called *People* magazine in New York and asked to speak to the reporter who had written the article, but she was out of town.

Val told the woman who answered the phone that it was an emergency, and the woman promised she would try to get a message through to the reporter, who was on assignment in Texas. Realizing that every hour was precious, Val even attempted to get a number for Al Zaponta, a Texas businessman linked to Cathy Mahone in the *People* article. But once again, she struck out. The next day, however, the reporter called from Texas and spoke with Val. Yes, she said, she had CTU's number in North Carolina. Val's hand trembled as she wrote it down on a scrap of paper.

"Mom," she said, after thanking the reporter and hanging up, "should I call now?"

A jumble of emotions, Barbara gazed over at her youngest

daughter. Val was the youngest only in age; in most respects she was the most mature of her three children. She had been ever since she was a teenager. But Barbara knew that this decision was hers, and hers alone, to make. The very thought of what they were about to do nearly overwhelmed her. She was numb with worry and confused by the magnitude of the decision at hand. After nearly three decades of marriage, it was almost impossible to think of making such an important decision without Bill.

She bit her lip and nodded her head. "Yeah," Barbara said at last, in a voice that was almost a whisper. Then, after another pause, she added, more forcefully: "Now!"

Val's hand still trembled as she stabbed at the buttons on the telephone. "Oh, my God," she thought to herself. "What are these people gonna be like? Are they going to think that I'm a nut case or something?"

# 2
# Rescues
# "R" Us

IT WAS a quiet Thursday afternoon in late October 1988 when Judy Feeney picked up the telephone at Corporate Training Unlimited in Fayetteville, North Carolina. The female voice on the other end of the line sounded shaky, but the tone was urgent. Before she knew it, Judy was buried by an avalanche of words. She tried to say something, but the caller just kept on talking—something about her sister, beatings, Tunisia, two weeks before she lost her daughter. Kids were screaming in the background, making it difficult to hear.

"Slow down. Slow down a minute," Judy interrupted. "Now, let's start over. What did you say your name was?"

"Valerie Holley. I'm calling from Lansing, Michigan. My sister's in terrible trouble."

Ever since the story of CTU's rescue of little Lauren Bayan had been carried around the world by the print and electronic media, CTU had received a number of calls from desperate Americans, mostly women, inquiring about rescuing loved ones in foreign countries.

"We heard about you guys several months ago," continued Val. "We don't have two hundred thousand dollars, but we really need your help."

"Why don't you tell me the story from the beginning," responded Judy in an even, collected voice, trying to calm Val down.

Judy took notes as Val described her sister's situation. Then Barbara got on the extension phone and they both began pouring out details of Laurie's life in Tunisia and information about the looming crisis that had prompted their call. Ever wary of crank calls or someone trying to set them up, Judy was circumspect, noncommittal. But in her mind she concluded that the two women sounded like the genuine article. Perhaps it was the screaming kids in the background and the disorganized and unrehearsed way Val and Barbara divulged the details of the case; it didn't seem like a put-on.

After a conversation lasting well over an hour, Judy finally hung up. She sat down with Don and Dave and relayed to them the facts she had taken down on her yellow legal tablet. When she was finished, everyone agreed that it was an interesting case but that more information was needed. There also was the issue of their fee. They had lost money on the Lauren Bayan case, and although some of the pleas for help tugged on their heartstrings, they were operating a business—and not a particularly healthy one at that. There was no financial cushion for taking charity cases.

Don wanted to size up Val and Barbara himself, and both he and Dave had a number of questions to put to them. In particular, they wanted to find out exactly how much time they had, if they chose to accept the case, to mount a rescue. Was the hearing date fixed in concrete or was there any leeway? Could they buy more time?

Judy placed a conference call to the Swints in Lansing, with both Don and Dave on the line, and they talked to Val and Barbara for another thirty minutes, drawing still more details from them—details that would be critical to any decision to proceed. Then they broached the issue of CTU's fee. They would need cash, and plenty of it, they told the women, to mount a rescue.

This was just the first of many calls that would flow between Lansing and Fayetteville in the next hundred hours, before the meeting with Barbara at LaGuardia.

## COURT OF LAST RESORT

Corporate Training Unlimited (CTU) is based in a yellow, barnlike building on a busy thoroughfare in Fayetteville, North Carolina. Fayetteville is a quintessential Army town, which takes its identity from Fort Bragg, home of the 82nd Airborne, the John F. Kennedy Special Warfare Center, and the 1st Special Operations Command. There are 5,100 buildings on the 142,000-acre installation. It pumps more than $3.2 billion annually into the local economy, and is by far the largest employer in a ten-county area. Around 41,000 active-duty military personnel are stationed at Fort Bragg, and the facility employs another 8,000 civilians. No crisis abroad fails, one way or another, to impact on Fort Bragg and Fayetteville. Men and women from Bragg have, most recently, served with distinction in Vietnam, Grenada, Panama, and Iraq.

Fort Bragg is also the home of the U.S. Army's supersecret anti-terrorist Delta Force, which is so clandestine that the Pentagon still refuses, more than a decade and a half after its creation, even to confirm or deny its existence. Hidden behind a high wall and coils of razor-sharp concertina wire, Delta's compound is off-limits to all but the initiated and an occasional high-ranking guest from Washington. Those in the unit are anonymous and never photographed, though Judy Feeney "always found it comical that no one was supposed to know that you were Delta. Your neighbor would be Joe Strach, hooah!, Airborne, SF. Then the next thing you know he's sporting long hair, a beard, and blue jeans to work. It could only mean one thing."

She believes that it "doesn't take a genius" to identify a Delta operator in Fayetteville if you know what to look for. During the days when Don was a member of Delta, she and some of the other wives would go down to the local mall, sit in the common area, and watch the shoppers and strollers go by. They could always pick the Delta operators out of the crowd. "Yep," they would conclude. "There goes another Deltoid."

Perhaps it was the way they carried themselves, the swagger they exhibited in their walks and the self-confidence on their faces. Delta men were different, no doubt about it. They liked to think of themselves not as soldiers, but as "warriors," a society of modern

Jedi knights dedicated to fighting evil, often against overwhelming odds. To this end, they perfected extraordinary skills. The average Delta operator is expert with dozens of weapons and explosives, can rappel off roofs and crash through windows, jump out of airplanes at altitudes so high that oxygen is needed or so low that there is barely time for the chute to open, ram hostile cars out of the way or throw a car into reverse and spin it around in the opposite direction. Action junkies to a man, most of the Delta men live from mission to mission, and the parking lot at the compound is filled with motorcycles and sports cars, a testimonial to their love of danger and excitement.

While most are family men, a few boast nicknames like "Chainsaw" and "Certain Death," and "need the fur shaved off of 'em in the morning before they put their clothes on," according to Judy. A closed community, "Delta hung with Delta." As a result, other military men considered them standoffish and stuck up.

Don had been the sixth man selected for Delta when the force was first formed. He grew up in the tough, largely Italian neighborhood in Brooklyn known as Red Hook, and by his own admission was "a punk headed for trouble before I joined the Army." His parents divorced when he was young, and he was raised by his mother. "We were poor, I guess, but we didn't know it," he remembers. "There always was food on the table."

He lived on the streets, part of a gang headed by a hunchback named Nunzie Russo. Nunzie was older than Don and his pals Whitey, Stevie, Sallie the Rat, and Dominick the Geep, and despite his disability, he was extremely tough and quick with his hands. "You'd rather jack off a wildcat with sand spurs than screw with Nunzie Russo," recalled Don.

When he was young, Don was one of the smallest kids in the neighborhood and, therefore, "wasn't a big-time fighter. But I was fast and could outrun anybody. So I figured, what the hell, if I could outrun 'em, why fight 'em." But Nunzie convinced Don that sometimes it was necessary to stand up for your friends and neighborhood. He taught the younger boys, like Don, not only how to survive on the streets but how to fight. The neighborhood was his domain and he impressed a very personalized style of order on it.

Years later, when Don ran into his childhood pal, Dominick the Geep, they reminisced about old times in the old neighbor-

hood. Dominick had read about some of Don's exploits, and reminded him that they once had had a pretty good brawl. Since he
was much larger, he had "beat up on [Don] pretty good." "If I'da
known you was gonna be this bad when you got older," Dominick
said, laughing, "I'da left you alone as a little kid. You probably
don't sleep at night, thinkin' o' ways to get even with me."

Don believes that the lessons he learned on the streets, and
the toughness and self-reliance that were part of growing up in an
ethnic neighborhood in Brooklyn, have been critical to his later
success as a Delta operator and as the head of CTU. He and his
buddies would go over to Manhattan on the subway and play a
game, for example, to see who could get to the highest floor of the
Empire State Building or some other office building without being
stopped. "I was probably thrown out of more buildings in New
York City than most people ever see," he laughs. "There we were:
eight raggedy kids in blue jeans and T-shirts, and we would see
how high up we could get before a guard caught us or a secretary
called the police. We would act nonchalant, like 'I belong here' or
'I'm so-n-so's son.' " It required the ability, he maintains, to stay
cool and bluff your way past anyone; qualities that later would be
invaluable in carrying out risky undercover assignments.

Don quit school when he was fifteen and went to work in a
butcher shop, first grinding meat and then later as meatcutter. It
was while he was working in the butcher shop that he decided to
join the Army. He was returning home one Saturday night after a
long day at work when he saw his pals Sallie the Rat and Dominick
the Geep standing next to a gaping hole in the cinderblock wall of
one of the neighborhood grocery stores. Evidently someone had
taken a sledgehammer and broken into the store.

"What the hell's goin' on?" Don asked.

"Someone punched a hole in the store," responded Dominick,
indicating the obvious. Then he reached inside, grabbed a Coke,
and handed it to Don. "Want something to drink?"

As Don took the Coke, suddenly two police cars, lights flashing, appeared at the end of the block. Not wanting to be found at
the scene of a crime, everyone took off at a run in different directions. The cops couldn't pursue all three of them, so they picked
out Sallie and Don to chase. With his pursuers gaining on him,
Don whipped around a corner and dove underneath a car. Now

Brooklyn cops weren't stupid, and if someone disappeared during a chase, they would get down on their hands and knees and peer down the street under the cars. "Well, a trick we had devised was as soon as you got underneath the car, you grabbed the chassis—hoping it was not hot from just being driven—and pulled yourself up," says Don. "Then you stuck your feet in the rear axle and hung there. When the cop looked under the cars, he'd see daylight all the way down the street."

The cops couldn't find Don and broke off the chase. Later, Don linked up with Dominick and learned that Sallie had been pinched by the other pair of cops and taken downtown. "Well, as I was standin' there, I started thinkin'," says Don. "I had nothin' to do with anything and I coulda really been in deep shit. It was only a matter a time until something happened an' I ended up in the slammer, or worse." The following Monday, on his seventeenth birthday, he joined the Army.

The recruiter said, "Hey, kid, give it a couple o' days. Think about it."

But Don had made up his mind and was soon en route to basic training. He adapted quickly to military life and earned his sergeant's stripes. After that he got his starched fatigues, Airborne wings, and Ranger tab, and went off to Bragg for Special Forces training. Prior to joining the Army, Don had spent his whole life on the pavement of New York and New Jersey; he would see a telephone pole and think he was in a forest. But after Ranger School and the Special Forces, he was as comfortable "in the boonies as the big city."

He was a member of a Special Forces "A" Team when he heard about a new unit being formed, and he volunteered to try out for it. Though he didn't know it at the time, it was Delta Force.

His years in Delta were the most challenging and rewarding of his military career. He thrived on the one-for-all-and-all-for-one spirit of the unit; it reminded him of the way things had been back in Red Hook with Dominick and Whitey and the gang. He was part of the mission in 1980 to rescue the American hostages in Iran, and survived the debacle at Desert One. He returned to the Middle East in 1982 as part of the U.S. ambassador's security detail in Beirut, and he and his men routinely came under hostile fire, on the average three or four times a week, from small arms to rocket-

propelled grenades (RPGs). He and another Delta operator orga-
nized the recovery of five American missionaries kidnapped by
rebels in the Sudan, tracking down the rebels with a Sudanese
special forces unit and rescuing the missionaries after a furious
firefight in which sixty to seventy rebels were wounded or killed.
During the 1983 invasion of Grenada, Don was part of the force
sent to capture Richmond Prison and prevent the execution of the
regime's political prisoners. The Blackhawk chopper in front of
Don's was shot down, and he and his men landed and pulled the
dead and wounded from the burning wreckage, then provided
cover so that they could be medevacked.

He left Delta in 1984, after refusing to accept disciplinary action when an audit discovered irregularities in conjunction with his
living expenses in Beirut. He was one of approximately seventy
Delta Force members with similar problems; but unlike many of the
others, Don didn't consider that he had done anything wrong and
refused to be a scapegoat for Army bungling. At the root of the problem was the fact that the Delta contingent had not been provided
with a large enough per diem to cover their daily needs. Beirut was
a city of scarcity; the civil war had driven up the price of everything,
especially food. Since their hotel bill was covered by the U.S. Embassy, Don made a deal with the hotel owner. He and his buddies
stayed in the same room, and the owner agreed to kick back ten
dollars a day to each man to supplement their per diem. It was the
kind of resourcefulness Delta instilled in its members, but the Army
preferred to view it as fraud, rather than address the issue of whether
military men living off the local economy in Beirut had been provided with sufficient resources to take care of their daily needs.

Although he left shy of retirement age, Don harbors no ill
feelings toward the Army. "I have no resentment toward the military; not an ounce. It taught me," he maintains. "It's like when I
was in the Ranger Battalion, knee deep in swamp and freezin' my
ass off, and all I had to look forward to was the sun comin' up and
maybe dryin' off half my body. I would say to myself, 'I could still
be sittin' on a street corner in Brooklyn worryin' about what I'm
gonna do tomorrow.' The Army gave me a career." Judy, however,
is not so charitable, and blames the Army for small-mindedness
and a lack of loyalty to those who had served it and their country
so well. She says she will never forget the stricken look on Don's

face the day he mustered out. "Babe, it was like leavin' home when they took my weapon," she remembers Don saying to her.

If he harbors any lingering regrets, it is for Delta's failure to accomplish its mission in Iran. For Don and so many other Delta men, Desert One remains what the poet George Barker called "the darkest altar of our heartbreak." Today, Desert One is never far from his mind, and Don believes that that failure has given him even greater impetus to succeed in rescuing other Americans held hostage.

## COSTUMES FOR THE KIDS

Since he had no pension or savings after his separation from the military, Don, together with his wife Judy, launched a day-care center in Fayetteville. It was a modest success, and soon they were able to open a second center. It was a long way from "duking it out with the scumbags of the world" and the supermacho life of a Delta Force commando. But it paid the rent and bought time for Don to decide what the future would hold.

In the back of his mind, he'd always dreamed of a firm of his own, where he could sell the skills that he had so meticulously honed over the years—skills that were increasingly in demand in a world beset by terrorism and crime. The way he figured it, there were probably lots of wealthy individuals and corporations out there that would pay big bucks for training, security, and bodyguard services. Perhaps the best news was that he had a virtually unlimited manpower pool to draw from, thanks to Uncle Sam.

Owing to the presence of Delta and the U.S. Special Forces, the Fayetteville area probably contains the largest aggregation of former special operations veterans in the United States. As Don knew, there were many other former "Deltoids," not to mention Rangers and Special Forces veterans, locally, whose pensions were too small to really support them and who would jump at the chance to earn some extra money doing the things they knew how to do best. All he had to do was pick up the phone.

CTU was launched around Don and Judy's kitchen table in 1985, after Don and four other ex-Delta operators polished off a case of Budweiser one evening. The following morning, Don moved the sofa and the other furniture out of the living room into his and Judy's bedroom, and turned the living room into an office. After agreeing on a name and ordering stationery, the problem of marketing loomed large. None of the men had any real business experience, other than Don's management of the day-care centers. During its first months, CTU was a seat-of-the-pants operation.

When she returned home in the evening from the day-care centers, after getting dinner for Don and their three kids, Judy would serve as the company secretary, typing and filing late into the night. In addition, she made certain the coffeepot was always full. After they got off work, the other wives also would come over in the evenings and pitch in.

The business grew slowly, but after six months enough small contracts had come in that they were able to move the office out of the house and into a nearby shopping center, next door to a shop called "The Bow Hunter." Its proprietor was Dave Chatellier. Within a year, Dave had closed The Bow Hunter and joined forces with Don, contributing his 60-acre farm outside of town as a training site.

Unlike Don and the others, Dave was not a former Deltoid. A retired U.S. Army intelligence operative, he had spent twenty years on the "dark side of the house," a soldier in the long twilight war against the Soviet Union and its surrogates prior to the collapse of communism.

While the firm hadn't started out to do rescues, both Don and Dave found them far more stimulating than the day-to-day contracts for training and security that were the company's bread and butter. They were, after all, real missions, with real people in trouble, and real consequences.

Thus, after the call from Valerie Swint Holley, everyone's adrenaline was pumping and there was a sense around CTU that this one might be a "go." But there were two problems: money and time. Don had informed her that the rescue operation would cost $80,000, and that they would need $35,000 in cash to get started. He estimated the chances of success at 20 percent, although he personally felt they were much higher; but he didn't want Val and her mother to have unreasonable expectations. Even the best-planned rescues required a quotient of luck, and if luck was not with them on that particular day, the mission could fail, with serious consequences all the way around. In addition, if they were to have any chance of pulling off a rescue operation before the custody hearing, there was no time to lose; they had to move at once.

Judy also had other problems on her mind—like costumes for their three kids. Monday was Halloween. Even if she and Don were going abroad on a mission they might never return from, they still had domestic obligations. So, along with maps, passports, and all of the other things they would need on the mission, she wrote down "costumes for the kids."

Don and Dave were poring over maps of the Mediterranean, searching for the best staging area if they decided to launch a rescue. Tunisia's neighbors Libya and Algeria were out of the question, but both Sardinia and Sicily lay some distance off the Tunisian coast. Sardinia appeared to be about 110 miles away, and Sicily about 90 miles across the Strait of Sicily. Both belonged to Italy. Even more intriguing, there was a tiny Italian island called Pantelleria no more than 45 miles from the Tunisian coast. That clinched it. They would fly to Rome, and from there to Sicily.

They needed someone, however, who spoke Italian and knew his way around Sicily. Don remembered a successful local businessman named Jack Domain (not his real name), who had pleaded with him on several occasions to take him along on a mission. Domain was a pilot and sailor, and had offered to accompany them for expense money alone. Forty years old, Domain had spent three years in the military and was in excellent physical shape. Dave was opposed to including an outsider, especially someone who wasn't a former special operator, on a mission. But they decided to sound him out. Domain indicated to Don that he was not only eager to go, but spoke some Italian. Even more potentially valuable, he told Don that his wife, Simone, had been born in Europe and raised for several years in Sicily. She spoke fluent, Sicilian-accented Italian, and still had many good friends there. In view of their knowledge of Sicily and Jack's other skills, which could come in very handy if they decided to bring Laurie and Leila out by sea or private plane, Dave reluctantly agreed to include them in the mission. It was a decision he wouldn't regret.

Barbara, meanwhile, was sitting down with Val and Jeff and discussing what to do. Even though the money still presented a formidable obstacle, there didn't seem to be any other option. Val called CTU and told them that they had decided to go forward. "I just hoped to God these CTU people could do it for us," says Val.

Barbara got on the phone and Don instructed her: "Come alone. Meet us Monday night at New York's LaGuardia Airport. Have your passport. We'll leave from there. Don't dress in anything flashy or wear jewelry that will call attention to yourself. When you get off the plane, someone will make contact with you. He'll be wearing a leather jacket. Don't leave the arrival gate. Just sit down and wait. Don't even go to the bathroom."

Then he impressed upon her the need for security. She wasn't to tell anyone what they were about to do, and certainly not speak of it over the telephone to Laurie. She was not to mention it even to her own brothers or to other family members. One slip, he told her, might lead to the failure of the mission or even to someone getting killed.

## "SHE'S FLOATING IN NEW YORK HARBOR"

Although time was short, Barbara didn't expect to have much trouble raising the $35,000 it would take to get started. Both she and Bill were salaried employees of G.M., and they had managed to save a little money over the years and even buy a summer cottage at Lake Odessa, which was now worth at least $35,000. Along with their house in a Lansing suburb and their G.M. stock, Barbara figured that it was simply a matter of going down to their local bank and liquidating some assets and taking a mortgage on their cottage.

But it was not to be. Everything, it turned out, was in both her and Bill's names. She would need his signature to do anything, and that was impossible. It was one contingency they hadn't planned for. Bill, in fact, was in Geneva, the first stop on his return ticket. Laurie had begged her father to leave Tunisia before something terrible happened to him, and Don had concurred, telling Barbara that Bill needed to "get out of the line of fire." Since he was under constant surveillance by the Tunisian authorities, it was vital that he leave so that they would drop their guard. If the rescue went forward, they would rendezvous with Bill in Rome. They sent word to him on Sunday to fly to Rome the following morning and take a room at the Ambassador Hotel. He was to wait there until contacted again.

After overcoming her initial shock at finding all of their resources tied up, Barbara turned to her and Bill's families for help. But Don had told her, in no uncertain terms, not to breathe a word about what they were doing to anyone. She would have to ask them to loan her the money on the strength of their family ties and devotion to each other, without informing them what it was for.

Her brother Neal agreed to co-sign a bank loan for $20,000 and Jeff volunteered to approach his grandfather Swint for the remainder of the money. Bill's father had always been extremely conservative with his money, but before leaving for Tunisia, Bill met with him. "If someone [from the family] comes to you and says they need money," he told his father, "please don't ask any questions. Just do it."

"Can I ask what it's for?" Grandfather Swint probed, disregarding Bill's admonition, when Jeff came to see him.

"No," responded Jeff, holding his ground. "I can't tell you."

His grandfather nodded in agreement and got his coat. Together they drove to the bank, and he withdrew $15,000 in cash and turned it over to Jeff.

"Are you sure you don't need more?" he asked.

"Not right now," Jeff replied.

"I know it has something to do with Laurie," his grandfather observed. "Well, good luck."

By mid-afternoon on Monday, October 31, there was $35,000 in cash spread out on the Swints' kitchen table, along with an airline ticket to New York. "Can you imagine what thirty-five thousand dollars looks like?" says Barbara, still in awe of the pile of money that represented so much hard work and so many hopes for the future.

As Jeff packed the money into Barbara's back brace and fastened it to her midriff, he cautioned her "not to talk to anyone. Not to look at anyone. Just keep to yourself. And don't take off the back brace until one of them asks you for it. Don't give it to anyone else." Knowing her mother's propensity for getting flustered when she was under pressure, Val wrote down a list of vital information for her to carry in her purse. The list contained things like Bill's full name and his date of birth, the names and birth dates of her three children and the grandchildren, and information about their parents and employer.

When it was time to leave for the airport, they all embraced and began crying. Barbara was about to embark on the greatest adventure of her life, to save her daughter and her granddaughter. Just a few days earlier, she had been an ordinary person pursuing life's ordinary tasks and pleasures, and now she was about to enter a world that was more like a movie than real life. She was deathly afraid that she would somehow "mess up," and though not a terribly religious person, she uttered a little prayer to herself that God would look after her and keep her, and allow her to be His instrument in once again reuniting the family safely in Lansing.

Bill, meanwhile, had done as he had been instructed and flown to Rome. But when he got there, he found there was no Ambassador Hotel. He located someone at the airport who spoke English and explained his dilemma.

"Ah," responded the man. "I bet you want the Diplomatic on Vittoria Colonna."

Bill took a taxi into Rome. The hotel fitted the description he had been given, and he went inside and checked in.

That night, when he called home, Val told him to stay put, that help was on the way. Barbara had left for New York to meet the commandos they had talked about, and had $35,000 taped to her body. Bill was stunned. When he had told them to "do whatever you can," he hadn't meant go out and hire commandos. In fact, he didn't know what he had really meant, because he had been so tired and discouraged, he wasn't thinking clearly; but a commando rescue? Ordinary folks from Lansing who worked on the G.M. assembly line didn't go out and hire commandos and carry out secret missions in foreign countries.

"Who went with her?" he asked weakly.

"Nobody," replied Val. "That's the way they wanted it."

"You didn't put your ma on a plane with all that money by herself?" he screamed into the phone. "How could you be so stupid? Next thing you know, we're gonna get a call that she's floating in New York Harbor."

Val held the phone away from her ear. When the tirade was over and she could hear her father sputtering on the other end of the line, she finally put the receiver closer.

"Shut up, Dad, and listen to me," she snapped, conscious of the role reversal. "Jeff says to tell you that if there is anyone in this world that can help, it's the people Mom is going to see right now," she explained, looking over at her brother, who was coaching her from across the table. "They're the only ones that can do something for you. And he says for you to have some faith and confidence in us. We wouldn't do anything to put Mom in jeopardy."

Chastised, Bill began to calm down. Val's calm demeanor and the strength in her voice were reassuring. Barbara would call him when she got to New York, Val said. He was to stay in Rome until he received further instructions.

## DECISION TIME

After Don, Dave, Judy, and Jack had listened to Barbara's story, they adjourned to another room to talk among themselves. Only Judy had reservations; the others found Barbara and her story convincing and felt they should go ahead with the rescue operation.

It was late, but everyone was hungry, so they decided to get something to eat in the hotel. Conversation over the meal was relaxed and there was little talk about the mission ahead. Afterwards, before going up to her room, Barbara took Dave aside and told him that she had promised to call Bill in Rome. Concerned about operational security, he said it would have to wait, and made her promise that she wouldn't call anyone that night. Reluctantly, she agreed.

For Barbara, sleep was virtually out of the question. She still had the $35,000 and, remembering Jeff's instructions not to give it to anyone until the people from CTU asked for it, she wore the back brace filled with money to bed underneath her nightgown. She lay awake most of the night, tossing and turning, wondering why Don or Dave hadn't talked to her about the money. As she reflected on the day's events, it occurred to her that they hadn't even expressly agreed to help. She had no idea what the sunrise would bring, and spent the night terrified of every bump and noise in the hall, fearing that she would be robbed before she even had the opportunity to turn the money over to the commandos.

It wasn't until breakfast that a visibly drained and weary Barbara finally raised the issue of the money.

"Don," she began, "when are you gonna ask me for the money? I've got thirty-five thousand dollars here, like you said, and I'm real nervous about it."

"If you want, I'll take the money now," responded Don. "I didn't want to say anything about the money until you were sure about us. How would you have slept last night if we woulda taken the money then? What assurance did you have that we'd be here this morning? I wanted you to trust us."

"Does this mean you're . . . going to help?" Barbara asked, an enormous sense of relief growing inside her.

"Looks that way," answered Don. "You can either stay here or come with us. We're goin' out this morning to get some airline tickets and then goin' over to my mom's for a while until our flight leaves."

Barbara didn't hesitate a moment, but responded, "I'll go with you," even though she didn't have a clue as to their eventual destination.

They went back up to Don and Judy's room. Don wrote out a receipt for the money, which Barbara gratefully handed over at last. It was wringing wet from sweat.

Before they left, Dave told Barbara to go ahead and call Bill in Rome.


## SEVENTEEN YEARS IN ROME

Following his arrival at the Diplomatic Hotel, Bill remained in his room for twenty-six hours straight, reluctant even to go downstairs for a meal in case he missed Barbara's call. "It felt like seventeen years," he reflects. When she didn't phone from New York as agreed, "All I could think about was that Barbara was in the drink someplace, floating." Like Barbara, he got little sleep Monday night.

When the phone finally rang late the next afternoon, he was in no mood to listen to explanations.

"Now, Bill, before you hang up . . ." came the voice on the other end of the line. Then, doing her best imitation of him, she launched into an angry litany of accusations: "Where the hell are you? What the hell's the matter with you? Why didn't you call me? I don't even want to talk to you!"

Barbara's mock outburst caught him off guard, and in a moment all the anger had dissipated and he was just thankful she was still alive.

"Bill? Bill?" she was saying. "Please listen to me. I've got someone who needs to talk to you."

She handed the phone to Dave.

"Bill, this is Dave," he drawled. "Now I want you to listen to your wife for just a minute and then I'll talk to you. Please listen," he repeated. "It's very important."

He turned the phone back over to Barbara.

"Barbara," Bill began before she could say anything, "you don't know what I went through in the last twenty-six hours. My whole world crumbled," he continued, his voice breaking, "and I rebuilt it and it crumbled again during that time."

"Bill, I'm sorry, but there are reasons that you'll understand later," she explained, holding the phone out again for Dave, who instructed Bill to get a flight to Palermo.

"Dave, I'd love to," Bill told him, "but I ain't got enough money to buy lunch, much less fly to Palermo. I left all my money for Laurie, at the embassy in Tunis."

"Okay, Bill, you just stay there an' we'll pick you up."

A day and a half later, Bill got a call on the house phone and went down to the lobby to find Barbara and Dave Chatellier. According to Bill, "I looked at him and I thought, 'Barb traveled all the way over here with that big animal!' It just kinda made my blood boil. But, you know, the minute he opened his mouth and started talkin', it was like someone turned a switch on and dialed you down. He's got that ability to make you believe him and relax. He almost sounds like a Baptist minister from the South."

After greetings were exchanged, Dave took care of Bill's hotel bill and the three of them left for the airport, where Don and Judy were waiting. They flew to Palermo, Sicily, and hired two taxis to transport them to the Hotel Azzolini, located in the picturesque coastal village of Carini, about a half-hour's drive from the airport under overcast skies. Olive trees lined the four-lane highway. Dave rode with Bill and Barbara.

"How long you be here?" inquired the driver in English.

"We don't know," responded Dave.

"A week? Two weeks?" persisted the driver.

"A year, maybe," snapped Dave, "if we like it. If not, we may leave tomorrow."

"Just asking," apologized the driver, eyeing Dave's formidable bulk in his rear-view mirror. "Just asking," he repeated. He didn't say another word for the remainder of the trip.

Carini was lazy and slightly decrepit, but not without charm. The buildings, many adorned with latticework balconies, were mostly brick and stucco, and surrounded by trees. There was little traffic, so the children played in the narrow, winding, dusty streets. Old women, dressed in traditional black, peered out from doorways and from behind filmy curtains at the strangers en route to the hotel.

The yellow stucco Hotel Azzolini was on a hill, overlooking a swimming pool and a sea of red-tiled roofs which spilled down to the water's edge. It was impossible to see Palermo, which lies about 17 kilometers to the east, because of a range of rugged mountains that juts out into the ocean. Three stories high, with sixty-seven rooms, the hotel was comfortable without being ostentatious. Tourist season was over, and there were only a few other guests, which made it difficult for the new arrivals to avoid attracting attention. Whenever they went in or out of the hotel, it seemed that every pair of eyes in the village was watching them.

Jack and Simone Domain, who had selected the Hotel Azzolini for its seclusion and modern communications, were waiting for them when Don and the others checked in. The Domains, however, were not staying at the hotel, but in nearby Palermo with friends. That evening, after a short meeting, Don came by the Swints' room and said, "C'mon, you guys. We'll get something to eat."

Bill, worry gnawing at his gut, tried to beg off. "I'm not really that hungry," he told Don.

"Bill, you gotta relax and enjoy it." Don laughed. "You're paying for it, so you might as well enjoy it."

Bill smiled for the first time since he had left home, and he and Barbara dutifully followed Don down to the dining room. Although Bill loosened up over dinner, tension hung over the table like an uninvited guest. After they finished, there was one matter yet to be resolved, and Don gingerly brought it up.

"Bill, Barbara?" he began softly. "You're funding this operation. What do you want us to do with Foued?"

"What do you mean?" responded Bill.

"Well, you said he might try to retaliate against you or Laurie or Leila or Val's boy, Jason. I mean, we could leave him with a little warning. Some broken ribs? Or a crushed elbow? A crushed elbow is something you live with all your life."

The thought crossed Bill's mind: "Let's take care of him. Take him out. After all, he's caused my daughter and my family terrible pain and cost nearly every dime we have in this world." But whatever Foued's crimes, Bill knew that he and Barbara weren't that kind of people. Violence just wasn't part of their vocabulary, although Foued had pushed them close to it. Bill looked over at Barbara to make certain she was in agreement, then shook his head.

"You're the boss," responded Don.

The following morning, after a good night's rest, Dave and Don left for the island of Pantelleria, to see whether it represented a viable escape route.

Judy, meanwhile, remained in Carini with the Swints. The hotel would serve as operations center for the mission, and Judy would be the chief contact point and conduit for information. She also was assigned to keep an eye on the Swints, because Don and Dave knew that uncertainty can have an extremely corrosivé effect on people. Operational security was critical. If the Swints became nervous because they hadn't heard anything, it was extremely important that they be prevented from getting on the phone to see what was going on or talking with Val back in the States. To this end, Judy served as a kind of informal tour guide, devising trips to occupy Barbara and Bill and keep them from dwelling too much on the minutiae, as well as the ups and downs, of the mission.

Pantelleria is a small, rocky, barren island, 2,743 feet above sea level at its highest point. It has no fresh water source and relies on catchments and water deliveries from Sicily. According to Dave, there are about 1,500 people living on the island, which has "a nice little settlement on the north shore with a good harbor." Once on the island, Don and Dave went down to the small port to inquire about renting a fast boat, powerful enough for the run to Tunisia and back. "There were three or four, a half dozen, boats sitting out in the port suitable for what we needed," recalls Dave. "We even looked at an eighteen-foot Zodiac with a twenty-horsepower motor. What we really wanted, though, was some kinda sea pirate with a pretty good-sized craft."

Many of the skippers on the island were engaged in smuggling, but were not eager to test the Tunisian coastal defenses unless they were extremely well paid. One of the captains they spoke with had a nice three-masted schooner with an inboard engine. He was a rough-looking character with two heavyset bodyguards, "both of them smoking camel dung rolled up in brown paper," says Dave. The captain indicated that he already had been arrested once for smuggling drugs from Tunisia, and that his first boat had been confiscated and he had spent several years in prison. "He knew exactly the consequences if he was caught again," relates Dave. "He told us flat out, you get picked up over there, you're going to jail and the boat's gonna be confiscated." Even if you're not smuggling drugs, added the captain, the presumption is going to be that you are, no matter what kind of story you tell them. Who knows, he went on, they may regard the smuggling of a woman and child out of their country, in contravention of their Moslem laws, as more serious than drug trafficking.

They finally agreed on a fee of $10,000 for the run; but later the captain had second thoughts and backed out of the arrangement. Nevertheless, he provided them with charts of the ports and maps of the coastline. They then learned that a friend of Simone's had what Dave described as "a super, super-high-speed boat, seventy miles an hour. The fastest thing that's ever been seen down there. It was an eighteen-footer, with a big two hundred–horsepower Black Max Mercury outboard." It belonged to the owner of a fishing fleet on Sicily and was in drydock on Pantelleria. "We figured even with rough seas we ought to be able to get this thing down there and back in three hours."

On Friday, November 4, after a day and a half on Pantelleria, Don and Dave flew to Rome. Everything pointed to an escape by sea, so they instructed Jack to rent the boat and get it out of drydock. They also told him to find enough cans of gas so they could carry plenty of extra fuel. The boat only had two six-gallon tanks, not nearly enough to get them across.

In Rome, Don purchased coats for Laurie and Leila. When it came time to make the break, Don knew that it was extremely unlikely that Laurie would be able to take anything with her.

Judy, meanwhile, was growing more and more concerned that the Swints were spending so much time in their hotel room, people were bound to talk. If they didn't start taking in some of the island sights, no one was going to believe they were tourists. All they needed was for someone to tip off the local authorities that a group of American "smugglers" or "criminals" had taken up residency at the Azzolini, and for the police to start poking around.

Although Barbara was game, Bill was in no mood to do anything. He felt "twisted into knots" and so on edge that he didn't think he could carry off the masquerade as a tourist. But Judy insisted, despite his protests. Saturday morning she drove them into Palermo. The chaotic traffic did little to calm Bill down, and only added to his irritability. Judy and Barbara, however, did a little shopping so they could return to the hotel with shopping bags. Some of the bags were empty but for wads of paper.

They took another excursion on Sunday, although Bill "swore he'd fight me if I started driving toward Palermo again," says Judy, with a laugh.

### "WE'RE SENDING THE PACKAGE"

Val called her sister at the safe house, but before she could get a word out, Laurie demanded to know what was happening.

"What's going on? How are you guys going to get me out? I can't take it anymore. I want to leave, now! Before the hearing."

Val was shocked. Laurie was throwing caution to the wind and talking openly on the phone. "Listen, Laurie," she explained. "We're sending the package. The package you've been asking for. It's going to come this week."

But Laurie kept rattling on as though she hadn't heard a word Val said.

"Don't you understand what I'm saying?" Val interrupted. *"We're sending the package!"*

Slowly Laurie began to calm down, but Val could sense that she sounded unconvinced. There already had been too many disappointments, and Laurie no longer trusted anyone. How hard it must be for her sister, Val thought, to be so alone, so afraid, with no one to lean on.

"Just a little while longer," she pleaded with Laurie. "The package is on the way. This week. *Wait for the package.*"

Don and Dave arrived in Tunis on Saturday morning, November 5. Tunis was "Indian country," hostile territory, and one slip could spell disaster. The first thing they did was to rent a beat-up dark-colored Renault at the airport. Then they set out to locate Laurie and Leila's hideout. It turned out that the information Laurie had provided her father contained many errors, especially with respect to the spelling of street names. After hours of effort examining maps and driving around, they finally found the house. There was no sign of Laurie but, under the circumstances, they hadn't expected to see her.

The next step was to decide how they were going to spirit Laurie and Leila out of the country. Since they had already ruled out overland routes, the only two remaining choices were by air or sea. They had Judy's passport with them, just in case Laurie might be able to pose as Don's wife and board a flight out of Tunisia. Since there was no Tunisian entry stamp in Judy's passport, or in the new passport that had been acquired for Leila, it would be necessary to bribe someone to look the other way; not an easy task in a country where they didn't have a local contact on the ground and didn't know whom to trust. The airport, moreover, was tightly policed, as it had been when Bill arrived, and the Immigration officers seemed to be reasonably alert and professional. Thus, everything pointed to an exfiltration by boat.

First, however, it was necessary to find a good pickup location on the coast, and then to figure out the best route to it from the safe house. Time was getting short; the custody hearing was only four days away. The roads leading to the coast were slow and congested, but once Don and Dave were driving beside the dark waters of the Mediterranean the crowds petered out and they came upon a number of stretches of deserted beach. But there were problems. Some sites had gently sloping beaches, where the water was so shallow that any approaching craft would run aground long before it got to shore. Others were extremely rocky, with heavy crashing waves. According to Dave, "We saw some beautiful scenery, but we just couldn't find a place where we could get a small boat, or any other kind of boat, in to make a pickup." They spent the night at a fisherman's bungalow and ate a dinner of fried fish and bread.

They were up bright and early the next morning, and started hitting the beaches again. "It took damn near fistfights between Dave an' me before we finally picked out just the right pickup point," laughs Don. "It was hard because we were rushed." They were starting to become discouraged when they spotted a trail leading off the blacktop road in the direction of the sea. The trail was rutted and bumpy, and more than once they debated turning around. But after nearly two miles they finally reached the coast and, in Dave's words, "Lo and behold, it was exactly what we needed. We could see a castle to the north and a castle to the south, and it looked like relatively good beach in between. Except for some animal tracks in the sand, mostly sheep, the beach was absolutely, totally deserted, and you could see for miles in each direction." The only negative was a Tunisian naval facility about four miles away, in the shadow of one of the castles; but they decided that it was the best place available, and they were fast running out of time to find a more suitable location. They pulled out their charts, pinpointed the beach, and took several coordinates that could be transmitted later to Jack in Pantelleria.

Tunisian coastal vigilance had increased ever since the April 1988 assassination of the PLO's number-two man, Abu Jihad, in a suburb of Tunis. Israeli gunboats had anchored off the coast under the cloak of darkness, undetected by Tunisian coastal patrols, and offloaded commandos, who rendezvoused with Mossad operatives on shore. They sped to Abu Jihad's house, and—after killing the chauffeur as he slept in his car in the driveway—broke into the house, stormed upstairs, and riddled Abu Jihad with bullets in his own bed, without touching his wife who was sleeping next to him. The whole operation, from the time they entered the house to the time they exited, took a total of only thirteen seconds. They subsequently retraced their route back to the coast, reboarded the gunboats, and slipped away. In the aftermath of the attack, the

Tunisian government and military came in for a good deal of criticism, and officials vowed to increase coastal patrols, both by sea
and by air.

Don and Dave returned to Tunis and took rooms at a local
hotel in the center of the city. It was an old, musty-smelling place,
with worn carpets and wallpaper peeling off the walls. Having
decided on a seaborne rescue and located their pickup site, Don
and Dave spent part of the next day watching Laurie's safe house
to make certain that she was not under some kind of surveillance.
They knew that Foued was combing the city for her, and they
didn't want any last-minute surprises.

In the meantime, Laurie—who was in regular phone contact
with Bill in Carini and Val back in Lansing—was becoming more
and more agitated and impatient. Her deteriorating mental condition was aggravated by a case of walking pneumonia. Foued had
sent a message to her via the U.S. Embassy, offering to sign Laurie's and Leila's exit permits if they would just come to the airport.
Through her father, Don and Dave advised her not to trust Foued,
and warned that it was most likely an attempt to draw them both
out into the open, so that he could grab Leila. The consular official
at the embassy agreed, but added that he didn't know if they had
any other options. Laurie, however, was growing more and more
desperate as the hearing date approached. She had little confidence that anyone was going to be able to help her, and at one
point said she was ready to try anything, including meeting Foued
at the airport.

"We thought she'd cracked for sure," remembers Barbara.
"She said, 'I've waited long enough. I can't take it anymore. I'm
going to do whatever I've got to do, but I've got to get out.' We
were so afraid she'd go to the airport and meet him."

But once again, her family prevailed on Laurie to trust them,
to believe in them. Something was about to happen, they told her.
The package would soon be delivered and then everything would
be all right. Just wait for the package.

# 3
# Escape
# from Tunisia

■ DAVE CHECKED in with Jack Domain on Sunday and learned that he had secured the boat and would soon have it in the water. He provided Jack with three coordinates in code which would enable him to reach the deserted beach, and they agreed on a two-hour time window for the pickup, between 4:30 and 6:30 P.M. If Jack didn't arrive by the time the window "closed," or if Dave and the rescue party hadn't appeared on the beach, it was decided that whoever was there would leave and return the following day, and try a second rendezvous during the same time frame.

"Yes, I understand," responded Jack at the end of the conversation. Without further ado, he hung up.

Laurie, meanwhile, had been told by her father that her "Uncle Jake" was coming by to take her and Leila on a picnic. She was instructed not to bring anything with her, so as to avoid tipping off anyone that she was going to make a break for freedom. She was not even to say goodbye to the people who were sheltering her, or indicate in any way that she wasn't coming back. The Tunisian family she was staying with—a husband, wife, and two sons—had treated Laurie very well. "I wanted so badly to be honest with these people because they were so good to me," Laurie remembers. "The boys would come home with ice-cream bars for Leila. The father—he spoke English—bought some little slippers for her, the kind they wear at home . . . But that day, when I got the call, I told them I was meeting a gentleman my father worked with, to have a picnic dinner. I've never been able to speak to them again."

There were only three days left before the custody hearing, and, like a cornered animal, Laurie was beyond reason and vowing under no circumstances to give up her daughter. She told an embassy consular official that she'd rather kill herself and Leila before she'd turn her daughter over to Foued and see her shipped off to Libya. Don knew that their plan had to work, and work the first time, otherwise there was no telling what Laurie might do.

After speaking with Jack, Don called Laurie.

"Laurie?"

"Yes?"

"This is Jake. I think your father told you the other day that I'd come and meet you and we'd have a picnic?"

"Yes," she said eagerly. "I'd love to."

"Okay," he told her. "Now listen carefully. Come out and turn left. I'll step out of another building and slip a coat over your shoulders. Walk with me, and we'll go to the picnic." He told her what time the following day she should leave the house and wished her luck. The call had taken less than a minute.

Monday, November 7, was overcast, with a slight chill in the air. Don and Dave were up early. They drove to the pickup spot and spent several hours surveilling it, concluding that nothing had changed that would dissuade them from "green-lighting" the rescue. They looked at each other and nodded. There was no turning back.

## "ARE YOU GUYS SURE YOU'VE EVER DONE THIS BEFORE?"

They drove back to Tunis and grabbed a quick bite to eat. Don was like a spring waiting to be released, tense, alert, ready for anything. He always had been a bundle of energy before missions, and it was all he could do to keep calm. In recognition of just how hyper he would become as a mission drew near, he was known around CTU as "Ricochet Rat." Once the mission was under way, by contrast, a calm seemed to descend over him and he could perform indefatigably for hours, if not days, as he spent the reservoirs of energy that had built up within him during the prelude to the mission.

Dave, by contrast, was called "Grandpa," both because of his age and the fact that he was always unflappable, with a certain nonchalant quality that could be mistaken for laziness or even slow-wittedness. It was Dave's ability to convince others to underestimate him that had often provided him with a vital advantage in a tight situation.

Dave was once described as the kind of fellow "who would walk a mile to spit." Where Don was impetuous and mercurial, Dave was cautious and deliberative, sometimes almost to a fault. According to Dave, "Donny wants to be told: 'This is the building—go kick in the door and kill everyone. That's the operation. Don't worry about anything else; just pack up and leave [when it's over].' Me, I'm a very slow and methodical person. I want to know every detail, to know which way the door swings, to know how many people are in there, so that I don't have any surprises when I go in. Donny's virtue is that he is very spontaneous and that makes us work well together."

After lunch, they drove to the safe house, taking care to ensure that they were not being followed. Once at the safe house, Dave parked the little Renault around the corner, and Don got out and walked up the street to a dark doorway, five doors up from the entrance where they expected Laurie and Leila to appear at 3:00 P.M.

Don took up a position in a dimly lit hallway, looking out at the street, a cashmere coat over his arm for Laurie. There was a padded purple jacket in the car for Leila. Several people passed him by and gave him hostile glances but did not speak or challenge him.

The street was quiet; there was no sign of Foued or anything out of the ordinary. Then, suddenly, a truckload of police rumbled down the street and came to a stop a short distance away.

"Oh, shit!" Don said under his breath. "They got us."

More than a dozen police officers climbed down off the truck and stood on the sidewalk. But they didn't make any hostile moves, and seconds later disappeared into a nearby building. Apparently, it was a police substation and a shift change was under way. Don breathed a massive sigh of relief.

Minutes later, right on time, Laurie walked out into the dull sunlight, clutching Leila in her arms. Don recognized Laurie immediately. He had seen pictures of her, but it was her hair that was the instant giveaway. "It's kinda hard to miss the color of her hair, especially in Tunisia," he observes. "It's not bright red, but it's red enough." She was also obviously pregnant from the neck to the knees, and had on a pair of white bib overalls, as she had promised.

Laurie looked around apprehensively, then, as instructed, began walking down the street. Her face was set, as if wearing a mask, and her steps were rapid, almost a trot. As she passed by the open doorway, Don stepped out of the shadows behind her and placed the coat over her shoulders.

"Hi, Laurie," he greeted her. "Just keep walking and don't stop or nothin'. Just act normal." He put his arm around her to reassure her and guide her, and he could feel her trembling slightly. The farther they walked, the more she leaned into him, as if it had taken every last ounce of strength she had just to get this far, and now she wanted nothing so much as to depend on someone else.

They turned the corner and Don helped Laurie and Leila into the back seat of the Renault, then stepped around, slipped in behind the wheel, and cranked up the engine. Dave was standing across the street on the corner "as blocking cover," countersurveilling the scene to make certain that no one had followed them. Don pulled the car forward a few feet, like he was leaving, but no one appeared to impede their departure. As Dave started to cross the street, a Tunisian man walked up to him and asked him if he was English. Dave said no, but the man seemed oblivious to his answer and wanted to know whether he knew an English rock star, and then if he had ever attended one of his concerts. Dave, whose taste in music ran more to country western, had never heard of the rocker but tried to be engaging, giving the man a friendly wave as he broke off and climbed into the Renault.

"Hit it, bud," he told Don.

They pulled away from the curb and Dave got out his half-glasses so that he could read the map. He and Don were arguing over a street sign when Don drove through a red light. A policeman immediately waved them over to the side. The officer, according to Don, "was dressed in little bozo pants with the flaps on the side and the boots up to his knees, standing there with a stick and a radio." From their earlier recon, Don knew that "If you ran any kind of traffic signal or didn't stop when they ordered, the cop would get on his radio and down the road about half a mile, they had four or five Jeeps, and they would stop you." Laurie was petrified and hugged Leila close to her. "I knew that Laurie had just absolutely pulled her top lip over her head," says Dave. As they had left in the car, says Laurie, Don and Dave "had told me that if we were stopped to only speak English, act like a tourist, and pretend we were cousins going on a picnic . . . I thought, 'Oh yeah—one with a New York accent, one with a North Carolina accent, and mine was Michigan.' "

Don eased the car over to the opposite side of the road and could see the officer reaching for his radio, thinking they were going to try and get away. Don hopped out of the car and ran over to the cop, waving his hands in the air and yelling, "I'm sorry. I'm sorry. I know I ran the light, but I didn't see it until the last second." Then he handed the officer his passport.

"Look, I'm from America," Don said apologetically.

The officer examined the passport and suddenly his eyes lit up and he broke out into a broad smile.

"Your name is Michael?" he asked. "Like Michael Jackson?"

Don's middle name on his passport is Michael. Everyone in Tunisia, it seemed, was interested in rock stars.

"Yeah," replied Don. "But I can't dance as good as him."

The officer laughed. "He is very great, yes?"

"Oh yeah, real great." Don paused, then changed the subject. "Say, I'm real sorry about the stoplight. Like I said, I'm an American tourist and I'm not too familiar with the roads an' all that over here."

"Oh, no problem," responded the officer. "Go ahead," he said, gesturing with a flick of his baton.

"Thanks a lot, buddy." Don waved and started back across the street, dodging traffic as he went.

"Michael Jackson," the officer called after him.

Don waved again over his shoulder.

When they were under way once more, it became clear that they were lost. Dave, reading glasses perched on the end of his nose, was muttering to himself, "Did we miss it? Yeah, I think we missed that one. No, here it is. No, there it was, we just passed it. No, that isn't the right one." Don was grinding the gears in the balky little Renault and cranking the wheel from side to side, trying to avoid hitting the pedestrians, donkey carts, smoke-belching buses, and other vehicles of every shape and description jamming the road.

Up to this point Laurie had been sitting silently in the back seat with Leila. But as Don and Dave began to argue over a particular turn, she leaned forward and asked, "Are you guys sure you've ever done this before?" Don and Dave stopped bickering and gave each other a knowing look.

"We always get lost once or twice," responded Don, trying to make light of the situation. "It's probably gonna take us a couple o' weeks to get where we're goin'."

Laurie settled back in the seat, not certain whether they were joking or whether she'd been rescued by the Keystone Cops.

Despite their navigation problems, they reached the pickup point in good time. Although it had been completely deserted on their previous visit, this time they found a herd of sheep and two shepherds moving down the beach, blocking their way. They waited for the sheep to pass, then parked the car near the edge of the sandy littoral and climbed out to stretch their legs. It was nearly 4:30 P.M.

There was no real cover or any place to hide, so they tried to look as casual as possible, as though they really were on some kind of pleasure outing. A short time later, they were surprised to see the two shepherds again. The two men plodded over to the ruins of a cinderblock house with no roof, located near the beach. They went inside, then reappeared a short time later in different clothes, carrying fishing poles, and they started fishing in the surf a short distance up the coast.

Not long afterwards, a Tunisian patrol boat from the naval facility near the castle cruised slowly by. They could clearly make out the men on the deck watching them, but the patrol boat didn't stop or make any effort to investigate their presence on the beach.

As six-thirty approached, there was still no sign of Jack and the rescue boat. Don and Dave were growing apprehensive, and Laurie was close to tears. She was sitting in the car, dejected, with

Leila clinging to her. The sun was going down and a gloomy pall descended over the beach. A storm was brewing in the sky behind them, and flashes of lightning were visible in the direction of Tunis.

When they had arrived at the pickup site, the sea was like glass, but now it was getting higher, with big, rolling swells. The shepherds had returned and were watching them, obviously curious as to what the little band of foreigners was doing on their deserted beach. Dave knew they couldn't remain much longer; they would have to go back to Tunis and try again the following afternoon.

But Don was not willing to call it a day. "Let's give it a few more minutes," he argued, as six-thirty rolled around.

The wind was rising, and with every passing minute it was getting darker and their lingering presence on the beach was becoming more and more suspicious. Don kept saying, "A few more minutes, just a few more minutes. I know he'll come."

Another twenty minutes passed and there was still no sign of Jack. "Okay," conceded Don at last. "He's not gonna make it today."

At that moment, as they were walking back toward the car, Don took one last glance at the sea and spotted a tiny speck on the horizon. "There!" he cried.

"Man!" exclaimed Dave. "I'll be . . . That's it!"

It was Jack. Standing at the controls of the high-speed boat, he homed in on one of the castles and then veered down the coast in their direction.

Don and Dave both started waving frantically. Laurie saw them, and ran from the car over to where they were standing, and all three of them began waving. The shepherds, meanwhile, seemed content simply to watch the scene with interest, without making any effort to alert the authorities.

Jack turned the boat sharply in toward the beach, and ran it aground in the shallow water. "I waded up to my knees," recalls Laurie, "in water so cold, carrying Leila. She wouldn't go to anybody else." The water became too deep for her, so Dave plunged in and carried first Leila, and then Laurie, out to the boat, losing his shoes in the process. Then, as they worked to get the boat unstuck and turned around in the right direction, they noticed the two shepherds watching them intently and apparently debating what to do. "Donny's getting ready to run 'em down and break their legs with his baton," says Dave, "so that they couldn't run off and warn the authorities." But they managed to refloat the boat and get the engine back in the water. The engine roared to life and Jack swung the vessel around in preparation for the run to Pantelleria. He now had three passengers aboard; only Don remained behind.

The combined weight of the new passengers and all the gas cans was too much for the small craft, and it began to take water in the back, so Dave climbed out over the windshield and lay down on the short front deck to "give it some ballast and keep the front end down." The swells near the coast were four feet high, but as they got into open water they rose to between five and eight feet, which made maneuvering the little 18-foot boat extremely difficult and meant that they had to travel very slowly, no more than eight knots maximum.

The sun had gone down like the drop of a curtain; it was a cloudy night and there was no moon. The lights of Tunis receded quickly behind them. They were running without lights and it seemed to Dave like they had fallen into a coal mine. "I mean, it was dark," says Dave. "You'd look out in front and it was absolutely pitch black. There was no glow behind us and no glow in front of us."

The roller-coaster waves made Laurie deathly seasick. She threw up constantly until there was nothing left in her stomach, and then she was beset by the dry heaves. Dave began to worry that she was becoming so physically drained by the ordeal that she couldn't hold on to Leila, so he climbed back over the windshield and lashed both of them to the boat. Leila was frantic with fear. "Anytime anyone got around Leila, she screamed like she was being killed," recalls Dave. "The poor child was just absolutely horrified of any man."

The water in the back of the boat was getting deeper, so Dave turned on the bilge pump, but it didn't work. He picked up a can and began bailing, but every time they went over a particularly high wave, the backwash would fill the rear of the vessel again. Dave realized that he still was weighing down the back of the boat too much, so once again he made his way back to the front deck and lay down, the waves breaking over him until he was drenched to the bone. The only good thing about the heavy seas was that they apparently had driven all of the Tunisian patrol boats into port.

After the rescue craft had slipped away into the gathering gloom, Don returned to the car under the watchful gaze of the two shepherds, and drove back to the main road and then on to the naval station. If they were apprehended by a Tunisian patrol boat, he reasoned, it would probably tow them to the nearest naval facility. Under cover of darkness, he backed the little Renault into a thicket above the naval station, where he could monitor the comings and goings. Everything was quiet and, given the stormy conditions, nothing was going in or out of the little harbor. "I saw the most amount of coastal patrol boats ever in port—two big ones and two little ones—so I figured they was all in," says Don. "They had come in and stayed in."

He waited in the cramped Renault, growing stiff and cold as the evening wore on. In time, he became more and more confident that his confederates and their precious cargo had made it. What could it take, he thought; two hours, three at the most, for them to reach Pantelleria? After a two-and-a-half-hour vigil, he decided to head back to Tunis. Since Dave had navigated on the previous trips from Tunis to the pickup point, Don began to laugh to himself as he wondered how many times he'd get lost on the return trip.

It was an extremely dark night and there were few lights or road signs. Don had to pull over three times and study his map in the headlights, and in one case he climbed up on the Renault's hood to compare the Arabic script on a road sign to a name on the map. After a while he came across several landmarks that he remembered passing earlier, and soon he was back in Tunis at the hotel. He immediately called Pantelleria, but despite the fact that almost three and a half hours had elapsed, Dave was not yet at the hotel.

Although worried, "being a good Ranger, you learn to eat and sleep when you can," says Don. "So the first thing I did after I couldn't get ahold of Dave was go to dinner." Every half hour he placed another call to Pantelleria, but he still couldn't reach Dave. Finally, after leaving a message for Dave to call him as soon as he came in, he climbed into bed, exhausted from the day's excitements, and fell into a deep sleep.

## RUN FOR PANTELLERIA

On the little boat, meanwhile, the situation was far from re-solved. With each jarring wave, Laurie's back slammed into the hard bench she was sitting on, raising large purple welts and bruises, and she was still gagging and retching, despite the fact that she had long ago emptied everything in her stomach over the side of the craft. There wasn't anything dry in the boat. She and Leila huddled together, shivering in the cold and wet, and wondering how much longer the ordeal would last. "Please, God, *please* get us home," Laurie prayed to herself. Her fear and misery, however, were rapidly eclipsed by rage. "I hope to God Foued suffers half as much as we have," she told herself, adding that, "I cussed and damned him. I thought to myself, 'I hope I have a son and he comes back one day and slaps his father across the face.' It might not sound like a very nice thing to say as a mother, but how could he have done what he did? How could he not love his own chil-dren? He had told me he would kill me before he would see me get even one hair of Leila's head. I just sat and cussed him."

"Oh, man," Dave groaned. Off to the left he could see running lights in the inky darkness, and he immediately suspected it might be a patrol boat. He turned to Jack and yelled, "Here comes a boat!" Jack cut sharply to the right in an effort to cross behind it. But instead of slipping by, it just seemed to keep coming, bearing down on them like an onrushing locomotive. Suddenly, Dave re-alized that it wasn't a patrol boat; it was a huge oil supertanker, several football fields long. Since they were showing no lights, no one on the tanker could see them, and the vessel was so large that no one on board would have noticed if they had run right over the top of the little boat.

Fearful not only of being run down but of losing their bearings for Pantelleria, Dave ordered Jack to cut the engine and stop dead in the water until the giant ship had passed. Then it took several minutes to ride out the heavy swells generated by the supertanker.

They stopped on several other occasions to refuel from the jerry cans in the back of the craft, each time buffeted by the waves until they could fire up the engine again. Given the unsteady rocking of the boat during refueling, it was impossible not to spill gasoline into the water sloshing around, several inches deep, in the back of the craft. Despite a stiff wind, the boat reeked of gasoline fumes that made Laurie and Leila even sicker. According to Dave, "Laurie was gagging and choking and dry-heaving, and it was just miserable. Absolutely miserable."

As the minutes dragged on, worry and doubt began to set in. Dave kept straining his eyes for any sign of Pantelleria. They had been at sea for more than three hours, and he knew they should have sighted the island some time ago. "I thought, man, either Pantelleria has no lights or we have missed that sucker," he concluded. He knew they didn't have enough fuel to reach Sicily, and the realization set in that, "if we don't find a port soon, we're gonna be driftin' out there in the Mediterranean." He didn't say anything to Jack, but Dave knew he had to be thinking the same thing.

As cold and wet as he was, Dave could feel the sweat breaking out on his forehead. Where was the island? Could they have missed it by that much?

Then, finally, a glow appeared on the horizon. Jack saw it at the same time and set a course straight for it. It took almost another two hours of plowing through steep waves and heavy seas before they actually reached Pantelleria. Jack swung the boat in a wide arc around the island, searching for the port, which lies near the north-western tip. On several occasions, they nearly slammed into large rocks and reefs jutting out from the dark foamy waters surrounding the little island.

"At last we found the opening to the port, near some rock jetties," says Dave. Jack guided the craft slowly up to the dock, beneath a medieval castle, and they received an emotional greeting from Simone, who had been waiting, with mounting anxiety, for hours. Once the boat was tied up, Dave climbed out stiffly and stood on terra firma for the first time in five and a half hours. He pulled Laurie out of the boat, then grabbed Leila by the back of the collar and hoisted her up onto the pier alongside her mother. They were too cold and exhausted to celebrate; instead, they just stared numbly at each other, the ground still reeling beneath their feet. According to Dave, "Laurie was just totally out of it. She had absolutely no idea where she was at or what she was doing."

Dave was white with salt from head to foot, his hair standing on end in spikes like a punker. "I looked like Frosty the Snow-man," he laughs. He was also badly bruised all up and down his right side, from the ankle to the shoulder. "I had bounced so much on the front of that boat. When a wave would run out from under the boat, it would drop seven or eight feet and just smack the water and I would hit the deck.

"Laurie was white as if somebody had just taken powder and covered her entire face and hair," says Dave. "And Leila was the same." Jack, too, was completely white, except for where his gog-gles had covered his eyes. His hair was spiky and reminded Dave of a porcupine.

Simone drove them immediately to the little hotel, where rooms were waiting for them. Everyone was starved, but all that was available at that late hour were pastries and coffee. Afterwards, Dave went up to his room and walked into the shower fully dressed and began to lather up. Slowly, the salt caked to his clothes and body and began to wash away under the assault of the warm water. The shower felt wonderful, but it soon dawned on Dave that the soap wasn't rinsing away. Then he remembered: there was no fresh water on the island. He was showering in salt water. "There I stood rinsing, rinsing, and rinsing, tryin' to get the soap outta my hair," he remembers. Eventually, he just gave up, toweled himself off, and collapsed into bed.

Laurie and Leila also showered once they were safely en-sconced in their room. While it was impossible to remove all of the salt and soap from their bodies, the warm water chased away the deep chill and soothed the bruises and scrapes. When she finished, Laurie dialed a number that Dave had given her and reached her parents in Sicily. They had been waiting all day for some word and were nearly frantic with worry. The conversation was short and devoid of emotion on Laurie's part. She and Leila were safe, she told them, and relieved beyond words to be out of Tunisia. "I still didn't feel a lot of emotions," says Laurie. "Just a lot of anger." Almost too exhausted to talk, and still dazed and ill from the rough crossing, Laurie said goodbye and told Bill and Barbara that she would see them soon.

At 6:30 A.M., Dave was awakened by the sound of the phone. It was Don.

"You're in. Didn't you get my message?" Don asked.

"No," Dave replied groggily. Usually an early riser, he was still feeling the effects of the previous night's adventure. "Everyone's safe. It took more than five hours," Dave told him.

"I don't have time to talk," Don interrupted. "I've got to get to the airport before they realize she's missing." He signed off, packed his bag, and checked out. Then he drove to the airport and turned in the Renault.

Don didn't care where the next flight out of the country was going so long as he was on it. There was no telling if the Tunisian authorities yet knew that Laurie and Leila were missing, but he didn't want to take any chances. The airport was chaotic as ever, crammed with passengers and baggage piled high on carts. There were extremely long lines in front of every counter and Don went from one to the next, asking in English where the flight was going and how soon it departed.

Finally, he approached a sales representative standing behind a counter and asked the destination of the next flight.

"Cairo," responded the man.

"Great."

"How soon?"

"Fifteen, twenty minutes."

"Fine, I'll take it," Don announced, relieved. The line was not very long, since most of the passengers had already been checked in. Don stepped to the end of the line and was just beginning to relax when he gazed up at the name of the airline above the counter: Royal Jordanian.

"Uh-uh," he said under his breath. CTU's first rescue had taken place in Jordan, and Don was pretty sure that he and Dave were still wanted by Jordanian authorities. Fortunately, he spied another airline with a flight leaving in about thirty minutes, and even better, it was going to Milan and then on to Rome.


## REUNION

Tuesday, November 8, dawned bright and sunny on Pantelleria. Leila woke up before her mother. She tottered over to the window and stared out at the little harbor below.

"What are you doing?" Laurie asked sleepily.

Leila was pointing at something, so Laurie slipped slowly out of bed, stretched, and joined her daughter by the window.

"What is it, Leila?" Laurie wanted to know, as she looked out at the boats tied up in their slips.

"Boat, Mama. No, no. No boat, Mama," Leila said with uncharacteristic firmness.

Laurie hugged Leila and assured her that there would be no more boat rides. They'd take a plane today.

Despite the fact that they were on Italian territory, "we knew we weren't quite safe," says Dave. "Surely an alarm had gone out that night before and maybe even a search party to find her." He also knew that Foued and his family were capable of virtually anything, including a counterstrike against them. If the two shepherds reported what they had witnessed to Tunisian authorities and Foued subsequently learned about it, it didn't take awesome powers of deduction to figure out their most likely destination.

They checked out and took a shuttle bus to the island's little airport, where they bought tickets on the next flight to Rome. Judy, Barbara, and Bill had left Sicily that morning and were scheduled to arrive in Rome a short time ahead of them, so they would be there waiting at the airport. For their part, Jack and Simone would remain behind to take care of the boat.

Dave, who hadn't brought anything with him, not even a toothbrush or a change of underwear, was still dressed in the damp, salt-stiff clothes that he had arrived in. As he had lost his shoes in the Tunisian surf, he was barefoot, so the first thing he did at the airport was to buy a pair of cheap plastic shower sandals. He had tried to comb his hair that morning, but it was still caked with salt and soap and standing up on end. Laurie and Leila were in the same fix, and in Dave's words, "We looked like first-class tramps."

Laurie was petrified that someone would stop them in the airport and did not settle down until the plane was actually airborne. Then the color began to return to her face and she appeared to relax for the first time since Dave had met her. "We're safe, and we're going home," Laurie told herself.

Dave cautioned Laurie that she and Leila were not entirely out of the woods until they were once again on U.S. soil. The reunion at the airport should be muted, he advised her. She shouldn't do anything that would call attention to them. He had given the same advice the night before to Bill, suggesting that he not tell Barbara until the last minute that they were all going to meet at the airport. He counseled Bill that Barbara was just too transparent to hide her emotions. "I'm afraid she'll let it out," Dave explained. "And when you do tell Barb," he continued, "you've got to somehow get her to understand she's not to show real big emotion if she can help it."

Accordingly, Bill didn't say a word to Barbara until a few minutes before the flight with Laurie and Leila on it was scheduled to land. Then, amid the hubbub of Rome's airport, he took her aside and said, "Now look, if we happen to see Laurie and Leila here, you've got to hold yourself together because we're not safe until we land in New York." Only then did Barbara realize that she was about to be reunited with her daughter and granddaughter. She promised Bill that she would keep her emotions in check because she knew he was right, adding that "I didn't really feel safe."

Judy was standing with Bill and Barbara at the luggage carousel when she glanced around and suddenly saw Dave behind her, a wide grin on his face. She was taken aback by his appearance. Normally he was so well groomed and meticulous, but today—his leather jacket white from the salt, his hair standing on end like Don King's, wearing floppy shower thongs and wrinkled trousers—to Judy, "he really looked like a bum. A beautiful bum, but still a bum." Then her gaze fell on Laurie and Leila, who were next to him. A lump swelled in her throat as she tried to say something to Barbara and Bill, but nothing came out.

Bill noticed the emotion in Judy's face and clutched Barbara's arm; they turned slowly around and there, not more than twenty feet away, were Laurie and Leila. No one moved. Barbara began to cry and Bill, for all his admonishments to her, couldn't hold back his own tears. Even Judy started to cry, and Dave's eyes misted over. Only Laurie remained composed. "I was amazed that she didn't run up and embrace Bill and Barb and just go crazy," observes Judy. "But she held herself very reserved and very serious in the airport." Dave attributes Laurie's reserve not only to his lecture on security, but to the fact that she was still ill from the boat ride, pregnant, and virtually dead on her feet, so completely spent that she could barely carry on a lucid conversation.

"It was a real tear-jerker," reflects Dave. "A long-lost daughter had come home, and the grandparents didn't know who to grab first . . . Laurie was pregnant, as big as a house, and all she could say is, 'We spent such a long time on that boat.' " After a brief reunion, they gathered up their luggage and departed for the city, where they would buy a change of clothing for Laurie and Leila and stay until Don arrived. Dave couldn't wait to take another shower and get into some fresh clothes. When they reached the hotel, they gathered in one of the rooms and, according to Judy, it seemed like everyone was trying to talk at once. Even Laurie joined in. Her face was animated, and Dave noticed for the first time what a pleasant smile she had.

Later they had a quiet lunch at the hotel, and then went shopping. But while the crisis was over for Barbara and Bill, Judy passed several anxious hours wondering when Don would show up. "I knew that he could take care of himself," says Judy, "but I just wanted to know where he was, that he was all right."

Don reached the hotel late that afternoon and they made arrangements to leave the following day for the United States.


## RETURN

Back in Lansing, Val was alternately angry and desperately worried because there was still no news. Don had said they'd be out of touch for between five and seven days, but it had been nine days since she'd put her mother on a plane for New York. The hardest part was the fact that she didn't have anyone to talk to. "You're just gonna have to sit there and wait and keep your mouth shut," Don had warned her. Well aware that loose talk could put both her family and the commandos in danger, she had remained absolutely mum, and the tension was beginning to get to her. She called her family doctor and told him she was "on the verge of losing it" and needed something to help her calm down. He gave her a prescription, and she continued her vigil by the telephone, waiting for word that everyone was safe.

Finally, she went out to shop for groceries. On the way home, she stopped to check on her parents' house and leave some milk in the refrigerator, just in case they returned in the next couple of days. Expecting to dash in and dash out again, Val told the kids to stay in the car. The phone was ringing as she walked through the door. It was her sister-in-law.

"Val?"

"Yes."

"Your dad just called."

Val's heart stopped. "Just tell me," she said. "Is it good news or bad news?"

"I don't know what's been going on, but it sounded like things couldn't be better."

"Oh, my God!" she said. "I'll talk to you later."

She returned to the car and started for home, 12 miles away. She was crying and shaking so hard that her kids kept asking, "What's wrong, Mommy? What's wrong?"

She spent the rest of the day next to the telephone. At last it rang, and Val clutched the receiver eagerly to her ear.

"Hello."

"Hello," came a faint voice on the other end of the line.

"Hello?" Val repeated.

"Hello," said the voice again.

"Listen, P.J.," snapped Val, thinking it was one of her girl-friends, "quit messin' with me. I need to keep this line open."

"Val, it's me."

"What?"

"How'd you like some company tonight?"

"Oh, my God. Laurie, is it you? Really you? Where are you?"

"New York. We'll be home tonight."

Val couldn't speak. The family's long ordeal seemed to be over. "I really believed the nightmare was at an end," she says.

## AFTERMATH

But it wasn't. While Laurie returned home to Lansing with Leila and soon gave birth to her second child, her life was still far from normal. A short time after her return, she received an official-looking communication in Arabic at her parents' address. She took it to a professor friend at Michigan State who speaks and reads Arabic, and he translated it for her. It turned out to be a summons from the Tunisian government, demanding that she present herself in Tunisia for prosecution and that she surrender her daughter to a Tunisian court.

"We got really upset and nervous about it," said Barbara. "Would our government actually make her go back? We didn't know."

Ultimately, they were advised to ignore the summons. But the Swints were still worried about Foued and looked to their own government for help. "Our congressman, our senator, everyone said, 'Once she's home, we'll help you,' " remembers Barbara. "But when we got her home, no one would help us." Even more outrageous, they heard that the U.S. government had formally apologized to the Tunisians for Laurie's escape. The Swints expected the State Department to stand up for them, not Foued, and to do everything possible to keep him out of the country.

A local court granted Laurie a divorce from Foued and awarded her sole custody of the children. Nevertheless, she still lives in fear that Foued will somehow get back into the United States and try to kidnap one or both of her children, or even one of Val's children. There is also concern that he might try to harm Barbara and Bill because of the humiliation he has suffered. So serious is the threat that Laurie is living with her children in another city, under an assumed name, and trying to put her life back together.

Foued has written her a number of times over the past two years, apologizing for his behavior and saying that he misses her. He even sent her a watch as a present. Unbelievably, it turned out to be the same watch that his sisters earlier had stolen from Laurie. In recent months, he has called the Swints, asking to speak with Laurie. Barbara won't talk to him, but Bill does, keeping his anger under control in an effort to learn what Foued is up to. Neither Barbara nor Bill trusts Foued, and both have concealed-weapons permits and regularly carry pistols.

"I really believe he would try to kill my daughter and grand-children without blinking an eye," says Barbara, adding that she would gladly use her weapon if she ever sees Foued near the house. Bill is not so much angry as bitter. "What's sad," he says, "is that we're here in America, the land we love and would die for, and we cannot have our daughter and grandchildren live with us."

Other families have contacted the Swints about the rescue. "My heart bleeds for all the other children in the same situation, and the mothers," says Barbara. "When they call here and talk to us, it tears me apart because I hurt for them, the way I still hurt for my daughter and family."

The story hit the local papers shortly after Laurie's return. "People were saying, we can't believe this has happened," Val says. "This is too much like a book." For a while, the personnel director at the Oldsmobile plant where Bill works received calls from journalists all over the nation wanting to interview him, but when she approached him with the offers, he demurred. All he wanted was for things to return to normal as soon as possible, and to banish forever the memories of Tunisia and the traumatic events that nearly cost the lives of his daughter and granddaughter.

More than any other reaction, according to Barbara, their friends and co-workers were "angry at our government, furious really, that we had to do what we did." As ordinary citizens, they couldn't understand why it was not the role of the American government to protect U.S. citizens abroad and to ensure their basic rights. "I said, this is what we thought, too," says Barbara. "But it isn't true. The baby [Leila] was born in America and is an American citizen. After she left the country, it seemed like she no longer was. People from our walk of life couldn't handle this."

The Swints calculate that it cost them $100,000 to bring their daughter and granddaughter home. This includes the money they sent to Laurie, legal fees, travel, phone calls, and the actual rescue. CTU's total expenses for the rescue added up to $56,000, of which $50,000 has been covered by the Swints. CTU has not pressed them for the balance. Laurie is deeply troubled by the financial and emotional distress she has caused her parents; but Bill is adamant about the fact that they would do it all over again, in a moment, if it were necessary. "We tell her that it's why God permitted us to have enough money to do something like that," Bill explains. "Barb and I made an agreement that when we got back here from Sicily, no matter how bad things were, the money would never be brought up again."

When asked about CTU, the Swints have nothing but praise.

They stay in touch with Don, Dave, and Judy, and recently visited CTU's headquarters in Fayetteville. They have no doubts that they did the right thing; that it was, in fact, the only option available to them to reunite their family. Their only regret, say Bill and Barbara, is that they should have hired CTU much sooner. "Don't throw your money away thinking a lawyer's gonna help you, or that our government's gonna help you," Barbara maintains. "Save the money and put it where it will help. This is the only way you'll ever get your children back."

# TWO
# Operation
# Lauren

# 4
# A Meeting
# in Dallas

■  CTU BEGAN rescuing Americans in trouble abroad not by
design, but rather by chance. On a cold afternoon in mid-
December 1987, Don was sitting at his desk in Fayetteville when
Everett Alvarez, Jr., walked in the door. An easygoing California
native with a broad smile, Alvarez is a former Navy pilot who spent
eight and a half years as a prisoner-of-war after being the first
American shot down over North Vietnam. Once he left the Navy,
he served as Deputy Director of the Peace Corps and then Deputy
Administrator of the Veterans Administration, and was rumored to
be in line for a possible cabinet post in a future Republican administration. But having drawn a government paycheck for more than
a quarter century, Alvarez retired from government service in
1986, seeking new challenges and an opportunity to make more
money, with which he hoped to provide a better life for his family.
He had met Feeney earlier in 1987 over a lunch in Washington
arranged by a mutual friend who thought CTU could benefit from
Ev's management experience and contacts.

Don asked Dave to join them, and introduced his burly partner to Alvarez. After discussing a number of other possible business opportunities, Alvarez finally brought the conversation around
to the real purpose of the meeting. Would CTU, he wanted to

know, ever consider conducting a rescue operation in a foreign
country?

Neither Don nor Dave was shocked by the proposal. Others
had, from time to time, broached the same subject. But for one
reason or another, none of the missions had ever materialized.
Rescues were the kind of thing posturers and phonies talked about
to impress civilians or pick up girls at a bar. Real-life special operators would sometimes raise the subject when they had had too
much to drink, but such ideas were usually discarded upon sober
reflection. Successful rescues—no matter how careful the preparation and planning—always were gambles and involved a great
deal of luck. Moreover, they were extremely expensive, and few
private citizens had the resources to mount rescue operations
abroad.

On the other hand, in contrast to others who had floated
rescue proposals before CTU, Ev Alvarez was no blowhard or
fantasist; he was a cautious and credible public figure. Alvarez
volunteered few specifics, but Don and Dave were intrigued. "We
told Ev that we were ready to consider the subject," recalls Dave,
"but it would depend on a number of factors: the given country,
the type of operation, who would be involved, and so on."

No novices to the world of shadows, Dave and Don also were
wary of being recruited under a "false flag" or for an off-the-books
CIA operation. A decade earlier, after all, renegade CIA and Navy
intelligence operative Edwin P. Wilson had come to Fort Bragg
and recruited active-duty military men for what they thought was
a government-sanctioned intelligence operation, which turned out
instead to be an illegal conspiracy to sell explosives and military
know-how to the Libyan government in support of international
terrorism. "We did a lot of work overseas," says Dave, "and had to
make absolutely sure that there was nothing gray or black in what
we agreed to carry out. It had to be white as the driven snow."

The meeting was inconclusive, and Alvarez returned to Washington. A few days later, Don received a call from a man identifying
himself as Al Zaponta. He said he was an oil company executive
and a friend of Alvarez's. He was calling from Dallas, he continued,
and knew a woman who had a "very serious problem" and needed
their help. He inquired whether they would be willing to come to

Dallas for a meeting. Don said they would get back to him. "We knew Ev," reflects Don, "who is well respected and well recognized. But we knew nothing about this guy."

Don contacted Alvarez in Washington, who confirmed that he had recommended CTU to Zaponta, and that he had made the inquiry about the rescue on Zaponta's behalf. Alvarez indicated that he had originally met Zaponta through Republican Party Hispanic political circles, and that while he didn't know him extremely well, he said the Texan appeared to be a solid and credible individual. According to Alvarez, Zaponta was a former Special Forces veteran who had headed an "A" Team in Vietnam and was still active in the Reserves. That was enough for Don, himself an ex-Green Beret. Reassured, Don called Zaponta back and asked him for more details on the case. Zaponta told him that he was trying to help a Dallas woman by the name of Cathy Mahone, whose seven-year-old daughter had been abducted to Jordan by her ex-husband, a Jordanian national. She had exhausted every possible avenue without success to secure her daughter's return, said Zaponta, and now—in desperation—was ready to mount some kind of rescue operation. Were they interested?

"Maybe," responded Don, who knew he needed to hear a lot more about the potential mission before agreeing to it. Nevertheless, he agreed to travel to Dallas as soon as possible. Four days before Christmas, Don and Dave arrived in Dallas, and were met at the airport by Zaponta and Cathy Mahone. Zaponta's short, pudgy stature belied his military background, but he and the CTU men established an almost immediate rapport. Cathy, on the other hand, was all business, uninterested in small talk, impatient to get to the problem at hand. A vivacious woman, with auburn hair and hazel eyes, Cathy was controlled, collected, but Don sensed she was at the end of her rope and had all of her hopes and dreams of recovering her daughter invested in the meeting.

They drove to a motel near the airport and, after saying goodbye to Zaponta, sat down with Cathy to listen to her story.

## "I KNEW . . . THAT HE HAD TAKEN HER"

Cathy's voice was flat, as cold as ice, as she described her plight, laying out the facts precisely, in chronological order, with charts, photos, and maps. Despite her calm exterior, it was evident to both Don and Dave that there was a fire burning inside of her. You couldn't see the flames or smell the smoke, but the fire was there nonetheless. She was cried out, and now her whole being, her every motion and thought, was focused on getting her daughter back—whatever it took, whatever the price.

She had met her former husband, Ali Bayan, in the mid-seventies, she told them, when she was working her way through college waitressing in a popular Dallas restaurant. Ali had come to the United States from Jordan in order to obtain an education, and worked, first as a dishwasher and later a waiter, in the same restaurant to support his studies. He had deep, liquid eyes, a shock of curly hair, and a winning smile, and she immediately fell for him. "It was an old-fashioned courtship," she told the men from CTU, adding that he had swept her off her feet. Eight months later they were married in a quiet Protestant ceremony.

At the outset, everything was fine. The young couple worked hard to build a life together and Cathy's family adored Ali. In 1979, Ali took his new wife home to Jordan to meet his prosperous and well-connected Sunni Moslem family. They lived in the town of Jarash, north of the capital of Amman, about 25 miles from the Syrian border. It was here that Ali had been raised, and it was in Jarash that he had first set his sights on moving to the United States to escape the tedium and relative lack of opportunity offered by his home town.

Before his death, Ali's father had maintained two wives in separate households, and sired twenty-four children between them. The current head of the family was Ali's older brother, Fwad Bayan, a wealthy pediatrician who operated a regional clinic under the patronage and protection of the royal family.

Although Cathy felt genuinely welcomed into Ali's extended family, she had traveled little before the trip to Jordan and was taken aback by the lack of hygiene and primitive living conditions that characterized life in Jarash. Like so many Western women, she had difficulty adjusting to the toilet, which was an open hole in the floor that one squatted over. After the novelty of the first few days began to wear off, she could see that life was hard in Jarash and that women counted for very little.

Cathy also began to notice subtle changes in Ali's behavior. He seemed, for instance, to regard her more as a trophy than as the loving partner she had been for more than two years. He was more demanding, less solicitous. He started spending most of his time with other men.

By the end of the visit, Cathy was looking forward to returning to Texas so that their lives could get back to normal. But it was not to be. They returned to Dallas, but when Cathy became pregnant, instead of sharing her joy, Ali exploded with anger and returned to Jarash. He remained there for seven months, reappearing just six weeks before the baby was born.

Ali was a changed man. By contrast to the tender and loving man Cathy had married, he was now distant, critical, and uninvolved in the things that meant the most to her. After the little girl, named Lauren, was born, he hung an Islamic medallion around her neck and informed Cathy that he wanted his daughter raised as a Moslem. Cathy, a born-again Christian, refused.

Six weeks after Lauren's birth, Cathy threw Ali out of the house and filed for divorce, which later was granted. The divorce decree issued by the District Court of Dallas County, Texas, dated December 30, 1980, appointed Catherine Phelps Bayan the "Managing Conservator of the child," and awarded her "all the rights, privileges, duties, and powers of a parent, to the exclusion of the other parent, subject to the rights, privileges, duties, and powers granted to any possessory conservator named in this decree." Ali was named "Possessory Conservator," with "reasonable access to the child." According to the court, "all such visitation periods shall be supervised by and in the presence of the Managing Conservator. The Possessory Conservator [Ali] is hereby ORDERED to surrender the child to the Managing Conservator [Cathy] immediately at the end of each period of visitation." Ali also was ordered to pay Cathy $175 a month in child support.

The divorce was, in most respects, amicable, and Cathy and Ali both seemed relieved to be free of the increasingly sour marriage. Cathy harbored no animosity toward Ali and, in fact, was genuinely grateful to him for fathering their beautiful daughter, Lauren, who rapidly became the focus of her life. Ali subsequently remarried, this time to a Jordanian woman named Maisha, who quickly bore him several more children. He continued to work in the restaurant business, and together with his brother Walid, bought a Dallas restaurant called "The Country Skillet." Cathy, too, remarried. Her new husband, Lytt Mahone, was the scion of an old Texas family and much older. She also opened an employment agency to service Texas's booming economy.

During this period, according to Cathy, Ali was "an excellent father," who visited his daughter, Lauren, on an almost weekly basis. Nevertheless, she had to take him to court on two occasions when he failed to meet his child-support payments. When Lauren was four years old, Ali asked Cathy if he could take his daughter to Jordan for two weeks to visit his family. Not wanting to seem unreasonable or to stand in the way of Lauren's maintaining a strong relationship with her father, Cathy assented reluctantly. But when Ali and Lauren did not return on schedule, Cathy became alarmed that he might have decided to keep Lauren and remain in Jordan permanently. She called Ali and his family repeatedly for an explanation and was assured that it was only a temporary delay. But one delay followed another, and Cathy was truly beginning to panic at the end of a month's time, when Ali returned with Lauren and all was forgiven in the joy of the moment. She had overreacted, Cathy convinced herself. However, she never forgot the incident, and it planted a seed of insecurity in her when she realized just how easy it would be for Ali to take Lauren one day and spirit her away to Jordon.

Over the next two years, Ali picked up Lauren on his visitation days and returned her, for the most part, like clockwork to her mother. Then, in late October 1987, Ali called to make arrangements for his regular visit with Lauren, but asked if he could keep her for an extra day over the Halloween weekend, returning her on Tuesday instead of Monday. He said that he wanted to take her to the State Fair in Houston, but would have her back in time to attend school on Tuesday. Cathy readily consented. Not only had the visits once again settled into a routine that seemed to suit everyone, but Cathy's marriage to Lytt was floundering and she was in the process of divorcing him. She figured that she could use Lauren's absence to tie up some of the loose ends and paperwork connected with the divorce.

Nevertheless, instead of enjoying a few days' respite from the cares of motherhood, by Monday Cathy was missing her daughter terribly. Although not scheduled to see her again until Tuesday after school, Cathy decided to drop in unannounced on Lauren for lunch at the elementary school cafeteria. Such visits were encouraged by the school administration as a way of increasing the involvement of parents in their children's education. Cathy looked forward to surprising her daughter.

The school was only four blocks from her home, and Cathy waited outside for Lauren's class to line up to go to lunch in the cafeteria. But when the children were all lined up, Lauren was nowhere to be seen. A sinking feeling gripped Cathy. "I knew," she reflects. "I knew in my heart that she was gone, that he had taken her."

Even though she lived nearby, Cathy stopped at the first pay phone she found and called The Country Skillet. Walid answered, but said he didn't know where his brother was. As an afterthought, he added, "He could have gone to New Jersey."

"What for?" she demanded to know.

"Well," responded Walid sheepishly, "he was going to see his wife."

"Since when does she live there?" Cathy exploded. "I didn't know that Maisha was there."

"He moved his wife and family to New Jersey two weeks ago," Walid explained.

Her head was spinning. Her stomach was doing flipflops. She tried to tell herself that it was all just a misunderstanding, some kind of mistake, but even as she dialed the number of Maisha's mother in New Jersey, she realized that Ali's move and Lauren's disappearance could mean only one thing.

Maisha answered the phone. Cathy told her what had happened and demanded to know where Ali was. Maisha, however, sounded confused and indicated that she thought he was still in Dallas. As they spoke, Cathy could tell that even Maisha was growing concerned.

She cut the conversation short and placed a call to Royal Jordanian Airways—Alia—in New York. The helpful saleswoman on the other end of the line confirmed Cathy's worst fears: Ali and Lauren had left for Amman at 9:00 P.M. the previous night. The plane had already landed in Jordan, and the daughter she cherished more than life itself was now beyond her reach, perhaps forever.

## "I'M NOT GOING TO GIVE UP"

In the days that followed, Cathy described herself as "an absolute wreck. I just totally lost it." She stopped eating and cried until she ran out of tears. She called everyone she knew who might be able to help, and repeatedly phoned Ali's home in Jarash, but no one would speak with her. She contacted two friends who were private investigators with good police contacts and soon learned that Ali, who had always been very careful with his finances, had accumulated a pile of debts and that the restaurant was failing. Shortly before skipping the country, he had purchased a new Honda with a down payment of only a few hundred dollars. In addition, he had gone on a buying spree, maxing out all of his credit cards, and shipping the goods to Jordan along with the car.

In retrospect, Cathy says that in the months leading up to the abduction of Lauren there were profound changes in Ali's behavior, but that she had chosen to ignore them. Although he was never particularly religious during the time they lived together, Cathy sensed that he had recently undergone a renewal of his Moslem faith. Sometimes when she called him to make arrangements for Lauren's visitation, Maisha would answer the phone and say that he would have to get back to her because he was praying. There had been other signs, too, signs that things were not well financially or at home.

Cathy initiated legal proceedings against Ali, even though she realized at the outset that legal avenues were going to be futile. She appeared before a grand jury and a warrant was issued for Ali's arrest. As she left the courtroom, the grand jury foreman stepped forward and handed her his business card. If he could be of any assistance, he told her, please call. His name was Al Zaponta.

She also contacted the State Department, but those she spoke

to couldn't offer her very much in the way of suggestions or encouragement. If the child is an American citizen, she was informed,
the State Department can provide legal advice and attempt through
diplomatic channels to secure the child's return. In addition, the
local U.S. Embassy is permitted to assist the parent in locating the
child and checking to ensure that he or she is in good health.
Beyond that, Cathy was told, there was little that they could do.
Despite the fact that Lauren was taken from the United States in
violation of the law, the State Department insisted that the case
would have to be governed by the domestic laws of Jordan, irre-
spective of the fact that Western mothers had few real rights under
its legal system. As in other Moslem countries, Jordanian courts
ordinarily give custody to the father instead of the mother, whatever the circumstances of the divorce or the father's character. "I
found out later," Cathy says, "[that] at the age of seven, according
to Jordanian law, a father has all legal rights to a child regardless of
reason. And so I had absolutely no right to her in Jordan. So
therefore there was nothing the State Department could do in
regard to helping me in bringing her [Lauren] back."

Outraged by her government's lack of responsiveness, Cathy
angrily vowed to the State Department official she was working
with that she was going to have her little girl back. "I'm not going
to give up."

But her words were greeted with skepticism and even deri-
sion. According to Cathy, "Their attitude was, basically, 'Lady,
who do you think you are? The U.S. government can't even get its
own hostages out [of Lebanon].' "

## PARENTAL KIDNAPPING

While the American hostages seized in the 1980 takeover of
the U.S. Embassy in Tehran and the hostages in Lebanon captured
worldwide attention, they represent only a tiny fraction of the
actual number of Americans held against their will in other countries at any one time. According to Shara Pang, an assistant to
Senator Alan Dixon (D-Ill.), 10,000 American children are currently "held hostage in foreign countries." Virtually all are pawns
in custody disputes involving one parent of American citizenship

and one of another nationality. In most cases, one of the parents kidnaps their own child, in violation of a U.S. court decree granting legal custody to the other parent, and then spirits the child away to his or her country of origin, or to a third country. According to Senator Dixon, "If the American parent tries to recover the child, a new custody proceeding is begun in the foreign country. In this way, the abducting parent is able to get a 'home court' advantage. Almost without exception, a foreign court rules in favor of their own citizen's case, even if the country is a close friend of the United States."

There are also cases involving American women married to foreign nationals and living abroad, who are prevented from returning to the United States or from taking their children out of the country in which they are residing. Many Islamic nations, for example, require the husband's permission for the wife to travel by herself outside the country or to take their children with her. In these male-dominated societies, the situation is especially difficult for women of other nationalities and religious faiths.

One particularly sad case concerns an American woman married to a Saudi man. They had two children and lived in the United States. On a visit back to Saudi Arabia, the husband was tragically killed in an auto accident. Unbelievably, the wife's brother-in-law went to court and applied for custody of his late brother's children. A Saudi court ruled that the desperate widow could have custody only so long as she remained in Saudi Arabia. In another case, the American woman went to Egypt with her Egyptian husband. While there, she was diagnosed with life-threatening cancer, and she returned to the United States for treatment. As a result of her illness, her husband decided to divorce her in Egypt and was awarded custody of their children. Now, as she combats cancer, the woman fears that she will die without ever again seeing her children.

Parental kidnapping is on the rise, according to two University of Maryland scholars, Geoffrey L. Greif and Rebecca L. Hegar. They suggest that there may be as many as 350,000 cases of child snatching every year in the United States, only a small fraction of which involve foreign locations. Fathers are more likely to abduct children than mothers, which may be attributed to the fact that fathers are significantly less often granted custody of children in a

"Taking down a bus" as part of a CTU training exercise, Fayetteville, North Carolina.

Although they never carry guns on their rescues, the CTU commandos provide firearms training to police, military units, and private-sector bodyguards.

The little harbor at Pantelleria where Laurie Swint Ghidaoui and her daughter finally docked after their harrowing escape from Tunisia.

OPPOSITE:
Safe in Rome after the rescue. From left to right: Dave Chatellier, Laurie, Leila, and Barbara Swint.

Swint family reunion in Rome. From left to right: Bill Swint, Laurie, Leila, and Barbara Swint.

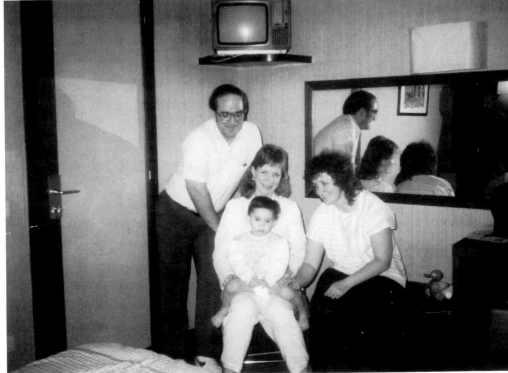

Cathy Mahone shows Don Feeney her missing daughter's doll collection during their initial meeting.

The city of Jarash, Jordan, where little Lauren Bayan was taken by her father. This photo was used by the commandos to help them find their way around.

The only clue to the location of the Bayan family home in Jarash was this photo of Cathy Mahone and Ali Bayan. The commandos used the Roman ruins in the background to find the house.

Part of the CTU rescue team that recovered Lauren Bayan in Jordan. From left to right: J.D. Roberts, unidentified man, Don Feeney.

Dave Chatellier in disguise during the rescue of Lauren Bayan in Jordan.

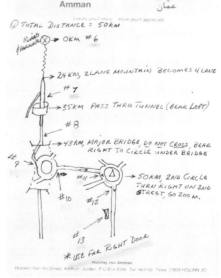

One of Dave Chatellier's hand-drawn maps showing part of the route between Jarash, where Lauren Bayan had been taken by her father, and Amman, Jordan.

Keli Walker Chowdhury, whose daughter Brittney was abducted to Bangladesh by her former husband.

Mohammed Chowdhury, who married and divorced Keli. He fled to Bangladesh with their daughter to escape formal deportation.

Brittney Chowdhury, after her rescue from Bangladesh.

OPPOSITE, TOP TO BOTTOM:
A flyer circulated to American Airlines employees by Jeannie Cripps, Keli Walker Chowdhury's mother, in an effort to raise money for Brittney's rescue.

Mohammed Chowdhury and Terry Smith riding in a Dacca pedicab after Terry returned to Bangladesh as part of the operation to rescue Keli's daughter, Brittney.

Don Feeney and his wife, Judy, posing as U.S. investors in Bangladesh. Judy's hair is dyed black.

Mohammed Chowdhury's family in their Dacca home. From left to right: Calpona, Mr. & Mrs. Chowdhury, Molutie.

September 15, 1989

TO ALL EMPLOYEES

## WE NEED YOUR HELP!!!

Jeannie Cripps' four year old granddaughter, Brittney Chowdbury, has been kidnapped by her deported father and is being held in Bangladesh, against court orders. That, in and of itself, is harmful enough, but Brittney has developed serious kidney/bladder illness and medical treatment is being withheld. There is no running water in the place where she is being held and there are fears that she is suffering from acute malnourishment.

There is an international agency which can rescue Brittney and return her to her mother, who has court-appointed custody. The cost of saving this child's life and returning her to her U.S. home is $25,000 (minimum). Needless to say, not many of us could afford such a fee. However, if each employee here gave as small a donation as $1.00 each, we in Tulsa could be responsible for approximately $10,000 of that fee. Some of us could give more; some less.

Please dig deep in your pockets and give whatever you can toward this rescue. You can make a tax deductible donation to the

One of Don Feeney's surveillance photos of Charlie Hefner's house and neighborhood in Guayaquil, Ecuador.

Kim Hefner, Jeremy, and Amy during happier days, before the children were spirited away to Ecuador by their father and then rescued by CTU.

divorce case. Greif and Hegar found that boys were slightly more likely to be kidnapped than girls, and that three quarters of all the children were six or younger at the time of the snatching, with the average age being two. Only 6 percent of the children were twelve or older.

According to a profile constructed by Greif and Hegar, 92 percent of the custodial parents were white and American-born. Fifty percent were Protestant, 25 percent were Catholic, 5 percent were Jewish, and the remainder did not indicate any religious affiliation. Two thirds of the custodial parents earned less than $27,500 per year, and female custodial parents tended more often to be in lower-paying, lower-status jobs than their male counterparts. Sixty percent of the custodial parents indicated that they had at least one year of college.

The U.S. State Department, in contrast to the figures assembled by Senator Dixon's staff, says that there are fewer than six hundred "active" cases of parental kidnapping involving foreign countries at the present time. However, the State Department only classifies cases as "active" for two years after they are first reported to the department; then they are removed from the list, unless a parent or relative remains in regular contact. The vast majority soon abandon contact with the State Department as a waste of time and effort. In this way, the department conveniently purges cases from the list as though they were somehow solved, whereas in reality few, if any, are ever resolved as a result of State Department intervention.

The largest number of parental kidnapping cases involve the United Kingdom, Mexico, Canada, and Western Europe, for reasons of geography as well as similarities of language and culture. There simply are more marriages between U.S. citizens and nationals of those countries. And because of compatible traditions and judicial systems, most of the cases involving these nations are resolved without fanfare or difficulty. By contrast, the problem of child theft is often extraordinarily thorny when it concerns the nations of Asia, Latin America, Africa, and—especially—the Middle East. In addition to the Arab states, Israel also has a relatively poor track record of recognizing the rights of non-Israeli parents, even if they are American Jews.

In an effort to address the issue of child abduction across

national frontiers, the U.S. government was one of the principal proponents of the 1980 Hague Convention on the Civil Aspects of International Child Abduction. Although the convention was opened for signature in 1980, it was not sent by the President to the Senate for ratification until five years later, and was not ratified until 1987. To date, only about a dozen countries have ratified the convention and none of them is in the Middle East, or for that matter in the Third World, where the problem is most acute. Thus, the convention has made little, if any, headway in addressing the problem of parental abduction of children to foreign countries, even though the State Department proudly points to the document when challenged over its impotence on the issue.

So ineffectual is the State Department that in two cases of parental abduction to Saudi Arabia, the only thing former Assistant Secretary of State for Consular Affairs Joan M. Clark could offer was a promise to press for visiting rights for the distraught mothers, including assurances that they could "enter and depart the country without incident." The U.S. ambassador, she continued in a memo, would "shortly be presenting to the Saudi foreign ministry the text of the Hague Convention and will be encouraging the Saudis to become a party to it."

## WHAT TO DO?

Refusing to accept defeat, Cathy spoke to other parents whose children had been abducted in similar circumstances. They confirmed her suspicion that the State Department was more interested in preserving cordial relations with offending countries than in assisting Americans in recovering children abducted in custody disputes. Some of the parents she contacted hadn't seen their children in years, she said, adding that "these people's lives were just devastated." Few of those she talked to could offer any hope. "I was just faced with a lot of negative, hopeless feedback," Cathy recalls.

One of those she met during this time was Holly Planells, who had formed a support group called American Children Held Hostage. Planells's case, it turned out, was very similar to her own. Like Cathy, she had married a Jordanian. They had fallen in love while students at the University of Tennessee, but Holly Planells's Prince Charming turned into an Arab Archie Bunker when they moved to Amman. He demanded that she be totally submissive to him, and even accused her of being a lesbian after she had lunch with a female friend. Once the marriage failed, she was forced to return to the United States without her young son. Today, the only way Planells can see her son is to travel to Jordan for short visits under her former husband's watchful eye. According to Planells, not only has the State Department been of little assistance, but a U.S. Foreign Service Officer at the embassy in Amman actually warned her ex-husband to be careful since his former wife was making "waves" in Congress and in the media.

Cathy asked Holly if anyone had ever rescued a child from a foreign country. Holly replied that the only successful attempt she knew of by an American mother to recover her child from an Islamic country involved Betty Mahmoody, who had been living in Iran and fled over the border to Turkey with her daughter. Mahmoody's story became a best-selling book and motion picture entitled *Not Without My Daughter*.

Around November 1987, although rapidly running out of options, Cathy was not about to give up. She turned to her faith for guidance, moving into a motel room, which she called a "prayer closet," to pray and fast and meditate. She went in exhausted and "totally confused," she says, and "cried out to the Lord to give me some answers." According to Cathy, she emerged after three days "a totally normal person," strengthened and restored. If no one would help her, she had concluded, she would take matters into her own hands.

She hatched a desperate plan to go to Jordan in disguise, and to locate and rescue Lauren herself. In the meantime, she wanted to make certain that she didn't do anything that would spook Ali or tip him off that she would stop at nothing to get Lauren back. She wanted to lull him into a false sense of security—especially since she knew he had relatives in Lebanon and might disappear with Lauren into that chaotic country if he got wind of any plan to rescue her. She called Jarash every day and babbled, often incoherently, to anyone who would listen, so that they would conclude that she was incapable of decisive action. Only once did Ali permit her to speak with Lauren, and then only for a few moments. Cathy also stayed in regular contact with Maisha, Ali's wife in New Jersey.

It was at this moment that she rediscovered the business card of the grand jury foreman, Al Zaponta, who had told her to give him a call if ever he could be of help. According to his card, he was an oil company lobbyist. If ever she needed a friend with connections, it was now. She picked up the phone and dialed his number. In the ensuing conversation, he urged her not to do anything rash and asked for time to explore some options.

Shortly before Christmas, Zaponta contacted her again and said that he might have located some well-qualified people who would carry out a rescue operation.

### "A REAL HEARTBREAKER"

As Don and Dave listened to Cathy Mahone's story, they grew more and more impressed with her single-minded commitment to recovering her daughter. Equally impressive was the briefing she had put together. It was almost military in tone and organization, and contained virtually everything they needed to know about herself, Lauren, and Ali. She had also compiled data about Ali's family, including the names of all his brothers, sisters, their spouses, their telephone numbers, approximate ages, physical descriptions, and personality profiles. She had even assessed whether they should be considered "aggressive" or "nonaggressive." There was a comprehensive description of Jarash that she had assembled from memory, noting the town's physical characteristics, roads leading in and out, the surrounding countryside, and what she believed was the location of the Bayan household, although she didn't have a record of its precise address. To the best of her ability, she tried to reconstruct the layout of the house, describing the bathrooms with the holes in the ceramic floors and the kitchen where the Bayan women cooked over propane gas bottles.

As the CTU men sifted through and examined the various photographs and maps she had brought with her, they both immediately seized on a photo of Cathy and Ali taken in 1979 on what Cathy remembered as the roof of the Bayan house.

"What's this?" inquired Dave, stabbing a thick forefinger at what appeared to be some kind of structure or ruins in the background.

"Those are Roman ruins," responded Cathy. "They're very famous."

"They shouldn't be hard to locate," injected Don.

"You're right," agreed Dave. "If we have any trouble finding the house, we can try to fix its location from the ruins."

Cathy was certain that Ali would be staying at the family home. That was where she had spoken with him, and it was where Lauren was when he had put her briefly on the line. She told the CTU men that while she was not completely familiar with Islamic customs, she knew that either Ali's mother or one of his sisters would have to be looking after Lauren because it would be inappropriate for a father to take care of a daughter's dressing, personal hygiene, and general upbringing.

Dave was particularly taken aback by her description of life in Jarash and the Bayan household. "It was hard to believe that a powerful and prominent family like the Bayans of Jarash would just straddle a four-inch hole in the floor to go to the bathroom," he reflected. "We're talking about a bath once a week on a Friday night," he added.

Both men were touched by Cathy's story. "[It] was a real heartbreaker," says Dave. Not only did it seem that right was on Cathy's side, but they were both fathers and could relate to the anguish she felt over losing her child. Moreover, what she was talking about was a real mission, the kind of operation they'd trained for all their lives and, in a few cases, had actually carried out. Don, in particular, could almost smell the cordite. He was tired of training cops and bodyguards, and missed the excitement and purpose that he associated with many of the missions he had carried out during his military career.

The only real problem was the money. They knew that they shouldn't consider the operation for anything less than $250,000. "We told her that we were looking, probably, for a sum in excess of a hundred thousand to do the job," says Dave. Cathy had sold her business and still had some of the money left, but $100,000 was beyond her reach, as she informed them. She indicated that she might be able to scrape together $50,000. According to Dave, "We told her that we needed at least one night to think about it before we could give her a decision." They promised to give her an answer the following morning.

It had been a long day, so the two men retired to one of their rooms to talk things over. The discussion lasted for several hours, as they debated the pros and cons of taking the job. Both men believed Cathy and found her case compelling. In view of her financial limitations, they also agreed at the outset that CTU would likely lose money on the deal. Then there were the risks to consider. Don and Dave had wives and families to think of, and neither had adequate life insurance or much of a financial cushion if something went wrong. Don didn't even have medical coverage.

Another concern was their lack of familiarity with Jordan. Although Don had spent time in Beirut as part of the Delta contingent protecting the U.S. ambassador, and had just returned, along with Dave, from a job in Israel, neither man had ever been to Jordan or spoke any Arabic. On the other hand, they were impressed with the wealth of intelligence that Cathy had provided them; it would save a good deal of time and effort. Their first goal would be to locate Lauren, then they would have to devise a plan to grab her and spirit her across the nearest border. The more they talked about the operation, the more feasible it seemed, despite the obvious obstacles.

In the end, their decision turned on emotional considerations more than anything else. They realized that Cathy was, according to Dave, in a "real jam" and didn't have any place else to turn. "I just felt like this woman did not deserve to lose her daughter," he says, explaining his reasons for wanting to take the case. "I also felt like the daughter did not deserve to be with a dirtbag like her daddy. Now we're talking about a car thief, a deceiver, a guy that stole money, plus a kidnapper. He had no use for that girl whatsoever. He knew he was taking her back to a life that she was totally unaccustomed to . . . to a world where she would no longer be an equal person, but a second-class citizen. Arabs treat their dogs better than they treat their women over there. I felt this little girl did not deserve it. The mother did not deserve it. And you could feel the heartfelt emotion of this woman missing her child. I mean, the child was her whole life. She had no husband, no job, no income, no support from anyone, and had lost the one thing in her life that she loved."

There was one other, perhaps more important, reason. In Don's words: "This was an American child, no different than any of the other Americans that had been abducted in Beirut or Tehran. This was an American child being held against her will in an Arab nation."

## CHOOSING THE TEAM

Cathy had gone to bed that night confident that Don and Dave would take her case. "Even before I met them," she said, "I had a peace about them . . . they were family men. They had children themselves."

The CTU men gave her the good news in the morning, but cautioned her that she shouldn't have any illusions about the mission. It was risky, dangerous, and there was no guarantee of success. All they could promise was to give it their best shot. Such operations, they continued, required careful planning and execution, as well as a large measure of luck.

Cathy indicated that she understood and would do whatever was required of her. They outlined various operational guidelines regarding security and communications, to which she readily acceded. In addition, she transferred $18,000 to CTU; the first of three payments that would total $50,000.

Dave and Don returned to Fayetteville to begin the operational planning and to select the team that would carry out the mission. As so many times in the past when they were in uniform, Christmas would take a back seat to the requirements of a mission.

It takes a special breed of man to make the grade in one of this nation's elite special operations units like Delta Force or its Navy equivalent, SEAL Team Six. Among veterans of such units there is an unspoken sense of fraternity and camaraderie, the result of having shared mind-numbing risks and extraordinary experiences. Many of the members of such units have traveled to the heart of darkness and back again in the performance of their duties, and are survivors of unsung battles and shadow wars. To such men, violence and death are not abstract concepts but are, or once were, their stock-in-trade. Theirs is a world of unspoken bonds and unwritten codes of behavior. And in a world of hype and hyperbole, their actions are often cloaked in mystery. Whereas their failures can be front-page news, their successes generally remain classified or attributed to other military units in order to preserve their anonymity.

It was from the pool of such men in Fayetteville that Don and Dave intended to recruit the other members of their rescue team. Considerable thought was devoted to identifying and assembling just the right mix of skills and backgrounds that would be needed. The first to be selected was a Tennessee native called James Daniel Roberts, better known as "J.D." A former Delta operator like Don, J.D. had worked off and on for CTU for over a year.

Forty-two years old at the time, J.D. is half American Indian and half Scottish. In celebration of his heritage, he carried a tomahawk on the raid into Iran to rescue the American hostages that ended at Desert One. A James Garner look-alike, with curly hair, an easy wit, and a broad smile, he has a warm exterior that hides lightning reflexes and an extraordinary capacity for controlled violence. Commenting on the contradictions in his character, J.D. concedes that he's easily moved to tears "while watching the flag raised or a movie like *Bambi*." By the same token, he adds, he'll "smash your face if you try to make fun of me."

According to J.D., he had never considered any other career but the Army. He enlisted on the same day that his father, a career Army man who had fought his way through Europe with Patton during World War II, retired. After boot camp, J.D. was shipped to Vietnam and celebrated his nineteenth birthday in the Mekong Delta.

Although a qualified sniper, he was selected to become the assistant to the battalion's chaplain. He had come to Vietnam to fight, not to pray, and J.D. was outraged. It wasn't until he learned that he was likely to see a lot more action as a chaplain's assistant than anything else that he began to calm down. The chaplain, he learned, moves from one scene of action to the next, ministering to the wounded and those in need. And sure enough, during the following twelve months, "I was in every battle the [First Battalion] of the 12th Cavalry was in." During his first tour of duty he won a Bronze Star, a Purple Heart, and other medals and citations.

Back from Vietnam, he went to the 101st Airborne Division, and then was sent to Officer Candidate School (OCS), graduating as a second lieutenant. Someone, however, read his orders wrong, and instead of being shipped off to the 10th Special Forces Group, as he had been assured, he was sent to the Army Special Services, where he "issued tennis shoes and basketballs for a year." His orders finally were straightened out and he joined the 10th Special Forces Group and was promoted to captain. He returned to Vietnam as a member of "Mike Force," but quickly ran afoul of an overbearing colonel who was poking him in the chest to make a point.

"I told him, 'Don't do that no more,' " says J.D.

But the colonel continued to poke J.D., who responded by decking him. "I poked him back," he explains with a grin.

In view of the seriousness of his offense, another colonel suggested that J.D. get as far away from headquarters as possible. He could arrange for him to take over a Special Forces "A" Team, he said, and J.D. readily agreed. He was flown out that night in a chopper to a fire base in the middle of the Delta. Tracers streaked through the night sky and flashes illuminated the flat landscape every few seconds as they drew closer.

As they swooped into the fire base, J.D. got out on one of the chopper's skids in preparation to jump off. But while they were still 12 or 14 feet off the ground, he felt a powerful blow in the small of his back, and the next thing he knew he was lying in the dirt, gasping for breath, in the middle of the fire base. The colonel had booted him in the back. As his wind began to return, he looked up into the twin barrels of a 12-gauge shotgun.

"Who the hell are you?" someone barked.

Before he could answer, an enemy attack on the fire base erupted. J.D. picked himself up out of the dirt and ran over to help man a mortar. When the attack finally petered out, J.D. introduced himself to one of the other men and, together, they walked over to the team house.

"What in the hell did they throw out of that chopper?" the team sergeant asked as they walked in the door.

"Our new commander," responded the man with J.D.

J.D. stepped forward and the sergeant shook his head. "I can't believe it."

"What do you mean?" asked J.D.

"We never had a replacement this fast before."

"Huh?"

"Look behind the bar."

J.D. walked over and behind the makeshift bar was the dead body of his predecessor, a young captain like himself. He had been killed earlier that day.

Although his debut was not auspicious, J.D. distinguished himself in the months that followed. It was a period of nearly nonstop combat, and at the end of his second tour he took pride in what he had accomplished. They had "run the tables" on the enemy many times, while suffering only light casualties in the many engagements. J.D. had established himself as a bona fide leader, who enjoyed the trust of his troops and the confidence of his superiors. He would have extended for yet another tour, but the war—for American forces—was winding down, and there were few billets available. Reluctantly, he returned to the United States.

After Vietnam, reductions in force were under way and there was no place for J.D., especially without a college degree, in the shrinking commissioned officer corps. Not wanting to leave the Army, he accepted a demotion to sergeant and for five years served as a Ranger instructor. When Delta came along, he went through one of the early selection courses and joined the unit. "I loved Delta," he reflects. "It was more than just a great unit: it was a family. Everybody had combat experience; all were Vietnam veterans. All of us were over thirty years old. All were married. In my squadron of forty-seven men, most of us were southerners or from the Midwest. Only one guy smoked. That's how evenly matched we were."

J.D. was with Delta's "B" Squadron, doing winter warfare training in the Colorado Rockies, when the U.S. Embassy in Tehran was seized by militants on November 4, 1979. B Squadron was ordered back immediately to the East Coast; however, they were told to cloak their movements in the utmost secrecy so as not to tip off the Iranians that they had been activated. As they returned to Denver, where a plane would be waiting for them, the rental truck carrying their gear broke down, so they rounded up seven station wagons and a small truck. The little convoyful of hard-looking, athletically built men, all dressed in similar clothing, arrived at Denver's Stapleton Airport, trying to look as inconspicuous as possible. Each vehicle was piled high with gear in large black military lockers with green military straps.

The plane that was supposed to pick them up was late, so they were forced to wait on the edge of the tarmac in their vehicles, with the engines running, trying to stay warm. At last, the chartered 727 arrived and a ground crewman began refueling it. However, after opening one of the wing tanks on the jet, the man disappeared. Soon, another member of the ground crew arrived on the scene, opened the fuel tank on the other wing, and began pumping fuel in. The transfer valves apparently were open, and as J.D. and his companions watched with horror, the fuel going in one wing began pouring out onto the tarmac from the open tank on the opposite wing. Soon there was fuel all over the tarmac and, when the mishap was discovered, fire engines were called in to foam the area and clean up the spill. This, in turn, attracted a local television crew, which began filming the incident.

The arrival of the TV crew produced tremendous consternation among the Delta commandos, well aware that the secrecy of the entire rescue mission would be compromised if the film crew had noticed the little convoy sitting in the shadows. While the television crew continued filming, the seven cars and one truck were quietly and inconspicuously backed around the corner of one of the hangars. Had the TV crew turned around, they surely would have spotted the Delta men and possibly scooped one of the biggest stories of the year. Instead, they finished their filming and departed, allowing the commandos to board the plane with no one the wiser.

J.D., Don, and the other Delta operators selected for the mission into Iran had spent nearly half a year at the CIA training facility known as "The Farm," near Williamsburg, Virginia. Their movements were restricted, and they were allowed to venture outside only when a Soviet satellite wasn't making a pass overhead. Finally, in late April 1980, "Operation Eagle Claw" was launched, with disastrous results. Too many of the choppers broke down en route to Desert One, the jumping-off point for Tehran, and the operation had to be scrapped. But during the refueling process at Desert One, in preparation for their withdrawal from Iran, one of the still-functioning choppers struck a C-130, causing a tremendous explosion that left at least eight American servicemen dead and a number severely injured, mostly with burns.

For J.D., like Don and the other survivors of Desert One, the memory of that terrible night in the Iranian desert is always with him. Although responsibility for the failure rested elsewhere, Delta was never the same after Desert One, says J.D. For J.D. and the other "old-timers" the fun was gone, replaced by the bitter reality of failure and the climate of accusation and denial that followed the abortive rescue mission. They were no longer "Jedi warriors," the elite of the elite, capable of taking on anyone or anything. They were mortal after all.

J.D. went on one more secret operation after Desert One, and narrowly escaped with his life. Tired and discouraged, he soon left the Army and retired to a family farm in Georgia on a $900-a-month pension. He decided that he would work the rest of his life toward the goal of getting a little place out west, someplace cold, perhaps in Montana or Colorado, where he could raise his kids quietly, cultivate a few acres, lay in enough meat every hunting season to sustain his family for the whole year, and maybe even do a little skiing.

When Don approached him with the offer to work with CTU, he quickly signed on. And when Don raised the possibility of coming along on the operation to rescue little Lauren Bayan, J.D. recalls that it took him "about three seconds" to consider the proposition before telling Don to count him in.

The final man selected for the team was Jim Hatfield, a husky six-footer raised in a small mining town in Arizona. The 30-year-old Hatfield has a laconic smile and penetrating eyes, and makes friends easily. Unlike the other CTU men, he says, "nobody ever shot at me." Discharged from the Rangers after being injured in 1984, he reenlisted and became an intelligence specialist with Special Forces.

Hatfield joined CTU as a firearms instructor and ultimately fell in love with and married Dave's daughter, Kayre. Everyone considered Jim a "steady hand"; but because of his lack of extensive operational experience, it was decided that he would be the "contact man" wherever they set up their operational headquarters, probably in either Israel or Cyprus, and would remain in reserve unless there was a real emergency.

## STUDYING OPTIONS

Now that the team was in place, the next step was to develop an actual mission plan. "Eighty percent of any mission," says Dave, "is planning. If the plan isn't good, the mission will most likely fail."

Don, Dave, and the other members of the rescue team worked virtually nonstop during the holidays, taking only a half day off to celebrate Christmas before returning to the office once again. In addition to travel arrangements and other preparations, their top priority was to develop a coherent mission plan. This effort once again underscored the differences between Don and Dave. According to Dave, "After Cathy left us that night, Donny said, 'This is a piece of cake. We just go inside, get the girl, and take her home.' But it was not going to be that easy. If it was going to be a 'piece of cake,' it would be because we turned every stone over in advance and looked at every option."

Soft-spoken and unflappable, Dave is CTU's professional "worrier" who, true to his training, analyzed every mission from every vantage point before settling on a course of action. The classic "intel" operator, he is both coldly calculating and extremely methodical. Although Don clearly recognizes the value of planning and blames the failure at Desert One, in part, on the fact that there was never a full rehearsal, he nevertheless feels that Dave can sometimes be so methodical that he loses the instinct for action.

Don argued that they didn't really have enough information to come up with a concrete plan of action. First, he said, they needed to put someone on the ground in Jordan to do a recon. Only then could they develop a viable rescue plan. Dave, however, was hesitant. While recognizing the need to get someone on the ground inside Jordan, he was adamant that they do as much work stateside as possible before heading off to the Middle East. In contrast to the unbridled enthusiasm of his colleagues, he knew that they were gambling the very future of CTU on the success or failure of one operation. Indeed, thoughts of possible failure, and its repercussions, haunted him.

While the rescue would be planned and executed like a military mission, the operation clearly differed on one critical point:

anyone captured would probably be tried as a criminal, or worse, as a mercenary, and sentenced to a long prison term. "We were concerned because of our military backgrounds," says Dave. "If anything went wrong in this operation, it would turn into 'American terrorists invade Jordan.' We were genuinely concerned that we would be labeled 'CIA,' or an undercover U.S. military operation. It would have given the Jordanians leverage against the United States, and it would probably have meant a longer jail term for us." It was unlikely, moreover, that the U.S. government would take any steps to intervene on behalf of the commandos in the event that something did go wrong, since Washington could be expected to distance itself from their actions as much as possible.

As Cathy would later observe, "They were risking their lives, because the Jordanians weren't going to let us walk out of the country with Lauren."

Since Ali had Lauren's passport, they initially discarded any thought of escaping from Jordan via plane, car, or boat, since all would require them to pass through border controls. They also rejected any method of leaving the country—such as ramming a Jordanian Army checkpoint with a truck—that might result in gunfire or place Lauren in jeopardy. It had to be a covert operation, discreet, and executed with precision. Prior to a reconnaissance of Jordan, the only plan of action that seemed to meet all their criteria was to grab little Lauren and "rucksack" her, that is, carry her piggyback, about 40 kilometers from Jarash to the Israeli border. It was, they knew, open country, sparsely populated, with little vegetation or water. Once at the border, they would make arrangements for the Israelis to provide them with safe conduct.

They didn't know it at the time, but their plan was hopelessly naive; the Israelis weren't about to permit anyone to cross their highly defended border on such a mission. In the end, Don was right: the mission plan would take far more knowledge of the area and Lauren's whereabouts before it could be finalized.

# 5
# "Is
# the Sun
# Shining?"

ON DECEMBER 27—only a week after first meeting with Cathy—Don, Dave, and J.D. Roberts departed North Carolina for Tel Aviv, where they had arranged to meet with several Israeli contacts whose help they would need in the rescue operation. To anyone outside their immediate circle, the CTU men would claim to be Hollywood moviemakers looking over Israel and Jordan as possible locations for a new motion picture. Since they previously had provided some of the security for *Rambo III*, which was filmed largely in Israel, Don was confident that no one would question their cover story.

Shortly after arriving in Israel, the CTU men sat down with their Israeli contacts to describe their real mission and outline their proposed plan of action. The Israelis, however, raised a number of problems. There was no way the rescue team could reach the heavily defended Israeli border without being mistaken for Palestinian infiltrators, they said. As to official Israeli cooperation, they were advised to forget it. The Israeli government was not about to take sides in a complicated custody struggle, especially when it involved former U.S. Delta Force commandos carrying out an illegal paramilitary operation in neighboring Jordan.

After being taken for a tour of the Israeli border and observing firsthand the security fences, tank traps, gun emplacements, and concertina wire, it was clear to Don, Dave, and J.D. that a different escape route was needed. "It was just impossible to cross the border between the two countries without being shot at by both sides," concluded Don. "And to take a frightened little girl with you on that path would just be suicidal."

Although no alternative plan of escape had been devised, it was decided that Dave should go ahead and reconnoiter Jarash to see if he couldn't discover Lauren's precise whereabouts, identify the various escape routes leading from the city, and get a general idea of the lay of the land. Dave was chosen for the assignment because he had the most extensive intelligence training and background, and had "lived inside the black envelope most of his life." He would travel using his own name and had secured a two-week tourist visa. If anyone questioned him, he would indicate that he was scouting possible movie locations, especially around the Roman ruins at Jarash. Once he had located Lauren, Don and J.D. would join him, and together, they would carry out the actual "snatch" and sprint the little girl to safety.

During this period, Cathy was advised to maintain her own counsel and not speak with anyone but Al Zaponta or someone from CTU about the mission. She was told to maintain her routine and to continue calling Ali, so as not to tip him off that something was afoot. Once Dave found Lauren—Don assured her—they would call and let her know, via a coded phrase, that her daughter was all right. As the signal, Cathy chose a phrase that had been suggested to her by Al Zaponta: "The sun is shining."

## GRANDPA

Like Cathy, Dave—or "Grandpa," as he was known around the firm—was originally from Texas. His roots are Cajun and Cherokee, although not much is known about his family tree. He recalls the solicitation one of his siblings received in the mail which began: "You come from a well-known and recognized French family, and this is your family crest. We'd like to trace your heritage . . ." "Well," he says, "she got all fired up by it and thought she'd be a social climber."

Inspired by the advertisement, Dave's sister went back to

Madisonville, Louisiana, a tiny Cajun hamlet with 799 residents, which lies directly across Lake Pontchartrain from New Orleans, to collect information about the family tree. What she found out was that their great-grandfather, on their father's side, was a Cherokee Indian who took the name Chatellier for reasons unknown. Little is known about the first member of the family to bear the Chatellier name, except that he was married to a German woman and died, after a short illness, in New Orleans. On Dave's maternal side, all of their relatives were of Cajun heritage, with names like Pelot, Goodeaux, and Badeaux.

His father was a ship caulker, but as wooden ships disappeared during the 1930s, he migrated to Orange, Texas, to look for work in the modern shipyards around Port Arthur. Orange lies on the banks of the Sabine River, across from Louisiana.

Dave was born in October 1939, in Orange, the youngest of four surviving children. He came to his parents late in their lives, just when they thought their child-rearing days were nearly over. One of his sisters was already married, and the next-closest sibling to Dave in age was a sister who was twelve years older.

His mother couldn't believe she was pregnant and went to the doctor, fearful that she had a tumor. The doctor informed her that "your tumor will be here sometime in October." Shortly after Dave was born, his family returned to Madisonville, where they remained for the next five years, until his father went to work again in the Texas shipyards. But a short time later he was injured in the shipyard, so he and his family returned yet again to Madisonville, where he farmed until his death in late 1946.

Dave's mother sold the farm and moved, for the third time, back to Orange, Texas, where she raised Dave. It was a marginal existence. His mother was a seamstress who made draperies, mostly for department-store customers. Dave was an average student and a good athlete, but he was more at home in the marshes of Texas and Louisiana than in school. His life, he recalls, "pretty much revolved around hunting, fishing, and trapping." He had started trapping muskrat and mink as a boy as a way to make extra money to support himself and his mother, and to pay for his school supplies and clothes.

By the time he reached high school, his favorite quarry was alligator and, true to his Cajun roots, he was becoming a successful poacher. A good alligator hide brought five dollars a linear foot, "which was big money in those days." In Texas, it was legal to hunt alligators but not so in Louisiana, which had a restricted season. "The problem was," says Dave, "there were no alligators in Texas. All the alligators were in Louisiana in game refuges, so that's where I did most of my hunting."

His regular hunting companion was another Cajun youth named Harold, who was from a family of poachers, and they would often go out all night in search of alligators in the Louisiana marshes. Their favorite hunting spot was about twenty-five miles— through marsh, swamp, and open water—from the Texas border, so when they killed a 'gator they would have to carry it back to Texas "to make it legal." They only had a small boat with a small motor, so "we had to be careful what size alligator we killed because you could only get so much in the boat with you and the rest of it you had to drag on the outside. And twenty-five miles is a long way by water."

There is an art to alligator hunting, says Dave. "You do it at night. You just shine your flashlight momentarily on the water, until you see the eyes of the 'gator. Then you go to him with your light out, get as close as you can, and ease up and hit him in the head with an ax." The danger is not so much from their enormous mouths and rows of razor-like teeth, he maintains, but their tails, "which can beat you to a pulp." What you do, says Dave, "is take your knife and run it down between its hind legs through the spine. That disables the tail, and then you can do anything with that ol' 'gator."

His mother, he says, was never neglectful of him, but being Cajun, didn't worry too much if he stayed out all night hunting in the marshes. To her, "frog hunting" was just something Cajun menfolk did. The only time she ever became truly angry over his exploits, recalls Dave, was on one occasion when he was a senior in high school. He and his friend Harold had gone alligator hunting, deep in the Louisiana marshes. It was late at night, and their light fell on several pairs of eyes poking up from beneath the water. They selected their target and went for it, but it turned out to be a much larger alligator than they expected, at least ten feet long. "It's hard to judge the size of a 'gator when you're just looking at the eyes sticking up," Dave laughs. He knocked the reptile in the head with his ax, then grabbed one of its rear legs and prepared to drive his knife into its spine. Although stunned, the alligator still had fight left in him. In the ensuing struggle, Dave missed the 'gator and plunged the knife into the top of his own thigh, all the way to the bone, where it stuck.

It took all his strength to pry the knife blade loose from the bone. Then he turned his attention back to the alligator, not wanting to lose a hide worth as much as $50. As Dave and Harold worked to pull the alligator into the boat, they were oblivious to the rising wind and the storm building off the coast. It was a hurricane. Soon the water began to heave and roll, even in the swampy marsh, and—as the storm built in intensity—large waves began to pound the boat. There was no way they could cross miles of open water, Dave realized. They would have to ride out the storm in the marsh.

By this time, his leg was beginning to throb and swell, with "the meat beginning to pucker out" of the two-inch wound. He tied an old rag around it as a pressure bandage and to staunch the blood.

As the full force of the storm hit the coast, Dave's mother became worried. She called the Coast Guard and the local game warden to advise them that her son and another boy had "gone frog hunting" in the marshes and hadn't returned home. As the fury of the storm began to dissipate, Dave and Harold started making their way slowly up the coast toward Texas, unaware of the fact that Dave's mother had sounded the alarm and that the Coast Guard and the game wardens were searching for them.

"Of course, Harold and I had an alligator in the boat and we didn't want anybody to find us," recalls Dave. Every time they saw a Coast Guard vessel or game warden's boat, they would slip back into the marshes and hide until it passed. As a result, it took most of the following day for them to return. When he got home, instead of being welcomed with open arms, Dave found his mother frantic with worry and fit to be tied. "She jumped on me like a rooster," he laughs. His mother was a tiny woman, not more than 5 feet tall and 110 pounds, but she whipped her 6-foot, 200-pound son "to within an inch of my life. I never thought a little ol' lady could whip anyone that hard."

As Dave approached his twenty-first birthday, color television was just beginning to appear in American homes and his goal in life was to be a television circuit-design engineer, "making thousands and thousands of dollars." He had spent three years at various colleges studying electrical engineering, but had run out of money and was forced to look for a job. However, the first question he was always asked was: "Have you completed your military obligation?" Companies didn't want to make an investment in someone who soon would be drafted. In order to satisfy his military commitment and pursue his interest in electronics, Dave joined the Air Force, the only service to promise him technical training and an appropriate M.O. (military occupation). Ironically, he had never had an ambition to fly. "I really felt that if God wanted man to fly, he would have given us wings instead of arms and legs," says Dave.

After a year of training as a "wires and pliers" technician, Dave was assigned to a secret unit that set up and maintained ground-based listening posts around the globe, which eavesdropped on signals and communications traffic in both enemy and friendly countries. He also married his high school sweetheart, but it was a rocky marriage, punctuated by Dave's frequent overseas assignments. His job, he says, "was not really conducive to good married life. The homecomings were great, but after that it was just a lot of tension as to, when are you going next time? Where are you going? And I'd have to say, I can't tell you, and she'd say, why do all these other guys get to stay here on the air base and you have to be gone all the time?" The arrival of three children, two daughters and a son, did little to solidify the marriage.

Soon he transferred to the Air Force's Special Activities Group, and after German-language instruction and additional training was sent as a case officer to handle agents in the Eastern bloc. In order to monitor shipping on the Baltic Sea, Dave would slip into East Germany, posing as a tourist, and recruit sailors from target ships to report on their cargoes. For several years his life centered on "dead drops" and high-risk clandestine meetings. After the defection of one of the unit's polygraph operators to Communist Czechoslovakia, it was assumed that he had "burned" all of the sources and case officers he knew, and so Dave was pulled out of Europe and sent back to Texas.

By his own account, Dave was a vastly different person in those days. In contrast to his present teetotaling, noncussing, born-again ways, during the late sixties and early seventies he was, by his own definition, "wild and woolly," rarely passing up a bottle or a good fight. Quick to take offense, he once got into a fight with a huge black airman who cut in front of him in the mess line. Dave hit the man so hard that he knocked him through a door and out onto the grass. On another occasion, he took on three sailors single-handedly, put one in the hospital, and ended up in jail. Fighting, Dave observes, was just part of life in the military thirty years ago. "You didn't go to the JAG officer and take out charges against your first sergeant or some of the troops. You fell out behind the bar-racks, and that's where you settled things."

He spent the years from 1967 to 1971 in and out of Vietnam, working as part of two- and three-man teams deep behind enemy lines to plant and maintain the listening devices used to monitor enemy troop movements and the Ho Chi Minh Trail. His unit was so secret that few knew what they were up to, and on more than one occasion, he and his team were caught in the middle of a firefight or pitched battle between the North Vietnamese and U.S. forces. "We would just be on a road or trail, and without the friendlies knowing we were in the area, and they would just start lobbing stuff in," he remembers.

After Vietnam, he returned to the States and found that his wife had "sorta reverted back to a teenager. Instead of getting older and maturing, she became a hip-hugging, mini-skirted, braless rock-'n'-roll queen." They soon divorced and Dave later got cus-tody of the three children. In 1975, he met his present wife, Diane, an Army lieutenant, and the following year they were married. Dave subsequently was transferred to Fort Bragg, where he worked as part of the ongoing effort to create an Army anti-terrorism capability, which ultimately became Delta Force.

After he retired from the service in 1981, he farmed his spread outside Fayetteville and worked part time with a "black hat" team, assessing security at Department of Energy installations. He also opened The Bow Hunter in a local mall, which he was operating at the time he met Don.

Those who know Dave are unanimous in one assessment of him: he's the kind of guy you want at your side in a crisis. His ability to take control of a situation is evident in an incident that happened a few years ago in North Carolina. He was walking in the woods with a deputy sheriff when the man's .38 Super Cal. pistol discharged accidentally. According to Dave, the bullet entered the top of the man's thigh, "next to his scrotum, and passed right through the femoral artery." He immediately passed out, his eyes began to dilate, and he turned a deathly gray. His breathing was shallow, almost imperceptible. Dave ran over to the deputy and stripped down his pants to find that the wound was gushing blood. He stuck his thumb down into the bullet hole to pinch off the artery, and began working to revive the man, a process that took nearly five minutes. They were more than a mile from the nearest vehicle and 15 miles from the nearest hospital, Dave told the wounded man. "I'm gonna carry you out on my back," he continued. "But you've got to talk to me the whole time 'cause if you lose consciousness, you'll go into shock.

"I doubled up his fist and stuck his thumb down the hole and then wrapped his fist over it," relates Dave. "Then I picked him up and put him over my shoulder, so that his body weight was on top of his fist like a pressure bandage." Dave managed to carry the wounded deputy out of the forest and keep him alive until a rescue team could get there and transport him to the nearest hospital. Although he had lost an enormous amount of blood, the man survived, thanks to Dave's quick thinking, medic training, and physical strength.

## JOURNEY TO JARASH

In January 1988, Dave flew from Israel to Cyprus, and then on to Amman, where he booked a room at the Amman Holiday Inn and rented a car from Avis. The following day, he drove to Jarash.

In antiquity, the city of Jarash was known as Gerasa, and was a member city of the Decapolis—one of the ten cities that served as a buffer zone between the Roman province of Syria and the independent Nabataean Kingdom remembered for the cities of Petra and Avdat. Located astride important trade routes, Jarash had prospered under Roman rule and been the site of an ambitious building program. Today, Jarash's Roman forum, theater, and Temple of Zeus are world-famous, listed in most guides as outstanding monuments of Greco-Roman culture and civilization.

It quickly became clear to Dave that doing a recon of Jarash would present a number of formidable problems. Few tourists, he learned, ventured into Jarash itself. The road from Amman leads to a police station on the edge of town, and to a nearby parking lot from which tourists are taken to the Roman ruins. "Most tourists never see Jarash," says Dave. "Tourists or foreigners rarely drive or walk through the streets of modern Jarash. Not only could I not easily locate the house, but my very presence in the city of Jarash was very unusual." In order to make himself less conspicuous, Dave donned an Arab headdress and grew a goatee.

To further complicate his task, Dave found that the streets of Jarash are, for the most part, extremely narrow, permitting only one car to pass at a time. Many of the streets have no apparent names and the houses are not numbered. There were no Western hotels or restaurants where he could easily blend in, so Dave resolved to commute each day from Amman.

His first task was to identify the Bayan house. This was made more complicated by the fact that he couldn't risk asking anyone for the address without the word getting back that a stranger was in town asking questions about them. All he had to go on was the photo of Cathy and Ali on the rooftop, with the Roman ruins in the background, and Cathy's vague recollection of where the house was situated. "What I had to do was go to the Roman ruins and shoot an azimuth back to Jarash," says Dave, referring to a navigation technique for calculating another location from a fixed point. But he soon discovered that Jarash had changed dramatically in the nearly ten years since the photo was taken: the city had grown in size; extensive new Roman ruins had been unearthed, making it difficult to identify the precise set of ruins in the photo; and new development had obscured much of the view between the ruins and the neighborhood where they expected to find the Bayan house.

Despite these obstacles, Dave threw himself into the effort with enthusiasm. On his first trip to Jarash, he pulled into the tourist lot and paid a fee of 1.5 dinars, which allowed him to park there all day. He spent four hours taking pictures of the ruins and the city of Jarash from the Temple of Zeus. From the ruins he also surveyed the city as unobtrusively as possible, using an eight-power monocular. Through the monocular, his eye fixed on a house that certainly appeared to be the Bayan residence. He couldn't believe his good luck, especially since a cold, freezing rain that chilled him to the bone was beginning to fall. He returned to his car and drove into the city in an attempt to locate the house he had spotted from the ruins, but the rain soon turned into snow, making driving treacherous and obscuring his visibility. Nevertheless, after more than an hour of searching he finally managed to find the house. He stopped and took pictures of the ruins from close by so that he could try to match the backdrop in the photo. He concluded the day by driving around the city and familiarizing himself with its streets, buildings, and potential escape routes.

Because of the heavy snow, few people were on the streets to take note of Dave's meanderings. However, as the snow began to pile up, he nearly got stranded in Jarash because there is no snow-removal equipment and the only effort local authorities make to keep the roads clear is to run army trucks up and down the highways. He made his way slowly back to Amman, arriving well after dark, but satisfied that he was close to accomplishing his objective.

The following day, he returned to Jarash to continue his reconnaissance. But his first discoveries hardly came as good news. Much to his dismay, there was a police station located almost directly behind the house he believed was the Bayan residence. Even worse, there was an army post at the end of the street. Not only would the nearby police and military presence make a snatch from the house very risky, but it meant that he would have to be extremely careful not to be spotted surveilling it.

Over the next day and a half, Dave watched the house without seeing anyone who resembled Ali or little Lauren, and began to wonder if he hadn't jumped too quickly to the conclusion that he had the right house. As the hours passed, his doubts mounted. To clear his head, he drove down to the city's central market and sat alone in his car turning the options over in his mind. Then, suddenly, without warning, he glimpsed a group of children being led through the marketplace by a woman who resembled one of Ali's sisters. The woman was holding a young girl by the hand, a young girl with blue eyes and a pug nose. It was Lauren.

In the days that followed, Dave never saw Lauren again. He continued to maintain his surveillance of the suspected house without success, and soon began to investigate other houses as well.

Gradually, he came to know the rhythms and routines of Jarash. The rush hour began around 6:00 A.M., when hundreds of buses converged on the city to pick up people and transport them to work, often in Amman. Between 7:30 and 8:00 A.M., school buses appeared on the streets. All of the children were dressed identically in school uniforms: blue for grade school students, green for middle school. Buses were segregated, with girls boarding one bus and boys another. Each bus appeared to have a chaperone. Dave never saw children alone or standing on the street. Generally, they waited until the school bus appeared, and only then left the house or protected confines of a walled courtyard.

At least he didn't have to worry about dogs, thought Dave, which are often a real nuisance when conducting surveillance. There were no dogs in Jarash; the only dogs Dave ever saw roamed in packs in the countryside. There were, however, lots of rats and, as a result, literally thousands of cats in Jarash. "We saw some major rats [in Jarash]," contends J.D. "Rats so big it would take four cats to whip one of 'em."

Initially, Dave was bothered by all of the stares he received from pedestrians as he drove around the city. Wherever he went, it seemed like people would turn and look right at him. He soon figured out that they were afraid that he was going to splash them as he drove along the rutted streets full of potholes filled with water. Indeed, most people in Jarash walked in the middle of the street in order to force traffic to slow down so they wouldn't be splashed.

To minimize the risk of someone recognizing the vehicle, Dave exchanged his rental car every two or three days. This required him to come up with a variety of novel complaints and excuses to get Avis to take back his old car and give him a new one. But Avis was very accommodating, and in the space of two weeks he used six different cars. Nevertheless, he continued to worry about attracting suspicion, so he generally parked and then prowled the city on foot.

Every day as he drove to and from Jarash, Dave was stopped at police checkpoints along the road, sometimes as many as three times in the space of 50 kilometers. At the checkpoints he would hold up his American passport and just start talking. If the policeman did not speak English, he normally would wave Dave through

just to get him to shut up. If he spoke a little English, and attempted to ask him for his license, Dave would plead ignorance,
and ultimately the policeman would relent and let him continue on
his way. The experience of dealing with the Jordanian police at
road checkpoints would later prove to be invaluable in helping
Dave understand their mentality and in ascertaining how much he
could get away with. Dave soon discovered that the Jordanian
police never set up a checkpoint in Jarash; they were always placed
outside of town on the highways and country roads. Another problem was that the green tags on Dave's rental car clearly announced
that he was not a local, and any time he pulled over to the side of
the road, he attracted unwanted attention. Invariably someone—a
soldier, a policeman, or just an ordinary citizen—would come by
and inquire if anything was wrong or just what he was doing.

## OTHER OPTIONS

In view of the difficulty locating Lauren, Don meanwhile was
actively pursuing other options in an effort to secure the girl's
return to her mother. At the suggestion of one of their Israeli
contacts, he met with a local journalist who maintained close ties to
Jordan's former queen, Dina. Dina had been King Hussein's first
wife and currently resided in London. The journalist Aharon
Barneha was planning a trip to London later in the week; he agreed
to meet with Dina and to see if she would be willing to contact the
Jordanian government on Cathy's behalf.

Don also went to the U.S. Embassy in Tel Aviv to learn what,
if anything, the American government might do to assist them. The
embassy official he met with provided him with little more than a
copy of the Hague Convention and the name of one of his coun-
terparts in Jordan, Thomas K. Brown [not his real name], whom he
said handled such cases.

Don passed along Brown's name to Dave in a telephone conversation, and Dave gave him a call on January 14, saying that he
was in Amman and wanted to discuss the case of a child that had
been abducted from the United States. Brown told him to drop by
the embassy, and a short time later Dave presented his passport,
for identification purposes, at the consular affairs office. He was

told that Brown would see him shortly and requested to take a seat in the crowded waiting room. While in the military, Dave had spent a good deal of time in U.S. embassies and generally viewed Foreign Service Officers as competent and helpful; he had no reason to doubt that Brown would be anything else.

After waiting for more than an hour, a tall, prissy man finally called Dave's name and he approached a bulletproof glass window. "What's the nature of your business?" asked Brown.

"I spoke to you on the phone," answered Dave, raising his voice in order to be heard over the din in the background.

Brown didn't respond.

"Isn't there someplace we can speak privately about this?" Dave suggested, not wanting to discuss such a sensitive matter in front of a room full of Jordanian citizens.

Brown still didn't respond.

"I've never been denied a private meeting with a U.S. consular official before," Dave pressed.

Brown answered that he was extremely busy: couldn't Dave see how many people were waiting for him? If Dave wanted to talk, said Brown, it would have to be in the waiting room.

Under the circumstances, Dave reluctantly explained that he wanted some advice about an abducted U.S. citizen.

"Is this a child you are talking about?"

"Yes."

"Well, I'll read this to you," Brown said, fumbling for a piece of paper. "I wrote this down somewhere. I think I've still got it." Finally, he found the paper and began reading from it, informing Dave that the U.S. Embassy could not get involved in matters relating to the abduction of children, even if the child was a U.S. citizen. He stated that if the child was with a Jordanian, the Jordanian had all the legal rights, and that he would not support the mother's claim because she did not live in Jordan.

"We're talking about an American citizen," Dave shot back incredulously. "Are you telling me that you will not help an American citizen?"

"No," Brown corrected him. "That's not what I am saying. What I am saying is that I cannot and will not help the mother. Regardless of where the child was born, and regardless of how it got here, if the child's in Jordan, it is considered a Jordanian resident." He then gave Dave a form letter pertaining to child custody disputes, and said that if he was formally requested to do so by the Department of State in Washington, he would perform a health and welfare inspection. But he would not do anything else. Brown recommended that the mother retain a Jordanian attorney and take the father to court. In closing, he warned Dave against doing anything that would violate Jordanian law, saying that if he knew what child Dave was making inquiries about, he would warn the father.

Reluctant to waste any more time, Dave thanked Brown and left. He hadn't expected a great deal from the embassy, but he had hoped for more than Brown had given him. Moreover, he went away offended by Brown's lack of compassion for the American mother and his willingness to side so unquestioningly with the Jordanian position.

Dave was now convinced, more than ever, that the only way Lauren ever would be reunited with her mother would be if they mounted a successful rescue operation. His primary goal now was to find an acceptable overland escape route. He ruled out any attempt to exfiltrate the rescue party through either Saudi Arabia or Iraq, since both borders were too far away. Jarash, however, was close to both Israel and Syria.

Dave checked out the southern Jordanian port city of Aqaba, which lies just two kilometers from the Israeli port of Eilat, first. The rescue team could easily reach the Israeli coast from Jordan with a small boat or Zodiac raft. But it took him eight hours to reach Aqaba from Jarash, and when Dave got there, he discovered a brigade-sized military force stationed in the city. Shtire armored vehicles, with 50-caliber machine guns mounted on the turrets, seemed to be everywhere. The streets were full of soldiers, and every major intersection had five or six policemen in it.

In view of the time it would take to drive to Aqaba, there was little likelihood that the rescue team could get there before the police and military had been alerted and placed on the lookout for Lauren and the commandos. However, even if they could reach Aqaba without being discovered, then what? They would still be in Jordan. Dave could see the Israeli city of Eilat in the distance, and even thought of swimming to it with Lauren on his back; but he soon gave up the idea as impractical. There was no way of knowing what kind of defenses the Israelis had in terms of mines and frog-man nets, and it would place Lauren in too much danger. Reluctantly, Dave abandoned Eilat as a possible escape route.

He returned to Jarash and decided to investigate the Syrian border. He drove northward toward Syria, but the closer he came to the border, the worse the road became. At times, he had to slow to a crawl because of the potholes and broken pavement. He knew the Jordanians would not expect the rescue team to escape via Syria because of its tight border controls and pervasive police state apparatus, but these same factors made such an escape problematic and very risky.

Thus, by process of elimination he knew that they would have to escape from Jordan by crossing into Israel at some point other than Aqaba. The only real option now left was the Allenby Bridge, linking Jordan and the Israeli-dominated West Bank. He would have to find the fastest route to the bridge from Jarash, and then worry about how to get Lauren across without the appropriate stamps in her passport.


## REINFORCEMENTS

Ever since the rescue team left for the Middle East, Cathy had sat by her phone in Texas waiting for the word that "The sun is shining." But it never came.

As the days passed without result, Don decided that they might need Cathy's help. He called her from Israel.

"Is the sun shining?" she asked expectantly.

"No," responded Don. He could almost hear her disappointment on the other end of the line. He asked her if she would fly to Cyprus, and she readily agreed. He told her she would be met by Jim Hatfield.

On Friday, January 13, Israeli journalist Aharon Barneha returned from London to Tel Aviv with the news that Queen Dina had flatly refused to get involved in the matter. It turned out that she had tried to help in an earlier case and had gotten burned, and therefore was reluctant to do anything to assist Cathy. As their other options dried up, Don—like Dave—was coming to the con-

clusion that only a rescue was likely to produce results. So, he and
J.D. left Israel for Cyprus, where they met briefly with Cathy
before continuing on to Amman.

She told them that a few days before coming to Cyprus, she
had finally lost her temper when speaking to Ali on the phone,
screaming that he was "no good," a "rotten wimp," and "a thief,"
and so on, until he hung up on her.

Don and J.D. rendezvoused with Dave at the Holiday Inn on
the 18th. According to Dave, "Donny felt that since I had seen
Lauren, we ought to just go take care of it. I felt, however, there
was a lot more to do before we could go and get her." Dave
convinced his confederates that their operational intelligence was
still incomplete and that more time was required in Jarash. While
the presence of three Americans would certainly increase the risk
of unwanted attention, the extra manpower would mean that they
could do the kind of surveillance required to produce results.

The three men drove to Jarash the following day and went to
work, but their presence certainly didn't go unnoticed. By now,
Dave was a reasonably familiar figure around Jarash. "Dave tried to
be covert and sneaky," observes J.D., "but when you are six foot
three and built like a small mountain, it's rather hard to do when
everyone else hits you chest-high." Don, too, had his problems.
Despite his efforts to blend in with the locals, kids would approach
him with a big smile and try out their English on him. J.D., who
has a dark complexion and was sporting a heavy black mustache,
fared only slightly better.

Time was running out. They could not count on their luck
holding forever; soon, someone was bound to get suspicious about
the foreigners in Jarash and mention something to the authorities.

It was now more vital than ever that they locate the Bayan
house. They continued to maintain surveillance on the house earlier identified by Dave. They also went back to the ruins and, now
that there were three of them, attempted to identify the right
house by means of triangulation. But the results were still inconclusive. Their frustration was mounting.

They finally decided to risk a close-up look at the house that
Dave had been watching, and under the cover of darkness J.D.
approached the house from the rear. It was late, and everything
was still. Suddenly he heard voices behind him. Searching around

desperately for someplace to hide, he slipped into a crack in a crumbling wall that bordered the alley. As he flattened himself against the wall in the shadows, two local men stopped just a few feet away, lit up cigarettes, and engaged in an animated discussion. They talked until their cigarettes were finished, then they ground them out and continued on their way. J.D. moved closer to the house, but there was no visible activity; nothing to indicate who lived inside. He waited for several minutes. Still nothing. Ultimately he rejoined his companions, discouraged and empty-handed.

It was now obvious that they were going to need Cathy Mahone's help. Not only could she probably identify the Bayan house, but the more they thought about it, she could provide other valuable assistance, too. Her presence would be needed to calm and reassure Lauren during the actual rescue. Although they had planned on showing Lauren photographs of themselves with her mother, they could not count on her reaction. Even if no alarm had yet gone out, two or three American men traveling with a terrified, or possibly hysterical, young girl was bound to raise suspicions at the various checkpoints they would have to go through.

After spending so much time in Jarash, moreover, Dave had concluded that the best place to grab the girl was on her way to or from school. From watching the school buses leave Jarash in the morning, he was convinced that she was not attending school in Amman, as Cathy had earlier been led to believe. But if her school was not in Amman, where was it?

It was time to call Cathy again.

Don placed a call from Amman, and in guarded language instructed Cathy to reestablish contact with Ali and to attempt, if at all possible, to learn where Lauren was going to school. "I don't care what you do," he explained. "Promise him anything. Grovel, beg, cry—anything. Just find out where Lauren is going to school."

Accordingly, Cathy placed a call to Ali and apologized for her earlier outburst, letting him assume that she was phoning from Dallas. She pleaded with him for news of her daughter. He told her that Lauren was all right.

"What do you mean, 'all right'?" she demanded. "She doesn't even speak Arabic."

"I've got her in a new private school here in Jarash," he responded. "She is learning Arabic and doing just fine." Then Ali put Lauren on the phone and she told her mother that she was the biggest child in the class.

Cathy quickly passed the information on to the CTU team, and after a few inquiries, Dave learned the location of the new private school in Jarash. He also found out from one of the local citizens that pupils rode to and from the school in a little orange school bus.

The following day, while Don stayed in Amman to handle other details, Dave and J.D. returned to Jarash. Both men are born-again Christians, and en route they decided to pray for God's help in "achieving their objective": locating little Lauren. According to J.D., the prayer went something like "Lord, we have been doing this for almost three weeks and have got no results. We need your help. It will not happen without your help. So please, if you want this thing to work, help us."

A little while later, as they parked along a narrow street in Jarash, a small orange school bus passed by, and there, in the front seat of the bus, was Lauren, "looking at me through the window," recalls J.D. "All I saw were these two big blue eyes and that pushed-up nose. But I had no doubt in my mind [who it was]." Dave was driving, and he took off in pursuit of the bus.

"Dave is used to covert stuff in Europe, spy versus spy," says J.D. "So he's trying to follow this bus, staying back two city blocks. That doesn't work well in Jarash. We lost the bus in five minutes." However, a few minutes later they spotted the bus again and continued their surveillance until it reached the school. J.D. worried that their car was too visible and that the driver would pick up on the surveillance. "We're in a red Nissan," he laughs. "I mean fire-engine red. It stands out like a maraschino cherry in a snowbank."

Fortunately, nothing happened. If he noticed the red Nissan at all, the bus driver didn't seem bothered by it.

Over the next several days, Dave and J.D. continued to follow the bus on its daily rounds. The driver took a highly circuitous route, sometimes doubling back on the same street twice to pick up children. Dave and J.D. were mystified, and only later realized that the children were never permitted to cross a street to board the bus; indeed, every child climbed aboard on the right side, after being handed over to the chaperone on board by a family member or household retainer. No child was ever allowed to be in the open for more than a few seconds. The practice had evolved as a result of blood feuds. In the Arab world, vengeance is sometimes visited on a family's children for alleged sins committed by parents and even grandparents. Thus, children are closely watched and protected, and never left out of sight.

While Dave and J.D. continued the search for the Bayan house in Jarash, Don was in Amman making arrangements to get across the Allenby Bridge when the moment came for them to escape. One of those he turned to for advice was the Assistant Regional Security Officer (ARSO) of the U.S. Embassy, Frank Baker. As a former Delta Force member and embassy protection specialist, Don was part of the "old boy" network and, when he traveled abroad, he often stopped by to get acquainted with the RSO (Regional Security Officer) and ARSO. Baker, a quiet and unassuming Marine veteran who had previously served in Beirut, had never met Don before, but he welcomed him and extended him the kind of professional courtesy he would to anyone with Don's background.

Don never told Baker his real mission in Jordan, but instead inquired about Jordanian security precautions and border controls. He asked Baker for the name of a trusted Jordanian citizen who might serve as a guide, and Baker introduced him to Adil Abdilhafiz Abdilrahman Abbadi, a part-time employee of the embassy who occasionally served as a guide and expeditor for visiting Americans. The thirty-four-year-old Abbadi is a former Jordanian military officer, a Boeing 747 pilot for Royal Jordanian Airlines, and a father of three children. Don hired him to assist in the rescue effort.

Abbadi's reach into the government was evident when he took Don and J.D. to the Ministry of the Interior to secure passes for the Allenby Bridge. He seemed to know everyone, and quickly obtained passes for the two CTU men. However, the ministry official would not issue passes for Cathy and Lauren until Cathy appeared in person at the ministry.

Now was the moment for Cathy to come to Amman. Don called her in Cyprus and told her, "You're going to have to come and help us." She took the first available flight to Jordan, "terrified that maybe my face would be on a poster at the airport." She was met by Don, Dave, and J.D., and they drove her straight to Jarash in a newly rented car. To avoid anyone recognizing them, the CTU men wore Arab headdresses and Cathy donned a scarf. They arrived in Jarash just before nightfall. She was to rely on her memory, they told her, to find the Bayan house; they weren't going to give her any hints. Initially, everything seemed strange and different to her; it had been, after all, almost a decade since she had last been in Jarash.

They passed through the city without triggering her memory in the least, and then decided to give it another shot. On the second swing through the city, Cathy suddenly remembered the house where Ali's aunt lived. It turned out to be the one that Dave and his companions had been watching for days. Then it all came back to her in a flood of memories: the pictures had been taken on the roof of the aunt's house, not on the roof of the Bayan family home. The CTU men had spent days looking for the wrong house.

She also recalled that the Bayan house had been located near a drugstore owned by Ali's uncle. The house was just around the corner from the drugstore, she continued. She remembered walking there once.

From all the time he had spent in Jarash, Dave knew that all of the drugstores and doctors' offices were located near the central business district, in a quarter that was a little off the beaten track. He drove her to the district and found a drugstore that looked familiar to her. They proceeded past the drugstore at a crawl until Cathy indicated a dark side street a short distance away.

"Are you sure?" Dave questioned.

"When I looked down the street, I got a cold chill," she responded.

Tension mixed with relief as they turned up the street and spotted, among the Mercedes sedans owned by the doctors in the neighborhood, a white Honda Accord with Texas tags.

Cathy began to tremble. "It's him," she said, indicating two men near the Honda. One of them was handing the other a transistor radio. "It's Ali!"

They continued on, trying to make themselves invisible by scrunching down in their seats. Fortunately, it was dark and Ali was engrossed in conversation. Cathy pointed out the Bayan family home. Unbelievably, the house was only a few hundred feet from the school, which was located on the other side of the street. Although she could have easily walked to school, Lauren was subjected to a lengthy bus ride every day because of the local preoccupation with security and the fact that it simply wasn't local practice for children to walk to school.

After days of fruitless searching and endless hours of surveillance, they had finally reached their objective. All that remained was to learn where and when Lauren boarded the bus.

## FINAL PREPARATIONS

The following morning, Abbadi took Cathy to the Interior Ministry to get the passes entitling her and Lauren to cross the Allenby Bridge. It had been decided that once they had grabbed Lauren, Cathy, Don, and J.D. would head for the Allenby Bridge. Since Lauren had entered Jordan on her Jordanian passport, and was going to leave using her U.S. passport, which had been brought by her mother, she would be missing a vital entry stamp. Abbadi assured them that for a little money the officials at the bridge would overlook the matter of the entry stamp. They agreed that Dave would remain behind to pay off Jordanian officials at the bridge, to return the cars, and to run interference in the event that there was hot pursuit by the Jordanian police or military. He would then walk or take a plane out later, depending on the circumstances.

In order to identify the quickest route from Jarash to the Allenby Bridge, Dave and J.D. combed the highways and back roads throughout the area. Because of the poor condition of most of the roads, they concluded that they would have to stay on the primary one leading to the bridge. There were only two checkpoints, but occasionally the police threw up random checkpoints which they could not anticipate.

If everything went without a hitch, it would take them approximately an hour to reach the Allenby Bridge from the city limits of Jarash. Dave and J.D. stopped at the bridge and checked the hours that it was open for crossing. That accomplished, they returned to Amman to get some sleep. They would have to be up bright and early the next morning, for they still lacked one last vital piece of information: did Lauren actually live in the Bayan household?

They were waiting for the bus when it appeared at the house the following morning. Dave and Cathy were in the car, its engine idling. Don and J.D. were loitering in an alleyway across the street. A minute or two before the bus chugged into view, the front door of the house opened and one of Ali's aunts appeared, holding Lauren by the hand. They walked to the edge of the street and the aunt stood with her hand on the girl's shoulder. When the bus pulled up in front of the house, the aunt physically turned her over to the chaperone. Lauren climbed on board and the bus continued on its rounds, traveling to the outskirts of the city and then back again until it reached the school. From door to door, Lauren spent approximately twenty minutes on the bus.

Without waiting around any longer, the CTU men left Jarash and headed for Amman. They had spent too much time in Jarash already and had been lucky that no one had grown suspicious. Now they had all of the "intel" necessary to do the job. The only real decision that remained was where to grab the girl.

On the way back to Amman, they weighed the various options. They could take Lauren from her aunt as they waited for the school bus in the morning, but the alarm would go out so quickly that they probably would be apprehended before they even got out of Jarash. They could blow up Ali's car in downtown Jarash as a diversion, and simultaneously stop the bus and grab Lauren. But such an operation, even if well planned and executed, ran the risk of innocent casualties. The CTU men did not want to be branded as mercenaries or terrorists, and thus ruled out any thought of using violence to effect the rescue. It had already been decided that they would not carry firearms on the operation.

Finally, the decision was made to snatch Lauren from the bus as it made its morning rounds. Initially, they thought about hijacking the bus, taking it to a remote location, taping the driver and the chaperone like mummies, and making a run for the border with Lauren. However, such a plan might result in some harm to the other children, and would certainly traumatize them. Other parents would be outraged, and the Jordanian authorities would surely view it as kidnapping. Also, there really wasn't any place to hide the bus near Jarash where it wouldn't be readily discovered.

The best plan, they concluded, would simply be to snatch Lauren when the bus stopped on the outskirts of Jarash to pick up the two children who lived furthest from the school. Lauren would already be on the bus, and they could leave directly for the Allenby Bridge without having to fight the traffic in Jarash.

When they reached Amman, Dave made reservations for Cathy and Lauren on Alia, the Royal Jordanian Airline, departing Amman at 10:45 A.M. for New York the next day. While he had no intention of putting them on the flight, Dave figured that the reservation might buy them some extra time during the actual escape. He had no way of knowing it, but his ruse would later prove crucial.

Two Nissans—one white and one red—had been rented for the operation, and Abbadi was advised to be ready. He would meet Don, J.D., Cathy, and Lauren at the Allenby Bridge and accompany them through passport control, where his brother-in-law was scheduled to be on duty. Once they were safely in Israel, Dave would pay Abbadi and give him the keys to one of the rental cars. Then he would take the remaining car back to Amman and leave the country by the best available method.

Now, at last, everything was in readiness for the final act. In twenty-four hours either a young girl would be reunited with her mother or they would all be in a Jordanian prison.

# 6

# "The
# Eyes
# of Texas"

JANUARY 28, 1988, was D-Day. All of their planning and effort had been focused on reaching this day, and now it was here. A little girl's future was on the line, and the next several hours would tell whether she would once again know her mother's embrace or, instead, be condemned to grow up in an alien environment a world away from the love and familiar things she had known since birth.

The rescue team checked out of the Amman Holiday Inn early in the morning, telling the desk clerk that they were going to the ancient Nabataean city of Petra and then on to Aqaba. A few minutes later, they gathered together in the parking lot.

"I have never done anything in my life without a pre-mission prayer and I ain't starting now," said Don, fixing his gaze on Dave. "Grandpa, make it short and sweet." Dave said a short prayer and they left for Jarash without further ceremony. Everyone knew what he or she was to do.

Don drove the white Nissan to the house in Jarash to make certain that Lauren boarded the bus on schedule. Dave, Cathy, and J.D. went directly to the house on the outskirts of the city where the actual snatch would be made. The site was a farm overlooking Jarash. There were two houses on the property, made of earth-colored stone and brick, which blended into the barren rocky hillside. At the top of the hill, parallel to the asphalt road that passed by the farm, was a stone wall, a clump of olive trees, and some old barns. A dirt road nearly half a mile long led to the houses, and the orange school bus normally pulled off the main road and stopped a short distance away to pick up the children. Once the children were on board, the driver backed the bus out onto the asphalt road, since there was no place wide enough to turn around on the access road.

Dave parked the red Nissan at the top of the hill, on the right side of the road near the turnoff to the farm, and he and the others waited. The cold, gray, overcast sky added to the somberness of their mood. No one spoke. Cathy, sitting in the back seat, moved her lips from time to time as if saying a silent prayer. The tension mounted with each passing moment.

As the minutes ticked by, it became evident that the bus was late. Ordinarily, the little orange bus ran like clockwork. During the surveillance, it had never been late before. Dave had a sinking feeling in the pit of his stomach: suppose something had happened? Maybe Don had been arrested, and the authorities were on their way to the farm to apprehend them.

They continued to wait, growing increasingly nervous. Then they heard a straining engine and saw Don's white Nissan speeding toward them. He screeched to a halt in front of them. Cathy and J.D. jumped into his car and they sped away, leaving Dave by himself. Dave wheeled his car around and headed back toward Jarash, passing the little orange school bus seconds later as it chugged up the hill toward the turnoff to the farm. Once the bus had gone by, Dave cranked the wheel of the red Nissan, swung it around, and followed the bus at a safe distance.

The bus made a left turn by the wall and stopped to take on the two schoolchildren who lived at the farm. But before the driver could back out, Don, at the wheel of the white Nissan, sped back down the road and screeched to a halt behind the bus, blocking its exit. Don, J.D., and Cathy then converged on the bus.

Don approached from the driver's side and tried to grab the driver through the window. J.D., meanwhile, shouted to the driver to open the door, which was operated by air pressure, but the driver was distracted by Don. So J.D. kicked the door open, bounded up the two steps, and took hold of the driver. He stuffed an envelope addressed to Ali Bayan into the driver's hands and, in English, growled: "Can you read this? Take it to Ali Bayan." He also thrust about $20 in Jordanian currency at the driver, saying that it was for him. J.D. then pulled the keys out of the ignition, showed them to the driver, and flipped them over the stone wall into a patch of grass.

Cathy, who was only one step behind J.D., ran down the aisle toward Lauren. All of the children were sitting in stunned silence, eyes big as saucers. Cathy gave Lauren a quick embrace and told the frightened girl to come with her. As they left the bus, they were followed by the nineteen-year-old female chaperone who, by this time, had recovered her wits and was not going to let Lauren go.

Cathy hustled Lauren into the back seat of the white Nissan, but before she could climb in behind, the chaperone grabbed Cathy by the sweater and they began to struggle. As Don stepped in to break it up, he saw a white taxi packed with men coming up the road. Two of the men were hanging out the window to see what was going on. "I said to myself," he remembers, "that we are in for a fight." He leaned heavily on the chaperone's shoulder and pinned her against the car, speaking all the while in a soft, soothing voice, telling her to hush. "Hush, lady." She started to scream, but Don explained to her in pidgin English that "this is Mama. She is taking her baby home."

"Mama?" said the chaperone, beginning to calm down.

"Yes, Mama," reaffirmed Don.

As the chaperone conceded defeat, the taxi passed by and disappeared over the hill. Don pushed the chaperone back toward the bus and yelled, "Let's go!"

The chaperone, stunned and forlorn, stood beside the bus, tears streaming down her cheeks, as the white Nissan pulled away. The bus driver, meanwhile, was rummaging through the grass on the other side of the wall for the keys, but as the white car accelerated, he looked up and seemed to make a mental note of the license plate.

## KEYSTONE COPS

Dave was waiting in the red Nissan, out of sight, only a short distance away. The white car, wheels smoking, pulled up alongside and Don, J.D., Cathy, and Lauren jumped out and piled into the red vehicle. Dave wished them luck and slid in behind the wheel of the white car. Once the switch was made, Don and his companions sped off in the direction of the Allenby Bridge, nearly an hour away. Lauren was stretched out on the back seat beneath a blanket, and Cathy and the commandos once again donned their disguises. Lauren was whimpering softly and muttering, "Mummy, Mummy." Later, as they passed through the Jordan Valley, Cathy dressed Lauren in different clothing.

Dave, meanwhile, drove the white car down to Jarash. He needed gasoline, so he pulled into a service station, topped off the tank, and waited for the bus. Seven minutes later the bus came roaring down the road, and Dave honked at the driver, pulled out in front of the bus, and raced away. Seconds later he doubled back and began his own run toward the Allenby Bridge. He was about fifteen minutes behind the red car, but unlike Don, he did not speed. Instead, he plodded toward the bridge at about 25 miles an hour.

As he entered the Jordan Valley on the two-lane road with no shoulders, he encountered some of the thickest fog he had ever seen. "I mean, it was thick, thick, thick," says Dave. "The road is real narrow and I'm praying to myself that I don't hit any roadblocks."

There were no roadblocks, but his rear-view mirror was suddenly filled with flashing red lights as several police cars loomed through the fog behind him. The Jordanian police were hanging out the windows and trying to wave him over. He pretended that he did not notice them, and moved to the center of the road so that they could not pass. The police then used a loudspeaker to order him over. Dave continued to ignore them, poking along as though on a Sunday drive without a care in the world.

As the police began screaming in the loudspeaker, Dave finally eased his car over slightly and rolled to a halt, still blocking the right lane. The first police car roared by on the left and stopped in front of him. Six officers jumped from the car and surrounded the white Nissan.

Dave was sitting munching on a Snickers candy bar, seemingly oblivious to the commotion. They shouted at him in Arabic, since none of them spoke English. Dave knew they wanted his passport, but he stalled for time, explaining—in English—that he was a tourist and on his way to the Dead Sea.

"No! No! No!" screamed the police commander. "Passeport! Passeport!"

Dave played dumb. "I'm a tourist going to the Dead Sea."

"Passeport! Passeport!"

At last, Dave indicated that he understood and fished his passport from his pocket.

Two more carloads of police roared up, one boxing in his car from behind, the other alongside. There were over two dozen policemen at the scene, and they had brought the bus driver along with them. The bus driver gazed at Dave and shook his head, indicating that he was not one of the abductors. The police tore through Dave's rucksack, which they found lying on the back seat of the car, but found only a pair of jeans, a souvenir plate from Jarash, and some dirty clothes.

"License! License!" one of the policemen shouted at Dave.

Dave handed over his driver's license and the rental car agreement, which was in Abbadi's name, and grinned at them. Now the police were totally confused. Traffic was backing up behind them, with people leaning on their horns and cursing the officers.

The policemen were arguing over whether or not they had the right car. One of the officers, from the first car on the scene, held a piece of paper with two Arabic numbers on it. Dave could see that they were the first two numbers of his license plate. The officer knew he had the right car, but the others weren't convinced, especially when they looked at Dave sitting like a fool, grinning at them and chomping on another candy bar.

Finally, they ordered Dave out of the car and pointed at the trunk. At their direction, he unlocked the trunk, which was completely empty and didn't even contain a spare. More than twenty minutes had gone by since Dave was pulled over, and he could see that the cops were becoming more and more agitated and confused. The horns behind them continued to blare, setting everyone's nerves on edge. Then a police radio crackled with the excited voice of a dispatcher, and the police gathered around to listen. Dave could not make out what the dispatcher was saying, but the word "Alia," the name of the national airline, was repeated twice. They were talking about the airport, he realized. Evidently they'd found out about the phony reservations.

The officer holding Dave's documents threw them back at him, and all of the policemen piled into their cars, did U-turns, and raced back up the road toward Amman, leaving him standing on the road with a long line of traffic behind him.

Dave returned to his car and continued on his way. A short time later, he picked up two Jordanian policemen who were hitch-hiking alongside the road. With the policemen as passengers, he passed through a half dozen roadblocks that apparently had been set up only minutes after the red car, bearing Don and the others, passed over the same stretch of road. Every time he saw a tall antenna, indicating a police or army post, Dave craned his neck searching for the red Nissan, in case the others had been appre-hended.

## DRAMA AT THE ALLENBY BRIDGE

It took Don and his passengers seventy-six minutes to reach the Allenby Bridge over the Jordan River. As they neared the bridge, named after the World War I British field marshal, most of the fog had burned away, leaving stark blue sky overhead. A light breeze was blowing toward them from the west.

The landscape near the bridge was very different from the barren hills of Jarash. The area is intensely cultivated, with banana plantations and truck farms that produce an amazing array of fruits and vegetables, including cucumbers, strawberries, and tomatoes. The village of Karameh, the "capital" of the Palestine Liberation Organization (PLO) in the late 1960s, which had once witnessed Yasir Arafat—dressed in women's clothing—fleeing from the on-coming Israelis, lies 12 kilometers northeast of the bridge. As the red car passed through the dusty main square, J.D. whistled to a group of children playing beside the road. When they looked up, he tossed a bundle of clothing out the window of the car. It was the clothing they had worn earlier, including the red-and-white-checkered kaffiyehs that the men had used to hide their features. As the car sped away toward the bridge, the kids converged on the bundle and began tearing at the contents.

Eight minutes later, the car pulled up at the Allenby Bridge bus terminal—a small, dusty, nondescript building that was once part of a British military camp. A few dust-laden banana and eucalyptus trees surrounded the terminal and the sun-baked parking area. Armed Jordanian soldiers blocked the road just beyond the building. The Allenby Bridge serves as the main crossing point between Jordan and Israel, and as the principal transit point for goods—chiefly agricultural produce—from Israel and the West Bank being shipped to the Arab world. Hundreds of people, mostly Arabs, cross the bridge every day. Prior to the onset of the *Intifada* and the subsequent Israeli crackdown, the number was in the thousands.

Don parked the car in a large lot next to the terminal building, and he and his passengers got out, stretched their legs, and retrieved their baggage from the trunk. Moments later, they were joined by Abbadi.

"Mr. Abbadi," said Don, stretching out his hand in greeting, "it's so good to see you. Is everything in order?"

Calm to the point of being laid back, Abbadi shook hands with everyone, even Lauren, and assured them that all was well.

Don handed the keys to the rental car to Abbadi and told him that "Mr. Chatellier will be coming very soon. He will take care of you and pay you." Then he injected a note of urgency into the conversation, realizing that every moment they wasted on cordialities placed them in greater danger.

Abbadi nodded and collected their passports and bridge passes. Then he disappeared into the shade of the terminal building. Don directed everyone over to an ancient, battered bus parked next to the terminal building, and they climbed aboard. There were three other passengers sitting patiently on the bus. J.D. positioned himself near the door, and Don guided Cathy and Lauren to seats near the rear. No one said a word. Minutes seemed like hours as they waited for Abbadi to return, the heat adding to their discomfort.

Finally, Abaddi emerged from the terminal and sauntered

slowly over to the bus. It was like they were stuck in a slow-motion movie, thought Don, who was trying to mentally will Abbadi to move more quickly. Don wondered why it was that there always seemed to be a bus in his worst adventures . . .

During the refueling operation in 1980 at Desert One, a busful of Iranians had appeared on the lonely road skirting the landing areas and was immediately surrounded by Delta operators, who began searching the passengers at gunpoint. Don, who was offloading cargo nets from one of the C-130s, was ordered to give the other men a hand guarding the passengers, so he jogged over to the bus and climbed aboard. The Iranians were beginning to "give us trouble," and Don walked up and down the aisle brandishing his silenced grease gun and jabbing anyone who got out of line in the ribs, forcing them back into their seats. Don screamed for someone who spoke Farsi so he could give some orders to the Iranian passengers, and another Delta operator named Eric Haney, a tall Georgian with a thick southern drawl, appeared. "Man, I didn't know you spoke Farsi," exclaimed Don. "Hell, yeah, I speak their language," said Haney, to Don's relief. Haney faced the wide-eyed Iranians and, in unmistakable English, roared: "Sit down, motherfuckers. Sit down!"

Now Don smiled to himself at the memory—one of the few humorous memories from an otherwise tragic night. He shook his head, and the images of the Iranian desert vanished, replaced by the reality of the heat and dust of the border crossing, and the growing sense of claustrophobia and imminent danger that was weighing on him like someone sitting on his chest.

Abbadi climbed up the steps into the bus, walked down the aisle, and handed Don their documents with a nod and a smile. "See," he said with a broad smile, "I told you. Everything okay."

"Where is the bus driver?" Don demanded.

"Everything is okay," Abbadi assured him.

But Don was insistent. "Where is the bus driver?" he repeated, more like an order than a question.

"Nothing to worry. He is having lunch."

"Lunch!" cried J.D., raising his voice. "Lunch! At ten-thirty in the morning?"

"J.D.," said Don calmly, turning to his partner, "it seems that we will have to get the bus driver."

Abbadi got the message and hurried away to the terminal, reappearing a few seconds later with an elderly man in tow carrying a glass of tea in one hand. The man finished his tea in one gulp and took his position at the wheel. The bus cranked slowly to life. Abbadi waved at them as they departed and yelled once again, "Everything is okay!" The driver pulled out of the parking lot, and the bus rattled down the road toward the bridge, which was obscured by the eucalyptus trees, pulling along a great cloud of dust behind them. Lauren was sobbing again and crying, "Mummy, Mummy." Cathy did her best to calm her.

They passed the shattered ruins of a number of buildings destroyed in one of the Arab-Israeli wars, and soon an enormous blue and white flag emblazoned with the Star of David came into view about 300 yards ahead. There is no Jordanian flag at the bridge. The bus shuddered to a stop next to what appeared to be an office building of some sort. A Jordanian officer came aboard and collected all of the bridge passes.

To the left of the bus was a two-story bunker with heavy-caliber machine guns aimed at the Israeli side of the river. Three soldiers loitered nearby, but J.D. could see that they did not have magazines in their assault rifles. Should everything come apart at the last minute, J.D. calculated how they could fight their way across the bridge. He caught Don's attention with his eyes and flicked his head in the direction of the bunker, indicating that he would jump off the bus, overpower the soldiers, and seize the bunker if necessary. Don, he knew, would spring forward, throw aside the driver, and steer the bus across the bridge.

Fortunately, J.D.'s contingency planning wasn't needed. The Jordanian officer returned, handed the bus driver the passes, and waved them on toward the bridge. Don looked over his shoulder and peered into the hazy distance but couldn't see any sign of pursuit yet. The bus started across the narrow bridge and chugged slowly toward the Israeli side, taking what seemed an eternity to transverse the relatively short distance. Everyone finally breathed a sigh of relief when an Israeli officer with a cockney accent climbed into the bus and welcomed them to Israel.

"I'm really happy to be here," J.D. said effusively, his body losing some of its rigidity for the first time that day. The Israeli officer, not used to such enthusiasm, studied him with a puzzled expression, but did not say anything.

The bus continued onward until it reached another terminal, and the passengers disembarked. Don and his companions were waved to a different line from the other passengers, and there, with a great big smile on his face, was their Israeli contact. After greetings were exchanged, Don saw that Cathy looked absolutely drained, almost on the verge of collapse.

"Sit down and relax," he told her. "The worst is over."

He escorted Cathy and Lauren over to a bench where mother and daughter could finally succumb to their emotions. Cathy no longer had to be strong and, once seated, she burst into tears and smothered Lauren with hugs and kisses.

The emotion of the moment was sensed by others in the terminal, including a group of African-American pilgrims on a tour of the Christian holy places. J.D. was approached by a woman from the group, who asked what had happened and if she could be of help. Normally tight-lipped, J.D. was positively bursting with pride over the happy scene in the terminal, and he told the woman that "this little girl was kidnapped from America. That's the girl's mother. They were just reunited. We're taking the little girl back to the United States to live with her mother."

Fascinated by the story, the black woman went back to her companions. A few moments later, they all returned, surrounded by Cathy and Lauren, and lifted their hands high in the air, singing "Hallelujah." J.D., the hardened combat veteran, was overcome and began sobbing like a baby.

## A NARROW ESCAPE

Dave pulled into the parking lot next to the terminal on the Jordanian side about forty-five minutes after his confederates reached Israeli soil. He was met by the ever-smiling Abbadi, who informed him that everything had gone smoothly.

"Where have you been?" inquired Abbadi.

"Oh, I got tied up down the road for a while," responded Dave, with typical understatement. He paid Abbadi, then told him that he wanted to go to Amman to catch a plane out of the country as soon as possible.

Taking his words literally and moving with uncharacteristic speed, Abbadi got into the red Nissan, pulled out of the parking lot with smoking tires, and headed for Amman at more than 110 kilometers an hour. Dave set off in pursuit in the white Nissan and was forced to flag Abbadi down and order him to reduce speed because they were likely to get pulled over by the police.

Halfway to Amman, Abbadi veered off the main road in a small village and stopped next to a police station. Dave couldn't figure out what he was up to. Fearful of being double-crossed, he stopped his car about 40 yards behind Abbadi and waited for an explanation.

Abbadi got out, stretched, and walked lazily back toward Dave's car. It was, thought Dave, as though he only had two speeds: too fast and very slow. Dave rolled down the window, and Abbadi informed him that "in all of Jordan, this is the best place to buy chicken. It is also the cheapest price. I'm going to get my wife some chicken."

Dave couldn't believe it. "You've got to be kidding," he protested.

"No, no, I'm not kidding," responded Abbadi, missing the entire point. "This *is* the best place for chicken."

For all Dave knew, every cop and soldier in Jordan was hunting them—and Abbadi wanted to stop and buy chicken. Before the CTU man could say anything more, Abbadi had crossed the road. He purchased some live chickens and put them in the back seat of the car.

Once they were under way again, Abbadi stopped to pick up a hitchhiker, and then an old man with a walking stick. Dave was beside himself with anxiety. He couldn't figure out what was going on. Surely Abbadi appreciated the serious nature of what they had just done. On the other hand, Dave concluded, maybe he was just an idiot.

But his troubles with Abbadi were not over. Not knowing precisely how to reach the airport, Dave was following the Jordanian blindly, counting on him to take the most direct route as he had been instructed. Instead, Abbadi pulled up in front of his house and invited Dave in for lunch. It was at this moment that

Dave exploded and told Abbadi, in no uncertain terms, that he wanted to go to the airport now, this minute, without further delay!

Abbadi finally seemed to get the message and proceeded to Amman International Airport without further protest or digression. When they arrived, they found that it was surrounded by so many troops and police that it appeared to be under siege. Abbadi flashed his credentials at the officers manning two checkpoints on the way into the airport, and they were waved on through. But once inside the terminal, Dave found that all passengers waiting to depart had been rounded up by armed military guards and taken to a cordoned-off area at one end of the airport. All flights out of Amman had been canceled. All, that is, but one. There was a Royal Jordanian Premier flight leaving within minutes for Paris. All of the passengers had been boarded and it was just waiting for clearance to push away from the gate.

Abbadi said he didn't understand what was going on and walked away to see what he could learn.

While Abbadi chatted with some guards, Dave strolled over to one of the Royal Jordanian ticket counters and, thinking quickly, said, "I hope I haven't missed that Paris flight. I need to get to Paris."

"Do you have a reservation?" the woman at the ticket counter inquired.

"No, I don't."

The woman scanned her computer screen. "We only have one seat on the flight, and it's first class."

"I'll take it," Dave responded, unable to believe his good fortune. He handed her his credit card.

"Have you got any luggage?" she asked when she was finished filling out the ticket.

"No, just this rucksack," he said, holding it up.

"The security officer will have to look through it, and you'll have to pay your airport tax."

Dave asked to whom he should pay the airport tax.

"The security officer can take it for you," she answered.

Dave had 40 Jordanian dinars left in his pocket, worth approximately $130. Although the airport tax was only 2 dinars, he handed all the currency to the security officer and said with a wink, "Will this cover the airport tax?"

"Oh, yes. That's just right." The security man smiled, stuffing the bills into one of his pockets. He spoke rapidly into his walkie-talkie, apparently to the plane, and then began to lead Dave to the gate without inspecting the rucksack.

At this moment, Abbadi returned.

"This guy is holding the flight for me," Dave informed him. "I've got to run and get on it. It's been nice knowin' you. I've really enjoyed it."

He pumped the speechless Jordanian's hand, then hurried down the jetway to the plane.

The flight to Paris was uneventful, but when he landed at Orly, Dave was detained for not having a French visa or a ticket on a connecting flight. Following a number of serious terrorist attacks in 1986, the French government had temporarily required that Americans and most other foreign visitors obtain visas before visiting France.

Dave was questioned by three different French security officials, and started becoming alarmed when they threatened to put him on a flight back to Jordan. Ultimately, he was able to strike a compromise with the French, whereby they allowed him to sleep overnight in the airport, and the following morning he purchased a ticket on the next flight to the United States from an American Airlines agent who came to the area where he was being held to sell him the ticket. "I was never so relieved in all my life," Dave sighs, recalling the moment the plane lifted off for the United States.

## AFTERMATH

It was only later that Dave learned how narrow his escape from Jordan had been. It turned out that the Jordanians had sealed the nation's borders and actually shut down Amman International Airport in a futile attempt to interdict Lauren and her rescuers. Within days of the incident, the hapless Adil Abbadi was arrested and jailed for his role in the escape.

The Assistant Regional Security Officer at the U.S. Embassy in Amman, Frank Baker, was removed from his position and resigned. State Department investigators allege that he knowingly "assisted directly or indirectly in the abduction of an American citizen child," and "illegally aided and abetted the efforts of American citizens in their attempts to violate host-government law." Although Don and Dave offered to submit written statements, on the penalty of perjury, that Baker had no knowledge of their real mission in Jordan, the State Department never contacted them and expressed no interest in their efforts to clarify the situation. Baker even agreed to take a polygraph examination regarding his knowledge of the abduction, but one was never administered. Today, he is happily back in the Marine Corps.

Despite the fact that Ali Bayan had illegally abducted Lauren and was wanted in Texas on that and other charges, the U.S. government expressed official regret to the Jordanian government over the incident. Ali Bayan even asked the U.S. Embassy in Amman for help in getting his daughter back.

In the final analysis, it is clear that Frank Baker was made a scapegoat for the State Department's failure to adequately come to grips with the problem of international child abduction. While incidents such as the rescue of Lauren Bayan certainly complicate the conduct of U.S. foreign policy, a desperate mother would not have felt the necessity of hiring commandos to carry out a risky paramilitary operation on foreign soil if the U.S. government had been more effective in enabling her to recover her kidnapped daughter.

Today, Cathy and Lauren have managed to start new lives and put the whole incident behind them. But Cathy still lives in fear that one day Ali will return and attempt to kidnap Lauren again. She hopes that the courage and resourcefulness she demonstrated will deter him, but she can't be sure. In the envelope left with the bus driver on the windy hill outside of Jarash was a note, in Cathy's handwriting, to her ex-husband. It contained a veiled warning. "You took my daughter," it read. "Now I have her back. Your brother and your wife are safe in the United States, for now. Don't come after us and don't give me any trouble. Remember, the eyes of Texas are upon you." It was signed Cathy Mahone.

# THREE
## Operation
## Brittney

# 7
# "I Knew She Was Gone"

IN THE MONTHS that followed the rescue of Lauren Bayan, a number of stories appeared in the national media about the incident. One of the most dramatic was captioned: "Rambo Raiders Save Tot." Initially, CTU denied all of the reports, but eventually decided to be more forthcoming because, says Judy, the reporters were "coming up with wrong information or information that could hurt other people." The media also were becoming a nuisance and disrupting the firm's regular business. According to Judy, "We had press hiding in the bushes at our office. There were news cameras set up across the road. We had locked our doors and were not speaking to anybody."

For a short while they became local celebrities. Their children were stopped by other kids who had seen articles about CTU in the paper and pieces on television. One day, Judy and Don's son, Buddy, was even approached by a friend who had read "about your mom and dad in the paper" during a trip to Australia. Their daughter, Stephanie, was asked by a teacher if "your dad's name is Don and your mom's name is Judy?" When Stephanie said yes, the teacher indicated that she had just read an article about them. For the remainder of the school year, whenever one of the kids in the class stepped out of line, the teacher would threaten them, "If you don't behave, I'm going to get the Feeneys after you."

Many of their Delta buddies were skeptical of the operation and all of the publicity it had generated; but others, having read wildly exaggerated reports about how much CTU had been paid, were eager to make Don and Dave aware of their availability. The firm was inundated with résumés and calls from ex-operators looking for work. Indeed, the large payments being bandied about in the media were accepted as gospel by many people, including relatives of the CTU operatives. "The family thinks we're rich," reflects Judy. "We get calls all the time for loans. They think we're pretty well off, when in fact it's just the opposite."

In actual fact, CTU not only failed to make a profit on the Cathy Mahone case but lost about $5,000 in actual out-of-pocket expenses. Cathy paid them a total of $50,000, but they spent $55,000 on the mission, not to mention the revenue lost by being unavailable to take other jobs. The firm was struggling in those days, and while Don and Dave were abroad rescuing Lauren, Judy remained at the office, juggling calls from creditors and bill collectors. The day after Don returned, he and Judy went to the supermarket. According to Judy, "All we had was a checkbook, knowing full well there was no money in the account."

"You know," Judy reminded her husband, "we're getting ready to write a hot check for food?"

"Yeah, I know," replied Don sheepishly.

"Well," continued Judy, "we can expect more money in from Cathy, can we not?"

"No," snapped Don. "Absolutely not. We won't be getting any more money."

Judy stopped dead in her tracks and turned to confront Don. "What do you mean?"

"Hey, she only has thirty thousand left in the bank," responded Don. "She's got to have enough money to live on."

Judy had always respected her husband's compassion, but this was too much. "Doggone it, Don," she said, a sharp edge to her voice. "Here we are taking food out of our kids' mouths. I don't know how we'll make our next house payment, and you're worried about her. She's got thirty thousand dollars left in the bank and owes us money, and you're worried about her welfare. I wish we had thirty dollars in the bank to get by until next week. What about us?"

Cathy had to have money, said Don, to carve out a new life for herself and Lauren, and that was that. End of subject.

Judy reluctantly dropped the matter and somehow they made it through the following week.

## EVERY MOTHER'S NIGHTMARE

The publicity CTU received generated a flood of calls from distraught mothers pleading with CTU for help in recovering their abducted children. Judy and the men were amazed by how many people seemed to be in the same predicament as Cathy. "We've had collect calls at home in the middle of the night," says Judy. "We've never refused to talk to anybody."

It seemed that every day a new package of unsolicited materials arrived at company headquarters, containing its individual tale of woe. Many were in longhand on lined paper. They come from across the country, mostly from women, but occasionally from men as well. The cases are so similar in many respects, says Dave, that "they look like they've been cut out with a cookie cutter." One letter describes a four-year-old girl abducted by her father, most likely to Greece. "She has survived being sexually abused and beaten by her brutal and dangerous father," begins the letter, which goes on to call the father a "monster." Another letter, from Washington State, asks for help in locating a missing baby, presumed to be with his American-born father in Central America. The former wife claims to have been the victim of "physical and verbal abuse, including being punched and kicked, and also being choked." Her ex-husband, she continues, has a "violent, quick temper that seems to erupt without reason," which she attributes to Post-Traumatic Shock Disorder arising from his service in Vietnam. The husband is an excellent shot, she goes on, and has a collection of approximately fifteen handguns and thirty rifles. "I feel helpless in my options for action. That is why I am asking you to consider helping me."

Another letter, which bore an eerie similarity to the Cathy Mahone case and was accompanied by a thick file, came from a grandmother whose two granddaughters had been kidnapped from Texas by the Jordanian father and taken back to his native country.

Her daughter, the mother of the two girls, "is a very wonderful person and one of the best mothers in the world," writes the grandmother, who also included a letter from the Jordanian father warning his ex-wife to "learn in this life not to cause a man to cry because real man [sic] will turn into a fierce giant and break everything in front of him." CTU also heard from the former wife of a Jordanian man who operated a tire company in the Midwest and disappeared with her two children during a routine visitation period. According to documents provided to CTU, the ex-husband is believed to be back in Jordan.

And the letters keep coming. All pull at the heartstrings. "Judy," pleads one mother whose daughter was abducted, "please help me find my little girl. Her birthday was Dec. 16th. She is now six years old. The holidays were very hard for me to deal with."

"I am a desperate American mother," begins another letter, which was forwarded to CTU by a magazine editor. "My two babies . . . have been abducted by their noncustodial father and taken to Iran . . . I know that somewhere in this great country there is someone who can help me. Perhaps you know how I might go about locating such a brave person? I do not expect a miracle. I only want someone to suggest a speedy alternative to the 'official' way of bringing my babies back home to the life that they deserve as American citizens."

Judy answers every inquiry to CTU regarding parental abduction cases. She responds to each appeal, generally by asking for more information—such things as court decrees, photos, affidavits, testimonials—which she methodically examines to ensure that the facts are as depicted by the person contacting them. Some cases are rejected as too old, others involve ambiguous facts or too little precise information about the current whereabouts of the children. Cases in countries like Iran, Libya, and Syria usually are dismissed as being too difficult and risky. However, when all is said and done, a majority of the cases CTU has been contacted about appear to have real merit and to be feasible candidates for rescue operations.

But if nearly every case has one thing in common, it is that virtually all of the desperate people who contact CTU lack the necessary financial resources to underwrite a serious rescue effort. Most are from blue-collar backgrounds, and without prosperous relatives who can be approached for financial help. Often they are divorced women whose former husbands have stopped paying alimony or child support, and who have been forced into low-paying service jobs in order to survive.

Thus, despite the viable nature of many of the cases, CTU hasn't been able to proceed on most of them because the necessary funds just aren't available. Only a few of the petitioners have been able to come up with enough money even to get started, that is, to underwrite preliminary meetings and a reconnaissance mission to the country in question. "We know there's no money in it, that it's not profitable," says Dave. "But when we get a call, it's in absolute desperation, and people have nowhere else to turn."

## KELI'S STORY

In June 1989, Judy received a telephone call from a young woman who identified herself as Keli Chowdhury and said she was phoning from Tulsa. According to Keli, she had not seen her daughter, Brittney, since May 7 of that year, when she had been abducted to Bangladesh by her ex-husband, Mohammed.

"I talked to her," says Judy, "and told her I'd need more information, which she promised to send."

A few days later, a thick packet of materials arrived at CTU's headquarters from Keli. The packet contained court documents, telephone records, Brittney's birth certificate, and personal data about both her daughter and Mohammed. In the neatly typed cover letter, Keli explained that "I have desperately been trying to get assistance from virtually every person or agency I could think of. I have run into one closed door after another." She concluded with a plea for CTU "to help me get my child."

Judy spoke regularly to Keli in the weeks that followed. Money, of course, was an issue. Keli said she was broke, but that she felt confident she and her mother could raise the necessary funds to mount a rescue. On that assurance, Dave traveled to Tulsa on October 5 to meet with Keli and her mother and size them up face to face.

A tiny wisp of a woman with dark, deepset eyes, Keli Walker Chowdhury was born in Tulsa, Oklahoma, and attended local schools until the twelfth grade, when she dropped out to enroll in cosmetology school. After graduating, she cut hair for the next four and a half years, and managed during that time to acquire her General Education Diploma and a husband.

Her first husband, Jamal, hailed from Abu Dhabi, the tiny oil-rich sheikhdom located on the Persian Gulf. He was studying at Tulsa University when they met. According to Keli, it was love at first sight. A fan of country western music who worships Patsy Cline, Keli says she was attracted to Jamal because "he could act as redneck as anybody from Arkansas or Oklahoma." When his older brother learned of the marriage, however, he "went into orbit," telling Jamal that their parents would never approve and that he would be disinherited. They had been married only a few months when Jamal reluctantly asked Keli for a divorce, to which she just as reluctantly agreed. "He cried. I cried," she recalls. "My mother had been divorced and it really hurt me. So my childhood dream was to get married and not ever be divorced. It crushed me, it just crushed me. I couldn't believe it."

In early 1984, she was enrolled in a religion course at Tulsa University, when she dropped by the annual international bazaar, which featured food and crafts from around the world. Standing in front of a table offering Indian cuisine, she tried a mouthful of something that didn't sit very well on her tongue. She was looking around for someplace to spit it out when a slight, dark-skinned young man approached her.

"Are you enjoying it?" he asked.

Unable to speak because her mouth was full, she smiled weakly, took a deep breath, and swallowed, forcing the evil-tasting concoction down.

"If you like that," the young man continued, "then why don't you try some of this?" He handed her a bite of something that tasted like spicy glue on cardboard.

"I-it's good," Keli lied.

He introduced himself, saying his name was Mohammed Chowdhury and that he was from Pakistan. As they talked, Keli noticed that he was extremely well mannered. He also seemed honest and straightforward, although she was later to learn that he was less than candid about many things. He turned out to be, for example, from Bangladesh, one of the poorest countries on earth, rather than Pakistan. Keli says that he was ashamed and embarrassed about being from Bangladesh, and always told people he was from Pakistan, where he had been born. He also "told me that they [his family] were wealthy, that he went to a private school, the very best school in Bangladesh, that his father had a high position in his country, and that they had servants." As Keli was later to learn, little of what he said was accurate.

Mohammed invited her to dinner, and soon they started dating on a regular basis. He loved to cook, and would often come over to her apartment and fix dinner, usually Indian fare. Despite her original distaste for subcontinent cuisine, Keli soon developed an enthusiastic palate for the spicy dishes Mohammed regularly whipped up in her kitchen.

Within weeks the relationship was on fast-forward. "Everything happened really fast," Keli recalls. "The love word came up really fast." They were married in July 1984, in Tulsa, at a wedding chapel. Keli's family was not enthusiastic about the union, especially in view of the earlier disaster with Jamal. Keli also says that her family, most of whom live in Arkansas, are "pretty closed-minded" about foreigners, and Mohammed's dark skin did not help.

Her mother, Keli says, was never rude to Mohammed, in fact, she was very kind to him. It was the disparity between their respective cultures that troubled Jeanne Cripps, Keli's mother. Jeanne counseled her daughter, "You were raised completely different. You don't realize the problems that you'll have in the future." Such considerations, however, never entered her mind, contends Keli. "I thought I knew it all. I was crazy about him . . . so I went ahead and did it."

Keli soon became pregnant. Although initially excited about the prospect of becoming a father, Mohammed quickly tired of her morning sickness and the other problems associated with a difficult pregnancy. She was no longer the fun-loving woman at his beck and call that he had married. Preoccupied with her pregnancy, Keli was far less solicitous of his needs, Mohammed complained.

According to Keli, however, the disintegration of her marriage was attributable to far more than just her pregnancy. The chief reason, she maintains, is that the better she got to know Mohammed, the less she liked him. "If I had not found out I was pregnant," she says, "the marriage would have been over in probably three months." In retrospect, Keli blames herself. She believes that she was looking for another Jamal, and had deluded herself that Mohammed possessed the same qualities she had found so attractive in her first husband.

By contrast to Jamal's strength, she says, Mohammed turned out to be a wimp. "He could turn on the tears like this," she maintains, snapping her fingers. She describes how he came home from work one day crying because "someone had hit him . . . I remember feeling like I wanted to get on my horse and go get the guy," Keli reflects. "You know, kind of like a motherly instinct, and he was like a child crying."

Mohammed's Moslem faith, which he barely mentioned during their courtship, was also increasingly becoming a source of friction. According to Keli, when she met Mohammed, he was far from a devout practitioner. "He didn't pray five times a day," she says. "He didn't visit the mosque. He didn't curb his cussing. The only thing he didn't do was eat pork." Mohammed wanted Keli to convert to Islam, and she had taken some instruction before they were married; but as the marriage continued to deteriorate, she quickly abandoned any thought of giving up her own Protestant faith.

Keli was amazed one day when her decision to take a visiting ten-year-old cousin from Arkansas to a local swimming pool outraged Mohammed and sent him "around the bend." He was livid that she would wear a bathing suit in public, and ranted and raved about her immodesty and lack of respect for him. She went anyway, and when she and her cousin returned, they found Mohammed lying on the floor crying. "I couldn't believe it," says Keli. "Waterworks. I told him, 'Get up from there. What are you doing?' I was embarrassed no end. Brian [the cousin] was only ten years old and he thought he was a nut!"

"She doesn't listen to her husband," Mohammed sobbed. Keli just ignored him.

On June 15, 1985, Keli gave birth to a daughter, whom she named Brittney. Keli was overjoyed, but her husband seemed to take only momentary pleasure from their daughter's arrival. Mohammed had been working as a cleanup man at a local Denny's Restaurant, but shortly before Brittney was born, he moved to Barry's Deli, where he had the opportunity to cook. Later, he moved on to yet another fast-food restaurant that paid better. Throughout this period, he continued to tell his family back in Bangladesh that he was going to school full time, though his attendance was sporadic at best.

In order to save money, they moved in with Keli's mother for six months after Brittney's birth. "Things were okay while we were there," Keli remembers, but when they once again rented a place of their own, "things got real bad, real quick." Mohammed, says Keli, "was very, very, very jealous of Brittney." He worked late hours, and when he got home, he often found Brittney sleeping with her mother. Their love life evaporated. "I didn't want to have relations with him," she says. "I just . . . didn't love him that way. Not the way you're supposed to."

"He was a much smaller, [more] self-centered individual than I had thought," she continues. Brittney was a major source of friction, and Mohammed increasingly became a "control freak," even refusing to allow Keli to go shopping. "He didn't want me out of the house. Period! I had no friends. Brittney was my life, which was fine . . . but when we needed diapers, I would tell him. 'Diapers again! Diapers again!' he would scream and yell. He would have a fit." And on one of the rare occasions when she did go out shopping and bought Brittney a modest toy, he screamed, "We aren't running a store here. Why did you buy all these toys?"

When he threw a fit, Keli would tell him to leave until he got over it. But he would just keep screaming, because "he seemed to get satisfaction out of it. He knew I didn't want him to scream, so he would scream even more, because it would make Brittney cry."

Mohammed became more and more bitter, and would call Keli's relatives to complain about her behavior. He phoned her mother, her aunt, and even her great-aunt. "My wife," he would tell them, "she has a sex problem. She needs to go to a mental hospital." Soon he began to complain that it was America that was the source of all his problems. According to Keli, "He would go outside and walk up and down the sidewalk, screaming at anybody who would listen about his wife, about America, about how he was being treated. . . . He would throw his finger in the air and yell, 'Fuck you, Americans! All you Americans! Only black people treat me right.'" In private, however, it was another story; "he always called them 'niggers,'" explains Keli.

Mohammed's grip on his emotions became ever more tenu-
ous, and soon he was fired from his job at the restaurant. He filed
a discrimination complaint, alleging that other employees had
made derogatory statements about him and had referred to him as
"an Iranian." He called the local newspaper and television stations
to complain about his treatment and received a small settlement
from the restaurant.

His rampages became more and more frequent, and ever nois-
ier. On several occasions, the Chowdhurys' neighbors called the
police. One evening, Mohammed threw all of Brittney's belong-
ings out the apartment door, including her stroller, pictures off the
wall, and a wooden horse. The police came and, as usual, Mohammed's rage and bravado quickly disappeared, revealing a frightened little man who started to cry and plead with Keli not to file
charges, telling her that terrible things would happen to him if he
went to jail. Touched by his tearful appeal and regarding him as
more pathetic than menacing, Keli, once again, refused to press
charges, and instead moved into her mother's home with Brittney.
As had so often happened in the past, Mohammed called every day
and cried on the phone, begging her to return.

Keli's mother urged her to leave him, but Keli couldn't bring
herself to break with him once and for all. In their earlier alterca-
tions, Mohammed had never physically abused either Keli or Brittney. But as time went by, he became more violent, throwing a hot
dog at Keli on one occasion, and pulling her down to the floor by
her hair on several others. Although of slight build, he was about
5 feet 10—tall for a Bangladeshi—and towered over Keli.

When Brittney was two, Keli and Mohammed finally separated. The incident that precipitated the break was a noisy row
witnessed by a maintenance man, in which Mohammed dragged
Keli to the floor by her hair with Brittney in her arms. The maintenance man called the police, and this time Keli told them she'd
file charges against him. Instead, Mohammed agreed to leave quietly. Keli subsequently went to court to obtain a protective order
against him.

Mohammed had other problems as well. Lee Diebel, the international student director at Rogers State College, where Mohammed was supposed to be studying, wrote his parents on July
20, 1984, explaining that their son wasn't attending classes and had

abused the parents' trust. The letter noted that during the fall semester of 1982, "Your son did not complete 12 semester credit hours. Violation of Immigration regulations." In the spring semester of 1983, Mohammed's performance had been even worse: "Your son completed no semester credit hours. Violation of Immigration regulations." The story was the same during the fall semester of 1983 and the spring semester of 1984. Diebel went on to observe that "Your son seems to be more interested in personal and social activities than he is interested in academic studies." He concluded: "The International Office is very much disappointed with your son. He has not attempted to become a serious and diligent student. Mohammad [sic] S. A. Chowdhury should return to Bangladesh in order to continue his education in your country."

The Immigration and Naturalization Service (INS) was also interested in Mohammed since he was in the United States on a student visa and could be deported for not going to school. Mohammed and Keli had not filed for a green card, giving him permanent resident status in the United States, after their marriage; they just hadn't gotten around to it. Now, faced with the prospect of being booted out of the country, Mohammed called Keli and begged her to help him file for his green card. Keli, as always, felt sorry for him and agreed to fill out the paperwork—omitting the fact that they were not living together and, technically, committing fraud. The months that followed, while Mohammed's application was being processed, were uneventful. "He didn't bother us," says Keli. "He didn't come see Brittney for several months, because he wanted the green card, and he didn't care about Brittney."

Keli began seeing a local construction worker named Jim, and Mohammed, who had obtained a temporary work permit allowing him to manage a local fast-food restaurant, enjoyed a cordial relationship with his estranged wife and her new boyfriend at first. Mohammed even seemed to take a new interest in his daughter. But soon the relationship began to sour once again, and in 1988, Mohammed filed charges with the police, accusing Keli of physically abusing Brittney and Jim of having threatened to "blow up my head." The allegations took Keli totally by surprise, and she was devastated, especially when the police came to their house and arrested Jim.

According to Keli, Mohammed called the night Jim was taken

into custody. He seemed distraught and confused. "Keli," he pleaded, "you've got to call them and tell them that I lied, and that I was just mad at you, or they're going to take Brittney away from both of us."

Keli angrily informed Mohammed that he was the only one who could straighten things out; it was up to him to call the authorities.

"No," he cried. "I'll go to jail! This is not my country. I'll get in jail and there's nobody to help me."

Mohammed called her again the following day and tried, in effect, to blackmail her. The only reason he wanted Brittney, Keli says he told her, was so that he could stay in the country. He offered her a deal: If she would consent to give him legal custody of Brittney, he would allow Keli to "keep her." "She [Brittney] could stay with me," Keli added; "we just wouldn't tell anyone."

"You're out of your mind," she responded.

Mohammed was desperate. He raised his offer. He said he would drop the charges against Jim and withdraw his child abuse complaint against Keli if she would just relent and let him have legal custody of Brittney.

"Of course, I cussed him," says Keli, "and he just laughed at me."

Mohammed filed for divorce in July 1988, requesting custody of Brittney. In his submission, he claimed that Keli and Jim had threatened him both with physical violence and deportation if he didn't withdraw his earlier charges.

By her own admission, Keli says that she underestimated how seriously the authorities would take Mohammed's charges. She couldn't imagine that anyone would believe him. But Mohammed had a good attorney and a sympathetic judge; during the court hearing he accused Keli of being a "drug abuser, an alcoholic, and a prostitute," but provided no hard evidence to support his charges. Keli and her mother were stunned when the judge awarded Mohammed temporary custody of Brittney, and only granted Keli weekend visitation rights. The judge also mandated psychological testing for Brittney, drug testing for Keli, and family counseling for both Keli and Mohammed. The divorce hearing was scheduled for May 16, 1989.

Keli fired her attorney and, with her mother's help, immediately hired a new, more aggressive lawyer. Mohammed, meanwhile, had met a young single mother by the name of Terry Smith, in what rapidly developed into an intense romantic relationship. However, when questioned in his divorce case as to Terry's identity, he described her as Brittney's "baby-sitter."

Although angry and despondent, Keli had no choice but to obey the judge's orders and give up Brittney to Mohammed during the week. According to Keli, Brittney hated going with her father after spending the weekend with her mother. When Mohammed came by to pick her up, "she screamed and cried, and would run and hide in the back of the house," says Keli. "She didn't want to go with him."

But Mohammed's lies were beginning, once again, to catch up with him. The court-appointed child advocate could find no evidence of child abuse and began to have doubts about Mohammed's real commitment to his daughter. In an affidavit filed on May 15, 1989, the child advocate, Brenda Stubblefield, indicated that Mohammed had refused to get Brittney medical treatment for an ear condition, and that "the minor child was fearful, refusing to go with the plaintiff [Mohammed] and became aggressive in actions and words toward the plaintiff." Informed by Keli that Mohammed's green card application was fraudulent, the INS started deportation proceedings against him. Fearing that Mohammed might skip the country with Brittney in advance of his deportation, Keli's attorney asked the judge to hold his passport, but the judge refused.

On Friday, May 12, 1989, four days before the divorce hearing, Keli drove, as usual, to Mohammed's to pick up Brittney for the weekend. When she got to his apartment, she knocked on the door, but there was no answer. She didn't panic immediately because the previous Friday he wasn't there when she arrived; he was at the laundromat, and she had to wait until he returned with Brittney. Rather than wait, she drove over to Terry Smith's house. No one was there, but everything seemed to be normal; nothing was missing from the yard. Nevertheless, Keli was seized by a growing sense of apprehension.

"I knew she was gone," says Keli, her eyes filling with tears. "I just knew it somehow." She went to the laundromat, not really expecting to find them, but still hoping. There was no sign of Mohammed or Brittney, so she drove by Mohammed's one more

time, then found a phone and tried to call her attorney, but he was
out of town. Then she phoned the police, but the officer who took
her call told her that they couldn't do anything until she obtained
a court order on Monday.

"Can't you at least go to his apartment?" she pleaded.

"No," the officer responded.

"Well, I'm going in," she affirmed, emotion rising in her voice.

"If you break into his apartment," the officer cautioned her
sympathetically, "I'll have to arrest you for breaking and entering."

"Okay," Keli told him. "But I've got to get in there. I've got
to find out for sure if he's gone."

The officer admonished her once more about the consequences of entering Mohammed's apartment illegally, then told
her that if he were in her shoes, he'd do the same thing.

When she got back to Mohammed's, it was dark. She found a
rusty steel rod in his tiny backyard, and broke one of the sliding
glass doors to let herself in.

"Everything was gone but the trash," she recalls. She went to
pieces when the full impact of what had happened hit her; she
might never see her daughter again. Brittney had been abducted
halfway around the world, to a country she couldn't even visualize.
When she tried to picture Brittney in Bangladesh, all she could see
was her child against a blank backdrop; perhaps that was the most
disquieting thing of all.

Keli called Mohammed's attorney, Mary Morris, with whom
she had become acquainted during the protracted court proceedings.

Morris was reluctant to take the call, but Keli pleaded with
her. "Mary," she sobbed, "I'm not calling you as an attorney. I
know that you have children, so please listen to me."

"Well, make it brief," responded Morris, relenting slightly.

"I'm at Mohammed's. He's not here. All his things are gone
and he has taken Brittney. Do you know where he's at? You've got
to help me. My attorney is out of town and I don't know what to
do."

"Don't get upset," Morris responded, trying to settle her
down. "Calm down and don't worry until you have reason to worry.
I'll try to get in touch with him, and then I'll get back to you."

After hanging up, Keli went back to Terry's and "banged on

the door, begging her to come out. But she was gone." Finally, Keli returned yet again to Mohammed's apartment, and located the manager.

With tears streaming down her cheeks, she told the manager that she was looking for her daughter.

The manager informed her that Mohammed had moved.

"W-what d-do you mean, moved?" Keli stammered.

"Monday," came the response. "They had a U-Haul. He and his wife and the two girls."

"His wife?" Keli growled. "I'm his wife."

At the divorce hearing on May 16, Mohammed's attorney, Mary Morris, admitted to the court that she had heard from her client and that he was in Bangladesh. The judge, however, was furious at having been taken in by Mohammed; he granted Keli a divorce and awarded her "the immediate permanent care, custody and control of the minor child, Brittney Begum Chowdhury." The judge also issued a civil warrant for Mohammed, with a $1 million cash bond.

## TERRY'S STORY

Mohammed had met Terry Smith standing in the checkout line at the Homeland grocery story in Tulsa, where Terry was picking up a few items for her daughter, Twila's, meals.

"You must have a child by the look of your groceries," he said as he stood in line behind her. He looked very young to Terry, although in reality he was two years older than she was.

"Yes," she responded, as she paid for the groceries and gathered up the sack. She walked out to her car and the young man followed her.

"Are you married?" he wanted to know.

"I was. But I'm not now."

"Are you dating anyone?"

"No," she replied, becoming a little uneasy at his interest in her and the directness of his questions.

"I used to be married, too," he continued. "I've got a three-year-old daughter."

"That's nice."

"Would you like to go out sometime?" he asked.

By her own admission, Terry's love life was "in the toilet." Until recently, she had worked as a bartender and the hours hadn't been very conducive to dating.

"I-I don't date very much."

"I don't either," he confessed. "I don't have many friends."

Terry knew that she should break off the conversation; he was, after all, a stranger and probably a foreign student, and she had heard a lot of bad stories about foreign students. But he seemed very pleasant and charming, and there was something reassuring about the way he spoke.

The conversation was noncommittal, but Mohammed introduced himself and they exchanged phone numbers. Terry promised to call him sometime. She didn't think anything more about the encounter until she reached her house. As she fumbled for her key at the front door, a pickup truck pulled up behind her car and Mohammed got out.

"I wasn't following you," he apologized, as he approached her. "I was going the same way and saw you turn, and I was curious to see where you lived."

Terry wasn't sure how to react. On the surface, he didn't seem like a weirdo, but these days you never knew. Actually, Terry's first impression of Mohammed was that he seemed vulnerable.

"Look," said Mohammed. "I live just two blocks down the street. Why don't you follow me over to my place for a minute, and I'll show you that I'm not some kinda crazy guy following you home."

Terry was intrigued. It had been a long time since any man had come on to her so strongly, and she was very lonely. She quickly put her groceries in the refrigerator and followed him over to his apartment. They shared a Pepsi and he told her that he had quit school when he had gotten married, and had worked in the restaurant business for a long time, but now was employed by a heating and air-conditioning firm. He had been separated for a year, he said, but his wife was trying to have him kicked out of the country, and if that happened, he would lose his beloved daughter forever. As a result of his wife's outrageous behavior and infidelities, he explained, he was trying to win custody of his daughter.

"I really felt sorry for him," recalls Terry. "He was very easy to like."

He took her to dinner the following night, and afterwards they went to a shopping mall where he bought her a new dress. Then they returned to Terry's house so that he could meet her daughter, Twila. "They seemed to like each other very much," she says.

They started seeing each other every day. As he had done with Keli, Mohammed often would come over to Terry's and cook dinner, usually Indian dishes with lots of curry. Then they would watch television, or occasionally go to a movie. According to Terry, during this period they were inseparable, especially after Mohammed once again lost his job.

Mohammed was the most attentive man Terry had ever met and it wasn't long before "I fell in love with him. It was, like, I couldn't get enough of this man. I loved the way he looked, the way he talked. Everything about him was perfect."

Initially, he had custody of three-year-old Brittney on weekends, and would bring her over to play with Twila, who was six. Despite their age difference, the two girls became fast friends. After the court awarded Mohammed temporary custody of Brittney, from Monday through Friday, he began relying on Terry even more to look after his daughter, usually for ten to twelve hours a day.

When he became unemployed, Mohammed began eating all of his meals at Terry's and went to the Department of Human Services and various local churches to obtain help in paying his utility and other bills. Finally, through a Bangladeshi friend he got a job with a local taxi company, without informing the INS. Although he was once again making money, Terry quickly realized that Mohammed had changed. No longer generous and solicitous, he didn't offer to help Terry with the household expenses and would ignore Brittney, often leaving her for long periods of time at Terry's. "I felt like I was being used," complains Terry. "But then he would turn on the charm and my heart would take over.

"If we had a fight," she says, "when it was over, he would cry. He'd come to my door, cry, and beg me to open the door. If I wouldn't do it, he would write suicide letters." Her neighbors and friends, Terry continues, "all thought: what a wimp!" Although she paints a portrait of a deeply troubled and unstable young man, Terry says she didn't see it at the time because he was a master of making women feel sorry for him. Nothing was his fault; everything bad that happened was the product of a conspiracy against him, or some kind of discrimination.

On April 20, 1989, he left Brittney, as usual, with Terry and drove to Oklahoma City to appear at an INS hearing on his case. Around midday, he called. He was crying.

"What's wrong?" Terry asked.

"I'm in jail," he sobbed.

"Why? What did you do?"

"I don't know," he blubbered. "They won't tell me."

Mohammed was being less than candid, since he had kept Terry in the dark about the real extent of his problems with the INS. In actuality, he had been "declared deported" at the hearing and taken into custody by Immigration officials. He was held for five hours before his attorney posted a $10,000 bond, which Mohammed later forfeited, allowing him ten days to file an appeal, which he subsequently did.

Mohammed and Terry spoke for a few more minutes, and then he promised to call her back again, but didn't. Instead, he arrived at Terry's house late that evening. "He was real upset, different," she says. He told her that the INS was trying to deport him and that he had posted a bond to get out of jail. His attorney, he reassured her, had said not to worry. "At this time," she says, "I had no idea what was going on. All I knew was that I loved him." Terry later learned that he had managed to pay the bond from savings he had amassed while she was supporting him.

They had a heated argument the following week, triggered by Mohammed's volatile and increasingly inconsiderate behavior. Terry decided she needed some time to clear her head and reflect on their relationship, so she refused to see him for a week. Mohammed called constantly, but she hung up on him each time. Undeterred, he drove to her house and pounded on the door, but she wouldn't let him in or speak to him.

On May 2, he called again and, before she could slam the phone down, pleaded with her to see him. "I'm gonna be leaving," he cried.

"What?"

"I really need to talk to you."

Terry reluctantly gave in, and he drove directly over to her house. A number of Terry's family members and friends were visiting, so she and Mohammed met out on the porch. He told Terry that he loved her, but that he was going back to Bangladesh and taking Brittney with him. He would give her his address and telephone number, he said.

"I couldn't believe it," says Terry. "All the feelings I had for him came back to me. He told me he loved me and to call him, and then he left." Terry burst into tears and was so distraught when she went back into the house that her guests thought something terrible had happened.

He called her later that night and "said again that he loved me and wished we could be together forever. I told him after his divorce, we could be." But Mohammed was adamant. That was impossible, he reminded her, because he was going to be deported. Then he gingerly brought up an idea that Terry now suspects had been on his mind all along.

"Why don't you come with me?" he offered. "You can marry me over there, and then I can come back on a visa and fight for my daughter, and not get deported."

Terry was speechless. Going to Bangladesh had never come up before; she didn't even know where Bangladesh was. Texas was as far away from home as she had ever been. If Mohammed had suggested traveling to the moon, the idea would have been no more fantastic than flying to Bangladesh. And while the subject of marriage had come up before, they hadn't discussed it in a while, and many things about the relationship had changed during the past few weeks.

"I-I can't do that," she stammered.

"Please," he begged. "Do this for me. You'll only be gone for a few weeks."

Terry said she needed time to think about it. She was full of conflicting emotions about Mohammed and his proposal, and she didn't know what to do. The product of a broken home, raised by a grandmother in Guthrie, just north of Oklahoma City, Terry had dropped out of high school and married young. It had not been a happy marriage, and the experience still haunted her. Other than the arrival of her daughter, Twila, few good things had happened to Terry in her life. She desperately wanted to be happy and to find some way to escape the hand-to-mouth existence she had known throughout her adult life, including periods on public assistance. Initially, Mohammed had seemed like the answer to her prayers, but now she wasn't so sure. Nevertheless, she finally decided to take a gamble and follow him to Bangladesh. She didn't know what lay in store for her, but she couldn't imagine that it could be any worse than her life in Tulsa. "If I could help him, bring him back, help him fight for Brittney, I thought, that'd work," she concluded.

"I'll do it," she informed Mohammed, who was ecstatic about her decision and immediately began making preparations for their trip. Terry applied for passports for herself and Twila, and Mohammed purchased four tickets to Bangladesh, charging them to his American Express card. The tickets for Terry, Twila, and Brittney were round-trip, with open returns. He bought a one-way ticket for himself, explaining that he might have to stay a little bit longer and could "buy a ticket cheaper in Bangladesh anyway." Terry assumed that Mohammed had obtained Keli's permission for Brittney to accompany them, and was not overly concerned about it since he had bought a return ticket for her.

Mohammed portrayed the trip as something of a vacation. They would have a great time, he assured her. He painted an exotic portrait of life in his homeland, and Terry's excitement grew as the time for their departure approached.

They set off on May 10, 1989. It didn't take long for Terry to discover that the reality of Bangladesh was far different than depicted by Mohammed. As their plane approached Dacca, the capital, Mohammed began to cry, and Terry realized that something was wrong. "He knew what was coming, you know," she says. "He was a mess.

"When we stepped off the plane, I realized we had just entered a new world," she remembers. "It was so hot. There was no wind at all; just the sun. I thought at least when we entered the airport it would be cool, but I got another surprise: there was no air conditioning, no open windows, just a few ceiling fans blowing the hot air around. All I could smell was body odor. People were pushing and everyone was staring at us. It took three hours before we got through Immigration and stepped outside the airport."

Mohammed's family, whom he hadn't seen in seven years, was

waiting for them. Terry was greeted stiffly by his parents, three sisters, and brother-in-law. Only his father and the youngest sister, Molutie, spoke any English. With their luggage in tow, they made their way through a sea of people to a small, battered van, which Mohammed's father had borrowed for the occasion. "There were people everywhere," she recalls. "Staring, pushing, touching you, begging for money. Twila and Brittney just freaked out. They were looking at everything and everybody and pointing because they had earrings in their noses."

Terry immediately detected hostility on the part of Mohammed's mother. "She just kinda looked at you, but didn't see you," says Terry. "She didn't like Americans, and Mohammed was her only son, so she took an immediate dislike to me."

They initially went to a rundown hotel with no air conditioning, and were taken to a filthy room where Mohammed and his father argued heatedly over where they would stay. Apparently Mohammed's father was ashamed of their humble house and wanted them to stay in the hotel. "The girls had to go to the bathroom," Terry recalls, "and the toilet was just a hole in the floor. There was no toilet paper and just a bucket of water to wash in. If this was a 'nice' hotel, I wondered what the house could possibly look like."

Finally, it was decided that they would go to the family home. But by this time Terry already was having second thoughts about the trip and what she had gotten herself and her daughter into. "It was like a bad dream," she says, "where I just wanted to wake up."

They traveled through the teeming streets of Dacca for about thirty minutes until they reached Mohammed's home in the Mirpur section of the city, "where they had never seen white skin before." The streets were dirt or crumbling blacktop, and most of the homes were ugly cinderblock or cement boxes, jammed together with no apparent rhyme or reason. The vegetation was stunted and ugly, not leafy enough to provide real relief from the blazing sun, and there was not even the hint of a breeze to carry away the fetid smell of rotting garbage and open sewers.

When they pulled up in front of a bunkerlike, one-story concrete house with a wall around it, a crowd gathered to stare at them. "I'm not ready for this," Terry thought to herself. "As I entered the iron gates that led to the house and saw the iron bars on the windows," she said, "I fought back my tears, even though I knew we were only there for a visit. As I entered the house, there's really no words anyone could say to describe it. The walls had not seen paint for fifteen years. The curtains were old, dingy material hanging in front of the windows. As I sat down, all I could think of was, why had Mohammed lied to me? His talk about the maids and his nice home; it was all a lie."

As at the hotel, the bathroom consisted of a hole in the floor with no toilet paper. The only running water came from a pipe behind the house, but it was available just once or twice a day and had to be boiled before it could be used. Some days there was no water at all. When water was available, there was a five-gallon bucket for bathing purposes. "You'd just stand in it and bathe yourself," says Terry. Electricity, too, was sporadic, available on the average for only two or three hours a day.

The walls and floor of the house crawled with cockroaches and other bugs. Lizards scampered up and down the walls and scuttled across the ceiling, but they were valued because they ate the bugs and were believed to bring good luck. Large black flies buzzed through the house and dive-bombed Terry and the girls.

Mohammed's family sat and stared at the visitors from America, and they soon were joined by dozens of neighbors who tramped through the house "just to see us, to look at our skin, to touch us. We were the entertainment." That evening the family had a meal of rice and curry, and a soup made from fish heads. Afterwards, when Mohammed and Terry crawled under the mosquito netting into bed, she says that she "could tell he was very embarrassed, but he did not say anything."

"Let's hurry so we can go back home," she whispered to him. He didn't reply. Instead, he just rolled over and went to sleep.

The following morning she awoke around 7:00 A.M. "It was already so hot, all you could do was sweat," she remembers. After a breakfast of rice and eggs, flavored with a little meat, people once again began passing through the house to stare at them. There was almost no privacy. Strangers would "even come into the bedroom while I was dressing to stare at me," says Terry. "And these were not even family members."

As the days passed, Mohammed paid less and less attention to

Terry and the two girls, preferring to spend most of the day with friends. He told her that they could not go out as they had in the States; in Bangladesh, women and children stayed home. There was little to do but sweat and play with the two children in the ovenlike bedroom.

Terry was also becoming concerned by Mohammed's harsh treatment of Brittney. The little girl had always been extremely fastidious and couldn't stand to be dirty. But when she had asked her father for some toilet paper shortly after they arrived, he slapped her across the face. When she mentioned her mother's name one day, he had slapped her hard and warned her never to utter her mother's name again. One time, Mohammed had dragged Brittney away from the table for some childish indiscretion and beaten her behind the closed door to the bedroom. All they could hear was the child's screams; the beating lasted so long that even his parents became concerned and tried, unsuccessfully, to intervene.

Mohammed's youngest sister, Molutie, made an avocation of tormenting Brittney. She terrified her little niece with stories of spiders under the bed that would attack her in her sleep, and other terrible fates likely to befall her. She and her girlfriends would goad and tease Brittney, sometimes locking her in a dark room, then running away and hiding. As long as she was in Bangladesh, Terry tried to protect Brittney and shelter her from Mohammed's wrath; but often her efforts were counterproductive and only made Mohammed more angry.

Three weeks had elapsed since their arrival, and Mohammed hadn't given Terry any indication he was preparing to return to the States, so she confronted him and demanded to know when he was going to obtain a visa. "You know that we have to get married first," he told her. By now, she had serious misgivings about the marriage but was desperate to return to the United States and figured that things would get better once they got back. If not, at least she would be home in Tulsa and could divorce him.

On June 11, Terry and Mohammed were married in a Moslem ceremony. She wore a pink sari with gold threads running through it, and gold embroidery, along with bracelets and other family jewelry. There was a little family celebration afterwards, but Terry was far from jubilant. "This was the day I had been waiting for, and now all I could think about was getting a visa for Mohammed and getting the hell out of there," she says.

When Terry subsequently raised the issue of his visa, Mohammed snapped at her that she should start behaving like a Moslem wife, and that he, not she, would decide when they were going to leave. "I couldn't believe it," she says. "The man I fell in love with and adored had turned into a monster. I felt so helpless."

He told her that they would wait a couple of weeks before going to the U.S. Embassy to apply for a visa. In the meantime, he said, her place was in the kitchen with his mother. She dutifully obeyed and each day spent hours helping Mohammed's mother and sister-in-law cook over an open flame in the sweltering kitchen. Then one day Mohammed informed Terry out of the blue that they were going to the U.S. Embassy. She says that "I felt like a stone had been lifted from my heart. The next day we were going to the embassy and soon we would be leaving. I told the kids we were going home." Terry was positively euphoric. That night, "we made love the way we used to, like we were in America and this nightmare had never happened."

As they departed for the embassy, Mohammed's father explained to Terry that he was pleased for her and the children that they would soon be leaving. Bangladesh, he went on, was not the right place for them.

They met with a U.S. consular official at the embassy and were given various forms to fill out and return the following day. Everyone was in high spirits that night as they completed the forms. At one point, Mohammed's father took Terry aside and told her that "he loved me like a daughter," and explained "how ashamed he had been when Mohammed came back to Bangladesh with no education. All of Mohammed's friends who stayed in Bangladesh had their degrees and he had nothing." Terry says that "I really liked Uhba [Mohammed's father]. I felt like he really cared for me. He took the time to talk to me, which Mohammed didn't do. At one point, Mohammed had told me he wouldn't talk with me any more until I could speak his language."

When they returned the forms to the embassy, they were told that it would take two to three weeks to process them. As the days passed, the rush of happiness Terry felt on learning that Mohammed was going to apply for his visa began to dissipate. Once again he was behaving indifferently toward her and the girls. He "just sat in the house, sometimes reading. He would talk to his family, but it was as if I was nothing to him. He would always talk about Americans and how they were no good." It was at this point, says Terry, that she realized that Mohammed "was no longer my life" and that the marriage was over, even if they got back to the States without further problem.

Although Terry couldn't understand it at the time, Mohammed seemed uninterested in learning about the progress of his visa application; it was as if he already knew what was going to happen. So, after two weeks, she called Vice-Consul David DiGiovanna, who told her to come to his office and to bring Mohammed along. It was then, says Terry, that she got "the shock of my life."

DiGiovanna explained to her that Mohammed had been deported from the United States, a fact that could not be erased by his marriage to Terry. Under the law, he continued, Mohammed could not even apply for a visa for two years.

Terry was stunned. "Are you sure?" she asked, fighting back tears.

"Yes."

She looked over at Mohammed, who avoided eye contact with her. "Did you not know about this?" she asked in an accusatory voice.

"N-no," he lied, jumping to his feet. He stood there, trembling with frustration and indignation, and began to cry. He accused DiGiovanna of "lying about me. Americans don't like me," he raged on. "I have not been deported. You're out to get me!"

Both in tears, they left the embassy with Mohammed still protesting that it was all a lie, that he could straighten everything out, that all he had to do was call his immigration attorney in Tulsa. Terry subsequently learned that once deportation proceedings had begun against Mohammed, the attorney allegedly had advised him to return to Bangladesh, marry a U.S. citizen, and then reapply for a new visa. What the attorney hadn't said—or perhaps what Mohammed had deliberately hidden from Terry—was that he was not eligible even to apply for a new visa for two years, just as the consular official had explained.

Mohammed's attorney suggested by phone that they try a new

application in India, but "Mohammed started dragging his feet," Terry says. "He didn't want to go. He just sat around the house and didn't want to hear about it, because he knew. He knew they wouldn't give it to him, and he didn't want to waste money taking me to India to find that out."

Mohammed's father subsequently began pressuring his son to leave, saying there was no work in Bangladesh, especially for someone who hadn't acquired an education. Accompanied by his father, they visited the British Embassy to see if Mohammed could get a visa to Great Britain. However, the British official informed them that a visa was impossible since Mohammed was wanted by the U.S. authorities for abducting Brittney. Mohammed and his father left the embassy, but Terry stayed behind, and soon a woman from the American Embassy arrived and inquired about Brittney's well-being. Terry described the fact that she had some health problems that were of growing concern, and a few days later two embassy representatives stopped by the house to check on her condition.

By this time, Terry and the girls all had worms and other ailments. Twila was particularly sick; she had a high fever and wouldn't eat and, as a consequence, was losing a great deal of weight. Mohammed dismissed her illness, maintaining that she was being cared for by local doctors and that they would make her well. But Terry regarded the local physicians as quacks. Their treatment of Twila was to massage her and "push the poison out of her with their fingers."

"These doctors are no good," Terry told Mohammed. "She needs an American doctor."

"No," responded Mohammed.

"We have to go home," cried Terry.

"You're not going anywhere!" Mohammed screamed at her. "This is your country now. You're not leaving here. You need to start acting like a Bangladeshi wife."

Terry glared at him. "I'm leaving," she said coldly.

"No! You'll never leave!"

"I'll leave here or die."

"Then die," he hissed. Terry was at the top of the stairs leading up to the roof, and Mohammed, fists clenched and full of fury, started up the steps toward her. "Go ahead and die," he ordered. "Go out on the roof and throw yourself off." As he came at her, she kicked him, knocking him down the stairs. He wasn't hurt and ran back up and started beating her with his fists, only stopping when his father and uncle dragged him off of her. His father was crying and trying to comfort Terry, repeating that he loved her like a daughter. He helped her to one of the bedrooms and she pleaded with him: "Help us. Please help us to go home!"

He agreed, but a few minutes later Mohammed entered the room and slapped her hard across the face and said, "No one's going to help you. You're here, and that's that." Then he threw two books at her, the Koran and a book in English about how to behave like a good Moslem wife, and stormed out of the room.

After Mohammed left, Terry pulled herself together. She went to the phone and called the American Embassy. "I need help," she told the Bangladeshi man who took the call. But at that moment, Mohammed returned and overheard her conversation. He grabbed the phone from her and slapped her again across the face. He slammed the phone back into its cradle and Terry ran from the room in tears. The following morning she discovered that he had put a lock on the phone.

It also was evident that Mohammed's father, however well intentioned, wasn't going to cross his son and give them any real help. In the weeks that followed, she stayed in the bedroom all day with the children, trying to make them happy and thinking about how they could escape. Twila's fever subsided, but Terry still had to force her to eat. Brittney was also losing weight. In an effort to get the girls to eat more, Terry tried cooking them American meals, but her efforts fell flat because few of the ingredients she needed were available in Bangladesh.

"I had to find a way out," Terry says. "I thought about sneaking out one night, but knew we would be caught. The section of Dacca we lived in was very dangerous. Everyone knew us, and there were no other Americans around. We were watched all the time, so I knew we couldn't just run away."

If she was going to escape, Terry realized that it was critical that she get Mohammed to drop his guard, so she reluctantly began playing the role of the chastised wife. She stroked his wounded ego with compliments and even started sleeping with him again. He had decided to raise chickens on the roof as a way to earn some money, and she told him "it was a wonderful idea and that I could help him." They enrolled in a chicken-raising course together and attended sessions daily. Each day Terry tried to size up the class, hoping to spot someone she could trust, someone who might help her. If she could just get in touch with the U.S. Embassy, she knew everything would be all right. But no one in the course seemed particularly trustworthy or dependable. If she tried again to leave and failed, Terry feared the consequences; there was no telling what Mohammed might do.

To further enhance her charade, Terry began zealously studying Islam, and let everyone know that she was in the process of converting. She prayed openly and visibly, which was especially gratifying to Mohammed's father. "Uhba, the father, was so pleased, because he is very religious, that he started to cry. He said, 'Here I [Terry] am, an American, trying so hard, and his son would not even pray to Allah.' "

The phone became her focus; it was her only lifeline. If she could just get a few minutes alone on the phone, she could contact the embassy and seek help. Every time she even went into the room where the locked phone was kept, other family members would congregate around her, watching, waiting for her to do something. From the bedroom, however, Terry could just see the phone, and she kept a constant eye on it, hoping against hope that someone would forget to lock it back up before they put it away or that she could discover where they hid the key. Finally, peering from the bedroom, she spied Molutie putting away the key after using the phone. Now that she knew the hiding place, she had to wait for everyone to disappear long enough for her to retrieve the key, remove the lock, dial, and reach someone at the embassy. "I had to wait until the time was right," says Terry. "I could not get caught this time. It was my last chance."

At last her chance came. The chicken coops were nearly finished, and Mohammed invited everyone to come up on the roof to admire his handiwork. All of the family members dutifully traipsed up the stairs; and Terry rapidly sized up the situation and decided that it was now or never. In a few moments they would miss her. She slipped out of the bedroom, took the key gingerly from its hiding place, and rushed to the phone. After stripping away the lock, she dialed the number of the U.S. Embassy. But nothing happened. The phone was dead. "I started crying and had to get control of myself," she says.

She tried again. "Jesus, help me," she prayed.

Suddenly, the line crackled to life and she could hear the number ringing. Vice-Consul David DiGiovanna answered.

"This is Terry Smith."

"Yes, Terry."

"I need your help," she blurted out. "I've got to get out of here. I'm being held prisoner in this house."

DiGiovanna knew where Mohammed lived and told her to "be ready in one hour." Help was on the way.

In the background, Terry heard Molutie approaching. "I've got to go," she said, and returned the phone to its cradle. There was no time to put the lock back on, so she quickly jammed the key into its hiding place and prayed that no one would spot the unlocked phone before DiGiovanna arrived.

While she waited with Twila and her suitcase, Terry took Brittney aside and told her, "Twila and I have to leave for a while."

"Am I going with you?" the little girl asked.

"No, honey," Terry said, folding her arms around the child and hugging her. "I'm afraid not." Terry knew that Brittney was Mohammed's daughter and that she had no legal right to take her. "But I promise you," Terry pledged, tears running from her eyes, "I'll be back for you. I promise."

Brittney began to sob quietly, not comprehending why she had to remain behind.

At twelve noon, she heard Molutie scream, "Americans! Americans!" as a van pulled up in front of the house and DiGiovanna and several other men from the embassy got out. Because vehicles other than carts and pedicabs were such a rarity in the Mirpur district, a crowd quickly gathered.

As the men approached the house, Mohammed ran down the stairs and confronted Terry, who was holding on to Twila with one hand and clutching a hastily packed suitcase in the other.

"You're not leaving," he screamed.

"Yeah," she responded as calmly as she could. "This is it."

"You're not leaving," he repeated, his family gathering behind him. "You're my wife."

Mohammed forced Terry back into the bedroom, which looked out onto the porch where the embassy men were standing.

"Don't leave me," she cried to them.

"You need to hurry," they shouted back over the din now erupting inside. "There'll be a riot in no time at all. We have to get out of here."

In the meantime, Molutie hustled Brittney, who was confused and crying that she wanted to go with Terry and Twila, into a back room and slammed the door. Another family member took up a position in front of the door.

The crowd outside was swelling by the minute, and the embassy van was engulfed by people.

Summoning all of her courage, Terry bolted for the door with Twila. Mohammed and his family tried to physically restrain her as she clawed her way to the door, but she pushed them away and began tearing at the locks. Each time she got one unlatched, they locked the other.

Then Mohammed dragged Terry, screaming and pleading, away from the door, and Molutie pulled Twila from her mother's grasp back into the bedroom. Terry broke free, jerked Twila away from Molutie, and once again attacked the locks on the door. This time she managed to unlatch both locks and to push the door open just a crack, before Mohammed threw his weight against it. She pushed her arm through the narrow opening and Mohammed, his face contorted with fury, yelled that he would break her wrist if she didn't stop.

"Go ahead and break it," she snarled back at him.

At that moment, the men from the embassy leaned hard into the door from the outside and propelled it open, knocking Mohammed and the other struggling members of his family backward.

DiGiovanna appeared in the doorway and gazed into the house. Terry was standing to one side of the door, holding Twila in her arms, jerking with sobs as she tried to catch her breath. Mohammed, disheveled and panting from the struggle, stood in the center of the room in the midst of his wild-eyed family.

"Hi," he said, recovering quickly and trying to seem as nonchalant as possible. "Come on in. We're just having a little quarrel."

DiGiovanna didn't move, but addressed Mohammed from the

doorway in a calm voice, barely audible over the din coming from the street and the excited jabbering of Mohammed's family.

"Mohammed," he said, "I know she's your wife. But she's also an American citizen, and if she wants to speak with us, she can."

"Ah, oh sure," Mohammed responded, trying to avoid the man's reproachful gaze. "Come on in."

DiGiovanna and his colleagues wouldn't come into the house but held their ground while Terry explained that she wanted to leave immediately. She quickly gathered up her things and, with Twila in tow, walked rapidly out of the house toward the waiting van, cursing Mohammed as she left.

Since there was no flight to the United States for two days, the embassy put Terry and Twila up in a safe house until it was time for their departure. The secrecy was necessary because Terry had been married in Bangladesh and was, in the eyes of the local authorities, little more than her husband's property. If Mohammed had been able to discover where Terry was hiding, he might have been able to get the local police to detain her. DiGiovanna told Terry that it was fortunate that she had not acceded to Mohammed's desire to legally adopt Twila. If Mohammed had adopted her, he explained, he would have been her primary guardian under Bangladeshi law and she could not have left the country without his permission.

Terry's joy in escaping Bangladesh was mixed with the sorrow of leaving Brittney behind. The little girl was like a daughter to her, but since she had no legal claim to Brittney, there was nothing she could do. "I'll get Brittney out someday, somehow," she vowed. "God will show me the way."

# 8
# The
# "Angel from
# Oklahoma"

TERRY WAS enormously relieved to be back in Tulsa, but there were many things to attend to immediately. They had been gone for more than three months, and Twila had already missed the beginning of the school year. Twila had lost 20 pounds while in Bangladesh, a considerable amount of weight for a six-year-old, and both she and her mother had intestinal parasites, head lice, and other ailments.

There were people looking for Mohammed, Terry discovered, mostly creditors. He had stiffed American Express for $11,679.26 for their tickets and other expenses, and his account had been turned over to a Dallas collection agency. At least three other agencies also were trying to recover more than $2,000 in charges.

Terry, however, was totally unprepared for the call she received on her third day back in town. It was from Keli.

## ENEMIES BECOME ALLIES

Since Mohammed and Brittney's disappearance, Keli had driven by Terry's house every day to see if there was any sign that she had returned. She had already been by the house once this particular day and had spotted no activity, but her mother, Jeanne, suggested that they take another pass by it.

Keli argued that it was a waste of time, but Jeanne was insistent.

They drove by the house, which didn't look any different. Then Keli's dog started whining, indicating that he needed to be walked, so they pulled over to the side of the street.

As Keli and her mother walked the dog, Keli glanced over at Terry's house and, much to her surprise, the front door was open. A moment later, a woman appeared.

"My God, Mom. That's Terry!"

Jeanne Cripps stared at the woman for a moment and shook her head. "No, that's not Terry."

The woman in the doorway was thinner than Keli remembered and her hair was a different color, but she was positive it was Terry. She strained her eyes to get a better look, and at that moment Twila appeared. The young girl also had lost a good deal of weight, but there could be no doubt as to her identity.

"What should we do?" Keli asked her mother.

"C'mon," Jeanne replied. "I think we'd better go."

Keli didn't want to leave, but her mother was adamant. When they got back home, Keli called Judy Feeney, who counseled restraint. Don't tip your hand, she advised; wait until Dave gets there the following week, then you can decide what to do. Keli reluctantly agreed to hold off on any direct approach. However, as the afternoon wore on she couldn't stand it any longer; she had to find out what Terry knew about her daughter. She quickly found Terry's number and dialed it.

Terry was totally taken aback by the call. She had never before spoken to Keli and all she knew about her was what Mohammed had told her. Mohammed had described Keli as a "whore," who "slept with blacks, used drugs, and was an alcoholic." He always portrayed himself as the aggrieved party in the breakup of the marriage, and had complained that his wife "had cheated on him and all he ever did was try to make a good living for her."

"I know you've heard every ugly thing about me possible," Keli explained, anticipating Terry's apprehension. "And I realize you have no reason to trust anything I say, but I love my daughter.

Even if you won't talk to me about anything else, please tell me how Brittney is."

"She's okay," responded Terry, still uncertain as to whether or not to trust Keli.

"Are you sure?"

"Yeah, she's okay."

But the more they talked, the more open Terry became. And the more she divulged. "By the end of the conversation," says Keli, "I had found out that Mohammed had been beating Brittney, that she might have a kidney infection or a damaged kidney, or a bladder infection, since after Mohammed beat her on one occasion she was urinating every twenty minutes. It scared me to death."

As the conversation wound down, Keli still didn't have a firm idea of where Terry stood. She knew from the State Department that they had gotten married, but reading between the lines, Keli sensed that Terry had had a miserable trip and that something had happened between her and Mohammed. Terry seemed genuinely devoted to Brittney, so Keli decided to take a chance and see what the other woman's reaction would be.

"Will you help me?" Keli asked.

"How?"

"Just information for now." She asked Terry if she would be willing to get together and talk. Terry indicated that she would.

Terry's last words before she hung up chilled Keli to the bone. "If you don't get her out of there," she warned Keli, "she's not going to live to see another birthday."

## "BABY, PLEASE COME BACK"

In the meantime, Terry received a letter from Mohammed, dated only nine days after her flight from Bangladesh. In it, he told her, "my heart is broken real bad" and asked her "why did you do this to me? Don't you know how much I love you and how much I am missing you?" He went on to say that he had gone to the airport "to give you a happy goodbye," but "you were already in the plane." Then he chastised her for not seeing "how I felt at that time. Your selfish, cruel mind didn't even look back for a second.

Didn't even say—'Mohammed, you are my husband, I love you forever, I am going to miss you.' "

A few days later, Terry received a second letter. Written in the same turgid prose as the first, but dated twelve days after her departure, the letter opened with Mohammed's observation that the twelve days had passed "like twelve years. My inside is burning like a fire-flame and I am screaming, 'Terry, come back to my heart.' " He told her that he was "very lonely and scare [sic] without you." He blamed his dilemma on bad advice from his lawyer, who had urged him to return to Bangladesh, and he pleaded with her to "help me to get out of this mess." In another letter, dated September 21, Mohammed closed by saying, "Baby, please come back. We will be very happy. Because we need each other."

These were the first of many letters Terry received from Mohammed in subsequent months. On first reading, his words always seemed so sweet and sincere; but then Terry would reflect back on the miserable weeks she spent in Bangladesh with Mohammed and his family, and all of the warm feelings conjured up by the letters would evaporate.

Soon Keli and Terry moved in together, drawn by their common hatred of Mohammed and their mutual commitment to somehow bring Brittney home. They talked a lot about Mohammed, comparing their experiences and laughing at his photographs in the picture albums. "If he could have seen us," laughs Terry, "it would have been his worst nightmare."

The biggest problem they faced, however, was money. Any effort to recover the little girl would surely cost tens of thousands of dollars, and neither Keli nor Terry was working; both were drawing public assistance. Keli turned to everyone she knew for money, but no one had the kind of money a rescue would require, so in desperation she wrote to talk-show host Oprah Winfrey, Wal-Mart billionaire Sam Walton, and country music king Roy Clark, seeking funds. All three sent back form letters turning down her request.

It was at this point that a remarkable woman appeared on the scene, a woman whom Judy would come to call the "Angel from Oklahoma."

## THE GOOD SAMARITAN

In 1989, Amelia Smith (no relation to Terry) was a $41,500-a-year systems and procedures analyst in the communications department of American Airlines, where she had worked for the previous fifteen years. A life-long Republican and community volunteer, Amelia was a short, pleasantly plump woman in her late fifties with a million-dollar smile and a mile-a-minute delivery when she talked. She was sitting at her desk in late September 1989, when one of her co-workers pointed out a flier in her in-box.

"Look at this," said the co-worker, reading the flier. "Have you heard about this?"

Amelia took the flier and was immediately struck by "this picture of this adorable little girl." Dated September 15 and addressed to all employees of American Airlines, the flier was headed: "WE NEED YOUR HELP!!" Circulated by friends of Keli's mother, Jeanne Cripps, who worked for American, it described how Jeanne Cripps's granddaughter, Brittney, had been kidnapped to Bangladesh, where she was suffering from "acute malnourishment" and a "serious kidney/bladder illness." "An international agency," the circular went on, was willing to rescue Brittney and return her to her mother, but it would cost a minimum of $25,000. "Needless to say, not many of us could afford such a fee. However, if each employee here gave as small a donation as $1.00 each," the employees in Tulsa alone could raise $10,000. The donations were described as tax-deductible, although that was incorrect.

The first thing that went through Amelia's mind was, "If this is a secret operation, why are they making it so public?" She was also suspicious of the claim that donations were tax-deductible. Nevertheless, she had just inherited a modest house and a little money, and was inclined to make a donation, perhaps $100.

On a whim, she decided to call Jeanne Cripps to get some answers before she wrote out a check. Jeanne described her granddaughter's plight, and how she and Keli had made contact with a group of commandos—at a firm called CTU—that were willing to attempt a rescue of Brittney. The more they talked, the more questions Amelia had. Just who were these CTU people? What were their qualifications? Had they ever performed such a mission before? And if these people are bona fide, she asked, wasn't it rather dangerous to advertise what they were preparing to do in a plea for donations? "After all," she told Jeanne, "we have a lot of these international students training with American and coming right on our base. Some of them are from the same country."

Despite these doubts, Amelia's emotions were taking over. The story of the little girl spirited away to a strange and inhospitable land, far from the mother who loved her, touched the core of her soul. Without giving it any more thought, she told Jeanne that "I would like you to take the appropriate course of action and for me to participate." She really didn't have any idea as to the size of the commitment she would be willing to make, but in the space of a twenty-minute phone conversation she had crossed the line from casual bystander to potential bankroller of an international rescue effort.

The following day, Jeanne Cripps called Amelia back. She explained that she had spoken with CTU and they confirmed that it was a bad idea to mention a potential rescue in any fund-raising effort. Consequently, Jeanne indicated that they would not be distributing any more fliers. However, while appreciating the need for secrecy, Jeanne was at a loss to understand how they could raise the necessary money to underwrite the rescue. In her mind, it was something of a Catch-22: if they publicized the case in order to fund the rescue, they risked the operational security of the mission. On the other hand, if they didn't publicize the case, there would be no money with which to mount the rescue.

"How much do you figure it's going to cost?" Amelia wanted to know.

"Twenty-five thousand dollars, minimum," Jeanne replied.

"Let me do some checking."

Amelia called her adult daughter and explored the possibility of funding the rescue. Referring to the relatively small nest egg she had inherited, Amelia figured that "it's part of my retirement, so if I don't have enough, she has to take care of me, I guess." In addition, her daughter wanted to go back to school to earn her Ph.D. and was hoping that her mother would help financially.

Her daughter was cool to the idea but understanding, since she knew her mother could be very impulsive when it came to helping others. Amelia's long-time boyfriend, Joe, by contrast, was adamantly opposed to any thought of such generosity. In his mind, "these people were probably nothing but deadbeats, I would never see my money again, and how hard can it be to go get a child out of Bangladesh? I mean, you get on a plane and go pick her up and bring her home."

"But the child's in danger," rebutted Amelia. "Her health is bad and she's not getting medical care. If I spend too much time analyzing this thing, something could happen to her." It was evident that Amelia had already made up her mind, and Joe knew better than try to argue with her.

Amelia's emotions were on autopilot; in less than two days she had become totally immersed in Brittney's case with such intensity that the little girl almost seemed like a relative, or even her own granddaughter. With characteristic efficiency, she read everything she could about CTU and made some inquiries on her own about the firm. "I wasn't interested in hiring mercenaries," she says. "But the CTU organization, from what I had found out about them, were people with a lot of integrity . . . and weren't going to go in and do really illegal things. They weren't going to kill this guy and bring Brittney out; violence was not to be part of it."

Like most other people, Amelia had only a cursory knowledge of Bangladesh. "I probably knew about their monsoons every year," she recalls, "and that they're such a poor country." The one thing she was certain of was that it was no place for a little Oklahoma girl stolen from her mother. In this regard, she empathized closely with Keli's anguish. "I can imagine the terror that could strike the heart of a mother if her child was gone, was across the ocean, to one of the poorest countries in the world. It was just horrifying."

What no one else knew at the time was that Keli's suffering had touched a raw nerve in Amelia's subconscious, dredging up long-suppressed memories of her own agony as a mother more than two decades earlier, when her former husband had threatened to take their daughter away from her. "I guarded her all the time," says Amelia, choking back tears. "I sacrificed child support and moved here and lived with my family two years until I could put her in a nursery where there was total security." To Amelia, Keli's story was a replay of her own desperate years after separating from her husband. She had little money and few friends in those days. What she would have given, she told herself, for someone to have helped her, who would have eased her burdens; it would have meant everything. Now that she had the wherewithal to help another young mother in the same terrible situation, she wasn't going to shirk the responsibility.

Not more than a half hour had gone by since Jeanne Cripps had spoken to Amelia, and she wasn't expecting Amelia to call back for a day or two, if ever. More than one person she and Keli had turned to promised to help and then didn't deliver. She had never even met Amelia, and wasn't very optimistic about some stranger lending a significant hand. Besides, even if Amelia came up with a thousand or two toward the rescue, they'd still have a long way to go to fund the operation.

So, when Amelia called back and offered to advance the $25,000 needed for the operation, Jeanne was stunned. Amelia intended it to be a loan, but was prepared to fund the rescue even if Keli and her mother were unable to pay it back. After thanking Amelia profusely, Jeanne phoned Keli to tell her the good news, and then they called Judy.

As in so many other cases, the lack of money had been the chief impediment to mounting a rescue operation. Now that the money had been found, Judy assured Jeanne and Keli that Dave would travel to Tulsa within a week to take stock of the situation and gather the necessary information to go forward with the case.

## RECON IN BANGLADESH

The meeting in Tulsa between Dave and Keli and her mother, Jeanne, went well. But while both women liked the CTU operator, Dave Chatellier was less certain about them. "My impression of Keli was that she was a very naive person who had lost her child and really did not know what to do. She had done everything she knew to get the child back, tried everything she could. She had gone to the State Department and the local courts, but she had gotten absolutely no satisfaction anywhere, and she was just at wit's end."

Still, Dave found Keli's story compelling. As far as he was concerned, it was a do-able mission, and one that CTU should undertake.

Once back in Fayetteville, it was decided that Dave would go

over to Bangladesh and "do a recon, try to locate her and the house
and pick out some exits, and modes of transportation." Given what
the CTU operatives had heard from Keli, they didn't expect to find
Mohammed very intimidating, and thought there might even be a
possibility of pulling off a rescue similar to the one of Lauren Bayan
in Jordan. If everything looked good, Dave speculated, he could
tell Don to come on over and bring along a little muscle, and they
could improvise a rescue on the spot. It would certainly be the
cheapest way of doing things, and money clearly was a consideration.

Dave bought a plane ticket to Bangladesh through one of
Don's buddies in New York, a travel discounter with a rather
unsavory reputation. Dave had asked the discounter about visas,
and was assured that American citizens didn't need visas for either
India or Bangladesh. But when he got to Kennedy Airport in preparation for boarding the Pan Am flight to India connecting to Bangladesh, he was told that both countries required visas (Bangladesh
for stays longer than fifteen days) and that he would not be allowed
to travel without one. Dave visited both consulates and was granted
visas.

He finally left New York on the evening of November 9 and,
with layovers, arrived in New Delhi at 2:30 A.M. on the 11th. The
terminal was practically deserted and his connecting flight to Bangladesh was incorrectly noted on his ticket: it didn't leave later the
same day, as Dave believed, but rather the day after. Not wanting
to lay over a day, Dave was told he would have to return to the
airport in the morning, after the reservation counters opened, to
book another flight. In the meantime, he was ordered to clear
Immigration and Customs and leave the terminal.

Owing to the late hour, there were no cabs, so when two men
approached him and offered, for a price, to take him to an international hotel, he agreed. But he didn't like the look of things, so
he took his telescoping police baton out of his suitcase and stuck it
in his pants. They had a small, beat-up English car, and started off
down a blacktop road with Dave in the back seat. "All of a sudden,"
Dave recalls, "the guy turns to the right and heads down a dirt
road, and pretty soon he pulls up in front of a couple of shacks and
starts to jump out." Dave grabbed him by the collar and demanded

to know what he was doing, and the man said that he had to tell his sister where he was going.

"Hold it," growled Dave. "You're not going anywhere. You're gonna take me to a hotel."

The driver's companion started to come to his assistance, but Dave pulled the baton from his trousers and flicked it to extend the shaft. When the second man heard that, he froze in his seat.

"All right, guys," Dave repeated calmly. "We're going to a hotel."

The two would-be muggers dutifully drove Dave to the nearest hotel and he gave them the fare they had originally agreed upon so he could not be accused of ripping them off. He took a room, after haggling with the desk clerk for three or four minutes over the price, and started up the stairs. But the two punks materialized again and began to follow him. They were demanding a "tip" of $40.

"Okay, okay," said Dave, flicking his head. "Come upstairs."

They followed him into his room and he grabbed the driver and put him up against the wall. "Look," he told him softly, "you're lucky I'm gonna let you live. In fact, I oughta take back the money I already gave you."

Because of his size, Dave could have snapped the driver's neck in one clean motion, and the man knew it. The driver glanced over at his partner, terror in his eyes, and began crying, "No, no, no, no, no."

Dave held him for a moment longer, then pushed him away, saying, "I'm gonna let you live, but I don't ever want to see you again. Get in your car and get out of here."

The two men fled as quickly as they could, banging into each other as they went through the door, and tripping over people sleeping in the hallway.

After a restless night, Dave bribed the clerk to get him a regular cab, but even so it broke down twice on the way to the airport. The second time, the driver had to stop by the road, remove the floorboards, and repair the transmission. At the airport, there were beggars and thieves everywhere, trying every device in the world, says Dave, to "get their hands on my luggage." He flew to Calcutta and, thanks to an Asian woman he met in the waiting area, learned the prevailing etiquette for securing a ticket on local flights, which were on a first-come first-serve basis. "You must force your way up front," she told him. "They move back and give you room if you're forceful. But if you are not aggressive, they'll run all over you."

With her coaching, he managed to get one of the last tickets on an afternoon flight to Dacca, which finally left at about the time it was scheduled to arrive in the Bangladesh capital. He was hungry, but the "in-flight meal was a handful of some kind of seeds that looked like caraway seeds." When at last he reached Dacca, he took a room at the local Sheraton and "crawled into a hot shower."

The next day, Dave decided to take in the city and get his bearings. Nothing, however, had quite prepared him for Dacca. What little he had seen of India was wretched, but Bangladesh was even worse; traveling from Calcutta to Dacca was, Dave felt, like jumping from the frying pan into the fire. He had read a good deal about Bangladesh before leaving the States, and knew that it was one of the poorest countries on earth, its 120 million people engaged in a perennial struggle to eke out a meager existence on a low-lying floodplain the size of Wisconsin.

A nation in extremis, ravaged by the disease of overpopulation, Bangladesh is a paradise only to those who love misery; the nation has one of the highest infant mortality rates on earth and one of the shortest average lifespans. But numbers don't really tell the story, Dave discovered; they are too sterile, too abstract. Bangladesh was something you had to see with your eyes to believe. The scale of the poverty and human misery was absolutely breathtaking. The smell, too, was overwhelming. With one of the highest average rainfalls in the world, everything stank of mildew and decay; but it was the fetid malodorousness of the open sewers lining the streets, beneath clouds of swarming flies, that most assaulted Dave's nostrils. Owing to the lack of sanitation facilities and the fact that as much as a quarter of Dacca's population lived on the streets, people urinated and defecated in the open, including just beyond the grounds of the Sheraton.

It didn't take long for Dave to realize that moving around Dacca was going to be a problem. As a Westerner, he was literally mobbed wherever he went. "I looked kinda like a dog with fleas, walkin' around the streets, because I had so many beggars hanging around me," he says. "I didn't dare put anything in my pockets for fear that they would be inside them before I knew it."

Walking was out of the question, so he decided to hire a taxi. After the requisite haggling, he secured a driver who had a 1947 Morris Minor cab with no exhaust pipe or rear window. Once again, he was assaulted by beggars at every intersection. "They go to every stopped vehicle and stick their hands in the car," he says, shaking his head. "It was just pitiful. They have fingers missing, hands missing, arms ripped off; it's one of the worst things you've ever seen."

He spent the next two days exploring the city. He would approach the outskirts of the Mirpur section, where Mohammed lived, but whenever he tried to enter its narrow, congested streets, he attracted far too much attention. "There are no white people in Mirpur," he observes. "There are no visitors, no outsiders, so everyone watches you very close. I could not get in there, even in a taxicab, without being totally conspicuous." He subsequently attempted to get into Mirpur by pedicab, but that didn't work either.

In desperation, Dave decided to try again at three o'clock in the morning. In most cities, he says, there are few people and almost no traffic at that hour. But not Mirpur: "There's people everywhere. They're sleeping under anything: under leaves, under trash, any place there was room for someone to lay down. I just couldn't hardly believe it."

Dave decided to abandon his attempts to enter Mirpur, and focus instead on identifying the various escape routes in and out of the city. Once again, Dacca posed unique problems. He checked out how long it would take to get to the city's port from the edge of the Mirpur section, and discovered that it could consume the better part of a day. "It would take sometimes as much as an hour, in a taxicab, to get two city blocks," he says. "There was a lot of rickshaw gridlock. Everything in that part of the country is built for rickshaws and people on foot; it's not built for motor vehicles."

The same was true of the train station. Not only was it difficult to reach, but when a train came in, it was immediately surrounded by a crush of pushing, shoving humanity. The coaches filled within

minutes, with the overflow scrambling up onto the roofs and clinging to the sides of the cars. It was the same, he discovered, with
buses.

The nation of Bangladesh is carved out of the delta of two great
rivers, the Ganges and Brahmaputra, which flow into the Bay of
Bengal. In addition, the marshy delta is laced with scores of other
rivers, tributaries, and canals. So, in desperation, Dave decided to
explore the potential river exits, with the thought of snatching
Brittney, heading for one of the rivers, and getting a boat. But it
was the dry season, and most of the rivers were largely silt. He
discovered that only a flat-bottomed boat or shallow-draft skiff
could successfully navigate the nearly dry channels, and they would
be too unstable to cross the storm-prone Bay of Bengal.

That left the airport, but flying out of the city with Brittney
would be risky. Because there were so few Western travelers to
Bangladesh, Dave and the girl would stand out like "eskimos at a
luau."

Since he couldn't get close to Mohammed, Dave decided on a
gambit to draw Mohammed out of Mirpur. On November 15, he
sent a fax from his hotel back to his office in the States, confident
that it would be read by the staff and would buttress his "cover
story" if Mohammed did any checking. In it, he indicated: "Vacation is great. Weather fine." But, he went on, it was difficult to take
pictures and move around the city due to the swarms of beggars,
and because "British driving rules apply here." Thus, "I need a
local that has some education and speaks English to work for me.
Check our résumé files for a person or a source. Tour guides rented
so far are not acceptable."

Two days later, using what was by now his standard cover
story, Dave called Mohammed up and said that he was from D&D
Productions and was scouting locations for a promotional film. He
needed an English-speaking guide and had asked his hotel to provide one, he said, but they had been unable to do so (which, in
fact, was true). So, he had asked his secretary back in the States for
a list of English speakers in Dacca that could serve as guides—and
Mohammed's name had been on the list. He was willing to pay the
equivalent of $30 a day for the service, and wanted to know if
Mohammed would be interested in interviewing for the post.

Initially, Mohammed seemed very enthusiastic and agreed to

come by the Sheraton for an interview. But the following day he called back to change the time of the appointment, and asked a number of questions, saying that he didn't understand "how you got my name." Dave tried to assuage his concerns and, frankly, thought he had done so, but Mohammed never showed up for his appointment.

Dave had hoped that by giving Mohammed a job he could win his trust, and possibly even wangle an invitation to his home in Mirpur. If he could just see the family home, he knew there was a chance he might be able to lay eyes on Brittney.

But calling Mohammed clearly was a mistake and in fact would result in his becoming extremely wary of anything out of the ordinary and questioning anything that seemed too good to be true. The moment Terry heard, via Judy, that Dave had talked to her husband, her first words were, "Oh my God, he's blown it!"

On November 20, student riots broke out in Dacca, turning an already chaotic city into one of absolute anarchy. The streets were impassable, jammed with student marchers and thousands of police. There were clashes all over the city and many people injured. Dave spent much of the day dodging both rioters and police, trying to figure out the local ferry schedule and determine where various vessels docked. He learned that the ferries had no fixed schedule, and did not always even dock at the same pier.

He'd had enough. After two weeks in the country, he decided that "it was just time for me to get out of there." The following morning Dave flew back to the United States, "never so happy to get out of a place in all my life, and I've been in some really rotten, dirty, bad places."

## INTERMEZZO

After Dave's return, Bangladesh was put on the back burner for a while, due both to the press of other business at CTU and the discouraging results of the recon. Keli, however, stayed in regular touch with Judy.

The Christmas season came and went. It was the first Christmas that Keli had not shared with her daughter since her birth, and it was an unspeakably sad time. The Christmas decorations and carols that the little girl had taken such delight in in the past only made Keli more depressed and reminded her of the awful void in her life since Brittney was taken from her.

On January 16, 1990, Dave returned to Tulsa, at Keli's urging, to debrief Terry and learn what additional information she might be able to provide about Mohammed, his home in Dacca, and the family routine. She filled him in on the individual family members and provided him with a floor plan of the house. Because of the secluded life she had lived, however, she was unable to tell him very much that he didn't already know about Dacca. Nevertheless, Dave regarded the trip as useful, if for no other reason than having the opportunity to assess Terry's credibility and personality.

Terry had spoken to Judy on the phone, and was beginning to emerge as a critical participant in any future effort to rescue Brittney. It was vital, Dave told her, that she keep the line of communication open between herself and Mohammed, since that was the only source of information they had concerning his and Brittney's whereabouts. "Keep tabs on him," he explained. "Let him think that you're growing a little more sympathetic to him. You're his best ticket out of Bangladesh, and he knows it. Keep him talking."

Accordingly, Terry both wrote and called Mohammed frequently, never letting on for a moment that she and Keli had met and were living together. During this period, Keli and Terry spoke with Judy two, even three times a week, keeping her informed about Mohammed and his current state of mind. Generally they recorded Terry's conversations with Mohammed, and sometimes played them to Judy over the phone.

Initially, Mohammed permitted Brittney to talk to Terry and, especially, Twila, on the phone, but in the spring of 1990 he started becoming evasive about his daughter and regularly made excuses about why she couldn't speak to them. As news of Brittney dried up, Keli and Judy became concerned that something might have happened to her. Perhaps her health had taken a turn for the worse? Maybe she had been sent away to live with relatives? Even more disconcerting, in late spring communication with Mohammed all but ceased, leading to speculation that he might have left Bangladesh.

Driven by concerns over Brittney's well-being, on May 18, Keli and Terry flew to Fayetteville to brainstorm with Don, Dave, and Judy about what steps they should take next and what it would cost. Much of the original $25,000 provided by Amelia had already been spent on Dave's recon, travel to and from Tulsa, phone calls, and other expenses.

Separated from her daughter for so many months, Keli was on the verge of a nervous breakdown. She wanted some kind of action as soon as possible, but the CTU contingent insisted that there be a viable plan of action first. They didn't want another false start, like Dave's November mission. According to Don, it was absolutely necessary that they establish whether or not the little girl was still alive and then get a precise fix on her location.

It was at this critical juncture that Terry volunteered to go back to Bangladesh and draw Mohammed out into the open. "The only link to him, and maybe Brittney, is through me," she told them.

The two women had been nurturing the idea for some time. According to Terry, "We would sit and scheme all the time because I knew in my mind that I'd have to go over there. It was the only way."

Don, however, was adamantly opposed to using "civilians" in one of their operations and, quite frankly, was worried about what could happen to Terry if something went wrong. Mohammed was a wimp, but he was also unpredictable and, like so many cowards, capable of resorting to violence against those weaker than himself. Dave was undecided, but leaned against using Terry if there was any other option. Judy, by contrast, supported Keli and Terry, and she and Don had a heated argument after the meeting.

"What is the alternative?" she demanded. "Do you have any better ideas? Sending Dave over there sure didn't accomplish very much."

Don was forced to admit that he didn't have a better plan, and reluctantly agreed to use Terry as the bait to lure out Mohammed and get close to Brittney. Immediately after Keli and Terry returned to Tulsa, Judy sat down with a stack of long sheets of drafting paper and began laying out an operational plan for the mission. "It was," says Judy proudly, "the first time Don and Dave let me plan something." In the past, Judy had always played a supporting role in the background; this mission would mark her debut as a full-fledged operator.

## THE GIRL FROM BONNIE DOONE

The youngest of four children, Judy was an Army brat, born at Fort Benning, Georgia, in 1955. Her father was a compulsive gambler, womanizer, and an "abusive drunk, and my memories of him are not fond ones," she says. One of her earliest recollections of her father was of him coming home so inebriated that he couldn't find the bathroom and urinating in a basketful of freshly laundered clothes. "He spent as much of his Army career behind stockade walls as he did on the outside," observes Judy. "His career didn't go anywhere since he was constantly being demoted in rank and pay. And if Uncle Sam wasn't taking his pay, he was losing it in card games."

When Judy was seven, her mother sat her down with her sister and two brothers and explained that she was leaving their father, and "if we wanted to, we could move out with her and start over on our own. She told us it would be rough at times, and that we wouldn't be able to afford many of the things we were used to." Without hesitation, Judy and her siblings voted with their feet and left home with their mother.

They moved into a small, rusting trailer in Fayetteville's largest slum, an area known as Bonnie Doone, infamous for its drugs, prostitution, and crime. Judy's mother got a job as a waitress to support the family, and her older sister, Kathy, became a kind of surrogate mother to the other children. Her mother worked such long hours, says Judy, that it was not unusual for Judy not to see her mother for a week at a time, because she would be in bed by the time her mother got home. Her father was always behind on child-support payments, and was so unconcerned about his family's welfare that he never signed for renewals for his children's military I.D. cards allowing them access to medical and dental benefits. Finally, her mother abandoned efforts to take him to court because it required too much time off from work and ate into her salary and tips. "She just couldn't afford to fight him," Judy recalls.

There was little money for clothes, so the dresses Judy and her sister wore to school were made-over waitress uniforms. Judy's first pair of blue jeans came from a Salvation Army box. Despite their poverty, Judy's mother attempted to instill a deep sense of pride and dignity in her children. "Our home was always clean and our clothes were always pressed," Judy maintains.

The hand-to-mouth existence was too much for Judy's sixteen-year-old brother, Philip, who opted to strike out on his own. "He gave my mother an extremely hard time after we moved," says Judy. "Finally, she was just too tired to fight him any longer. She pulled the last bit of money she had from the pocket of her waitress smock and handed it to him. I'll never forget the look of defeat on her face. My brother took the money and left." Judy was devastated: "I felt like he was giving up on all of us." A year and a half later, he returned home, a little older and a little wiser. "It took him that long to realize that no matter how bad things seem at home, nobody is going to care for you like your family does."

When Judy was a teenager, her mother married a local salesman she had met in the restaurant, and the family moved out of Bonnie Doone. In many respects, however, the imprint on Judy of Bonnie Doone is indelible; she will forever be a child of the notorious Fayetteville slum. Although she vowed, on the day they moved away, never again to return to Bonnie Doone, Judy has been back many times. It gives her, she says, a sense of perspective: "Whenever I find myself feeling depressed about finances or the lack of something material, I drive out there. It hasn't changed an iota during these past twenty-eight years. As I drive through the neighborhood, I remember the poverty, the unhappiness, and sickness of the place, and I leave feeling much better about where I am and what I'm doing today. I've even driven my kids there to give them some perspective about what's really important."

Over time, Judy's stepfather earned her love and trust and became a real father to her in every sense. He has been married to her mother for a quarter century, and Judy says that "I can't imagine my life without him."

But the years without strong parental supervision left their mark on Judy. As a teenager, she was extremely rebellious and more interested in boys than school. She started hanging out at a local dive called "The Pink Pussycat" that boasted live rock music, wine, and beer, and fell in with a bad crowd. Drugs were plentiful and she was headed for trouble when, at the age of sixteen, she met a young soldier at the "Cat" named Don Feeney. He was unlike anyone she had ever met before, and they soon began seeing a lot of each other. Don was brash, uninhibited, and fearless, but he also had a warm and gentle side that appealed to Judy.

In view of her age and the fact that Don was a GI, Judy was afraid of what her parents would say about the relationship. But she shouldn't have worried. She and Don made plans to meet one night and go to the hospital to visit her mother, who was having some surgery. When Judy arrived at the hospital, Don wasn't outside as planned: he had already gone inside, introduced himself to her mother, and presented her with two dozen carnations. By the time Judy arrived, Don and her mother had become fast friends and she was won over.

Don's family was another matter, however. "Although his mother tried her best to like me," says Judy, "I was everything she hated. I was country, and I wasn't Italian." Having been raised in a military community, Judy wasn't used to everyone having a label. Don's ethnic neighborhood, where "you were Italian or Jewish or Irish or Puerto Rican, every nationality claiming superiority over the next," took some getting used to.

After dating for about a year, Don and Judy were married in a traditional Italian ceremony in Brooklyn. Judy's mother, stepfather, and one of her brothers drove up from Fayetteville for the occasion. After counting the "boot"—the money given by all the relatives to launch the couple on their new life together—she and Don left for a short honeymoon in Manhattan. When it was over, they returned to Fayetteville and moved into a trailer Don bought from Judy's stepfather. Don rejoined his unit, and Judy finished out her senior year of high school.

In the years that followed, they had three children, and Judy served as a dutiful military wife and mother, following Don from post to post, assignment to assignment, without complaint. She took great pride in Don's career and accomplishments, especially after he joined Delta. "I always came second to Delta," she says, without a trace of resentment.

Her worst night as the wife of a Delta operator was April 24/25, 1980. Everyone connected with Delta had long suspected that the unit was preparing an operation to rescue the American hostages in Iran. Don was away, and Judy knew that it was only a matter of time, in view of the political pressures building against the Carter administration in an election year, before Delta was given a "green light" to attempt a rescue. No one had to remind her how dangerous such a mission might be, but Don had gone on many dangerous operations before and had always returned in one piece. The possibility that something could go wrong, terribly wrong, was not something she or anyone connected with the unit spent too much time dwelling on.

She was awakened in the wee hours of the morning by the jarring ring of the telephone. It was one of the other Delta wives. She was crying.

"The news is bad, Judy," she sobbed. "T-they're all dead."

The fog of sleep quickly dissipated, and Judy sat bolt upright in bed. The other woman was still talking, but Judy wasn't listening; she knew intuitively that the operation had gone forward and that there had been some kind of problem.

Judy's eyes filled with tears as she hung up the phone. Seized with grief, but still holding back a little until the facts were confirmed, she peered down at the end of the bed and saw her six-year-old daughter, Stephanie. She had been awakened by the telephone.

"Don't worry, Mom. Dad's all right," Stephanie assured her.

Although "she didn't have a clue about Iran or what Daddy did for a living or why I would be crying," says Judy, Stephanie said it "so positively that I knew Don was okay."

Along with the rest of the wives, Judy stayed glued to the television set throughout the day, waiting for some word about the fate of their husbands. On April 25, President Carter addressed the nation from the Oval Office and described the rescue mission, attributing its failure to mechanical difficulties. He went on to praise the men who died when a chopper hit one of the C-130s during the refueling operation at Desert One.

Casualty information was slow in coming. There were eight confirmed dead and a number of injured. Although Judy had never spoken to her friends and neighbors about Don's work, "when Desert One hit the news, I was inundated with visits from neighbors inquiring about Donny's welfare. It was obvious that they had always known, despite the fact that Fort Bragg was still denying Delta's existence."

When a Delta representative came to the house for a morale

visit, Judy sent him on his way, saying "there were other wives who truly needed someone or something." Finally, she got word that Don was okay. She was relieved but terribly disappointed for Don. She knew the mission's failure had to be eating him up inside, and unlike many other Delta wives, who just wanted their men home, Judy secretly hoped that they would turn around, go back into Iran, and make a second attempt to get the hostages. But it was not to be. The survivors of Desert One returned, bitter and frustrated, convinced that they had been let down by both President Carter and the military high command.

The unit was never the same after Desert One. Something was missing. Everyone could feel it, but no one could quite articulate it. Once they had been the best-of-the best, the elite of the entire U.S. military establishment. But failure robbed the Delta men of their sense of being second to none, of their belief that they could "take on the world on behalf of God, country, and apple pie." Desert One was the unit's epiphany; after the debacle in the desert a sense of limitations set in, and the feeling, for the first time, that "they were just another unit in the U.S. Army."

After Don left the service, he and Judy worked together, first in the day-care business and later at CTU. She was expected, at CTU, to fulfill the traditional female role of secretary and receptionist. However, as time passed, she became more and more involved in the management of the firm, while "always remembering my place."

It was, after all, a totally male environment, made up of men with decades of special operations experience. Judy had not served in the military and was acutely aware of her own limitations. But none of the men, Don included, had much writing talent, so it fell to Judy not only to do the correspondence but the lesson plans for CTU's various training programs. Many of the programs were for police SWAT (Special Weapons And Tactics) units.

If she was going to do the lesson plans effectively, Judy told Don, she needed to "get out there and get the feel for what you're doing. Then I'll know what I'm writing about." At the outset, Don was not terribly enthusiastic about Judy's desire to go through the training programs they were running; but he reluctantly agreed, figuring that after she had a taste of it she'd be satisfied. He was wrong.

Judy loved the rigorous training and the chance to push her physical and mental limits beyond the safe precincts of the past. She soon mastered surveillance and countersurveillance, various firearms, evasive driving and ramming techniques, and all of the skills of close-quarter combat. Then, in 1986, disaster struck.

CTU was conducting a training program for the Fayetteville police department, rappelling off an 80-foot-high firetower. Rappelling is a mountain-climbing skill involving the rapid descent down a sheer cliff or surface using a double rope belayed both above and around the person's body, allowing them to control the rate of descent. SWAT and special operations units often have to rappel from helicopters to the ground or onto a rooftop, or they rappel down the face of a building until they reach the right floor, then crash through a window.

During the morning sessions, Don had welcomed Judy's participation because "if he put a female out, the guys couldn't chicken out." It would goad them into working harder. However, that afternoon Don decided to try out a new rappelling harness called the Petzel device. He was leery of letting Judy use it, since it required a high degree of skill and expertise; but she insisted, not wanting her courage questioned in front of the guys. Don relented, and Judy slipped on the harness and stood in the window of the tower, feet braced against the sides, ready to bound out backwards.

"It was my last rappel of the day and I was going to make it great," she says. "As I went out, I hit the device . . . but it didn't stop."

She fell all the way to the pavement below and landed on her back. She was only out for a few seconds. When she came to, Don was screaming, "Don't touch her! Don't touch her!"

They put her into a mountaineering rescue basket and rushed her to the hospital in the back of a pickup. Once she was at the hospital, Judy's thoughts were more on their fragile young business, and the impact her accident might have on it, than the pain radiating from her back. She told Don that there wasn't anything more that he could do. "Leave," she urged him. "Go to the range and carry on with the class. Don't worry about me. They'll take care of me here."

Shortly after he left, the doctors confirmed the worst: her back was broken. They put her in traction for a week until the swelling subsided enough to operate, and then removed numerous bone fragments lodged near her spine. They then took bone from her hip to repair the damage and inserted metal rods in her back. She was in the hospital for almost a month; when she left, the doctors warned her that she would probably never again be able to resume an active life.

But within two months Judy was back at work, and today she is fully recovered from the accident, although she still suffers from constant back pain. She doesn't rappel anymore but otherwise is "fully mission capable." She's a certified driving instructor and teaches both executive protection and firearms courses. When asked about her skill level with firearms, she calculates that "on a scale of one to ten, I'd say I'm an eight." Operationally, she thinks her surveillance/countersurveillance skills are her biggest contribution to the firm.

The fact that Judy has achieved parity with the male operators at CTU in many things gives her a good deal of satisfaction, although she feels guilty about the time she spends away from her three children (now in or approaching the teens) on missions or just helping Don at the company.

In the spring of 1990, however, as she worked on the plan to rescue little Brittney Chowdhury, the only thing Judy was feeling was the exhilaration of the chase. Don had described it to her many times: that rising excitement, that anticipation of the rush action junkies value so much, which comes before you go on a mission where the stakes are particularly high. But Judy had never before experienced it. Now she was savoring it for herself, for the first time, and loving every second of it.

## A CONSPIRACY OF WOMEN SCORNED

By the end of May, Judy had arrived at a plan that she was convinced would work. Keli and Terry were both on board, and Don and Dave had signed off on the essential details.

But now that they had a workable plan, they needed to come up with the remainder of the money to fund the operation. Keli and her mother, Jeanne, once again started calling people they knew for help, but succeeded in raising only a few hundred dollars.

Finally, Jeanne contacted Amelia and asked her if she knew anyone who might contribute to the rescue fund. Amelia said she might have a few ideas, and indicated that she would do some checking and call back shortly.

Instead, Amelia phoned Judy and asked, "What's it going to take to bring this child home?"

"Twenty-six thousand dollars," Judy responded, noting that it was about $16,000 more than they had on hand.

"Are you absolutely sure?"

"As sure as I can be."

"Well, I've got an IRA I can cash in, but it may take a little time."

Suddenly realizing that Amelia was volunteering once again to help, Judy demurred. "I felt very uncomfortable about taking any more of this lady's money," Judy says. "Other than the modest house she lived in and another rental property, it was nearly everything she had." In actuality, both houses were still tied up in probate and wouldn't formally belong to Amelia until the summer of 1991. It also turned out that Amelia would have to pay a penalty for cashing in the IRA early.

Judy tried to talk Amelia out of it, but she was insistent, and so Judy finally relented. Amelia then called Jeanne back and said that she would provide the necessary funds to mount the rescue, adding that it had better work this time because she was all tapped out. It took several days, but Amelia soon transferred $16,000 to CTU, and gave another $1,000 to Jeanne for Terry's expenses. Amelia justifies her generosity by saying that "the mission was still incomplete. I mean, all this work had been done and that little girl was still there." With the money remaining from the first payment, they had just enough to fund the operation.

Once the money was in hand, there was not a moment to waste. Under Judy's direction, they began implementing the plan. The key was Mohammed's greed. By appealing to his greed—Judy and the Tulsa women reckoned—they just might be able to draw him out of Mirpur and make him drop his guard.

Terry had injured her back the previous year, which had forced her to quit her job. She had filed a lawsuit for damages, which Mohammed knew about, but no action had yet been taken on the case. Nevertheless, working from a carefully drafted script,

Terry, in one of her phone conversations with Mohammed, informed him that she had received a $100,000 settlement in the suit.

Mohammed was all ears. In the conversations that followed, his tone was conciliatory, even charming, a quality that Terry hadn't perceived in him since their courtship. Earlier, she says, "he was so scared that I was trying to get Brittney back, but then the money took over with him. It was, like, 'Wow! I could have money.' But he was still scared, very scared."

Terry told him that she still loved him. The problem was Bangladesh, not him. She just couldn't live there. She went on to say that she wanted to help him get back to the States, and indicated that now that she had some money, it might be possible. "He just ate it up," Terry laughs.

Finally, he invited her to come back to Bangladesh for a visit so that they could work things out. Terry accepted, but told him that this time she would stay in a nice hotel rather than at his parents' home. He didn't object.

Mohammed had taken the bait.

# 9
# The
# Bangladesh
# Sting

ON JULY 21, 1990, Don and Judy left for Bangkok, which would serve as their base of operations for the mission in Bangladesh. They stayed there for two days, making preparations and adapting to the time change. In an attempt to better fit in with the local populace, they worked on their suntans by the pool in their spare time and Judy dyed her hair jet black. Dave remained behind in Fayetteville, running the office. He would come over when everything was ready.

On July 23, Don and Judy flew to Bangladesh. It was monsoon season, and from the air it seemed to Judy that the entire country was underwater. Her first impression of Dacca was that "it had a very evil and unhealthy look." That impression, she says, had a lot to do with her mood, which was very dark and apprehensive. Her apprehension was reinforced by the airport, which was "hot and filthy, absolutely filthy. And there was not a smile anywhere."

As they walked out of the airport, "people were grabbing us and touching our skin and pulling on our clothes and screaming and begging. There were women out there with skeleton babies on their hips, with their hands outstretched." The drive to the hotel was an eye-opener, even to seasoned world travelers like Don and Judy. The poverty and squalor were absolutely overwhelming, and brought a lump to Judy's throat. "Everything was very, very filthy," she remembers. "There were these skinny cows on the side of the road, and these skinny, skinny people. Men dressed in long skirts with flipflops, and they were just so skinny. Skinny in the face and toothpick legs."

Tears welled up in Judy's eyes, the product of too much travel, too much stress, and the grim human wreckage she observed along the road from the airport en route to the city. She turned to Don and told him, "I want to leave. I want to leave right now! I want to get out of here."

He squeezed her arm and she could tell that even the hardened Delta operator, who had seen so much violence and pain, was himself moved by the grim struggle for existence taking place outside the van, only a few feet away, and by the enormous gulf between their comfortable air-conditioned world and the reality of life in Bangladesh.

"But we can't," Judy intoned, mastering her emotions. "We can't leave without the baby we came to get."

Like Dave, they stayed at the local Sheraton hotel. Initially, Don had harbored suspicions that Dave had botched the earlier Dacca recon; it couldn't have been as difficult as he made it out to be. Both Don and Judy prided themselves on their ability to do undercover work, and were convinced that they would find a way to succeed where Dave had failed.

But, like Dave, they found the city hot, teeming, and inhospitable. And despite their efforts to blend in with the indigenous population, they quickly realized that they would never pass for Bangladeshi. Everywhere they went was a replay of Dave's earlier experience: they were constantly assaulted by beggars, and hundreds of eyes seemed to watch their every movement around the hotel and the city.

They also tried to drive through the Mirpur district, but were forced to abandon the idea after several false starts. It was on one of their trips near the outskirts of Mirpur that Don spotted an old brick tower, perhaps 40 feet high, north of the district. He asked what it was and was told that it was part of the city's Botanical Garden. He immediately directed their driver to take them there. Instead of the highly manicured botanical gardens of the West, the Dacca Botanical Garden was, in Don's words, a "slum jungle," overgrown with weeds, with little in the way of exhibits or explanation of the various plant species. The ground was soggy and steaming in the hot sun. As in the rest of the city, "there were crows everywhere," observes Judy. "Big, black, ugly, messy, noisy crows. They filled the sky and were in every tree. It was like the garden in *The Addams Family*, where Morticia would snip the buds off rosebushes; that's what it reminded me of. Very, very eerie and—with the crows—evil. I felt very uneasy."

Don and Judy mounted the stairway to the top of the tower and gazed down on the Mirpur district, which lay beneath a haze of cooking smoke and seethed with so many people that it looked like an anthill that had just been stirred with a stick. Both of them were soaked with sweat, and black dye was running from Judy's hair, trickling across her forehead and down her cheeks. Every time she mopped her brow to push the sweat from her eyes, she would get the dye on her hand.

With each passing hour in Dacca, Don and Judy grew more sympathetic to Dave and the problems he had earlier encountered. It was clear that locating and snatching Brittney was not going to be easy, and more evident than ever that Terry represented their only real hope of getting close to Mohammed.

They also did their own recon of the port and other possible exfiltration routes, to see if there was anything Dave had overlooked. The port area was so gridlocked that they couldn't get closer than several blocks from the water's edge, so Don ordered their driver to park by the side of the road and they walked the rest of the way on foot. "It was hot, filthy, and there were bugs everywhere," says Judy. "Because it was monsoon season, we had to walk through the muck and mud to get there. We kept losing our shoes. They'd get stuck in the mud and we'd walk right out of 'em." Like a car going down a dirt road in the country, pulling a trail of dust behind it, they soon attracted a following of hundreds of beggars and children, all clamoring for money.

They were assaulted by the river's horrible stench long before they could see the water. When they finally reached the wide, lazy, silt-filled river, Judy was amazed to find that it was chocolate brown in color and that there were naked children jumping from a pier into the fetid water. "They started showing off who could jump the highest and furthest away from the pier," she says. She took comfort that "kids are kids the world over, and it doesn't matter what nationality or color they are."

But, once again, at the end of the day, they could only confirm what Dave had already discovered: in Don's words, "there was only one way to move out of Dacca fast, and that was by air." Since much of the country was under water from the monsoons, by contrast to Dave's earlier recon, the rivers were now deep enough to navigate but they were treacherous, and being caught on open water during a squall or storm was not something Don wanted to chance. Driving west to India also was out of the question because there was no telling how far they might get before finding the road flooded or a bridge washed out. And to the east lay Myanmar, formerly known as Burma, a repressive police state suspicious of all Western travelers. But if they were to leave by air, it meant that they would have to be able to clear Immigration and Customs.

On the 28th, they returned to Bangkok, sobered by the task ahead and convinced that they needed someone who could pull some strings in Dacca. To this end, Don met with John Ingram (not his real name), an ex-special operator he knew from Latin America, who made his home in the Thai capital. John had spent time in Bangladesh and was willing to recommend a contact there who might be able to help; he called him only "the Professor." Carrying an introduction from John, Don would get in touch with the Professor when he and Judy returned to Bangladesh. They had not yet picked a date for their return. First, they had to wait for Terry, who was scheduled to arrive on the 29th; and second, they couldn't go before they cleared their American Express card.

As usual, CTU was in precarious financial condition, with Don and Dave juggling monies from one account to the next in a frantic effort to keep the company solvent. Although they were grossing $1.5 million a year, all it took was for one client to be late in paying for everything to come to a screeching halt as they reached their various credit limits. Not only were they spending far too much time on the Chowdhury case, which promised little, if any, return, but other clients had been slow in paying, and this had combined to create a temporary cash-flow shortage. Fortunately, the funds arrived at the end of the month, permitting Dave to clear the credit cards that would be needed in Bangladesh.

Terry arrived, as scheduled, on July 29. She had left Twila with Keli's mother, Jeanne, and Keli had driven her to the airport. Before she left, Terry had promised Keli that if Brittney was alive, she wouldn't return without her.

At CTU's instruction, she had secured a new U.S. passport in the name of Terry Chowdhury, and it was hoped that she might be able to leave the country with Brittney, posing as her mother. On the other hand, if real problems arose, it was possible that Keli also would have to come to Bangladesh, to exert her legal right to custody of Brittney. For that reason, Judy made certain that Keli had a U.S. passport and a visa to Bangladesh.

## RETURN TO DACCA

After Terry arrived in Bangkok and the credit cards cleared, Don and Judy took her shopping. In order to convince Mohammed that Terry had, indeed, come into money, it would be necessary for her to both look and act the part. She had bought new clothes before she left Tulsa, and now they needed gifts for Mohammed and his family. They purchased a color television for the family, along with blankets, bedspreads, lice shampoo, and clothes for virtually everyone, including the nieces and nephews. For Mohammed, they bought Reebok athletic shoes, shirts, razor blades, deodorant, and other toiletries that were impossible to get in Dacca.

That done, Don and Judy worked with Terry on the plan of action, rehearsing her story with her, and setting up the various signals and procedures they would use to communicate with each other. Finally, everything was in readiness for her departure. But at that moment, the operation was suddenly cast into jeopardy by events beyond their control. On August 2, Iraq invaded the oil-rich sheikhdom of Kuwait, producing a major international crisis and throwing the Islamic world, including Bangladesh, into turmoil. The United States condemned the action and immediately came to the defense of Saudi Arabia.

Don was committed to getting Brittney out, and concluded that if they were going to do it, they'd better move at once, for there was no telling what might happen in the weeks ahead. More-

over, according to Dave, back in Fayetteville, the crisis had cre-
ated a major demand for the kind of unique services provided by
CTU. Many Westerners were trapped in Kuwait, and their companies were eager to hire companies like CTU to get them out.
And given the war jitters throughout the region, the bodyguard
business was also booming. Dave advised Don to wrap things up as
quickly as possible because it looked like there was a great deal of
potential business coming their way.

It was now or never, Don concluded, as he walked out of the
hotel to find Terry, who was sitting by the pool with Judy.

"We're going ahead," he told her. "Day after tomorrow. You
know what you have to do."

Terry nodded in acknowledgment. Nothing else needed to be
said; she had long before committed to the operation, and from her
point of view there was no going back.

Because there was only one flight a day from Bangkok, they
couldn't risk traveling together, for fear that someone might draw
a connection between them; so it was agreed that Don and Judy
would arrive a day later.

Terry landed in Bangladesh on August 5, and found the
same country she had left less than a year earlier. There were
signs and slogans painted everywhere, calling for "Death to
America" and professing solidarity with Saddam Hussein. Mohammed was not at the airport, and Terry was met instead by his
father and brother-in-law. His father told Terry that Mohammed
was sick, but it was clear to Terry that he had chickened out and
hadn't been able to muster the courage to come to the airport.
"They hugged me and everything," says Terry, "but it was different. It was real tense."

Don and Judy had arranged for a van from the Dacca Sheraton
to meet Terry, and had made her promise that under no circumstances was she to stay at the Chowdhury home; she was to go
directly to the hotel, otherwise they would have no way of com-
municating with her when they arrived. As scheduled, the driver
from the hotel was waiting for her, but after talking to Mohammed's father and brother-in-law he started to leave.

"Where are you going?" cried Terry.

"You're going with the Chowdhurys," he informed her. "So
I'm leaving."

"Yes," said the brother-in-law, "you must come to the house because Mohammed is sick."

"No, I'm not," she said forcefully, looking about for the man from the hotel. She grabbed him by the arm and told him in no uncertain terms: "I'm going to the hotel and you're gonna take me there."

Then she turned and addressed Mohammed's father and brother-in-law: "You tell Mohammed that I'm going to the hotel and I'll be there if he wants to see me. If not, I'm going back to America."

With the help of the man from the hotel, all of Terry's luggage, including the gifts for Mohammed and his family, were loaded aboard the hotel van. A short time later, she checked in at the Dacca Sheraton, where she was met again by Mohammed's father and brother-in-law. Once again they tried to persuade her to come home with them, but she flatly refused.

"You people have put me through enough," she told them. "I'm surprised that I even came over here again but, you see, I love Mohammed. Now I'm going to my room."

With that, she departed, leaving them standing in the lobby. Not more than an hour had passed when there was a rap on the door; it was Mohammed.

"He didn't look sick at all," says Terry. "In fact, he'd gained more weight." They embraced and kissed, and Terry invited him into the room. They talked awhile, but Terry carefully steered clear of any mention of Brittney for fear of spooking him.

Mohammed wanted her to go home with him, but she refused, saying she was not used to conditions in Bangladesh and would feel far more comfortable in the hotel, with its Western amenities. He didn't really protest very much, she says, because he was eager to join her and take advantage of the good life available at the hotel. He was delighted with his presents, although he was critical of her for not bringing him more.

After Mohammed had been there for about an hour, his father and one of his sisters arrived, and she gave them their gifts. His father tried yet again to convince her to come home with them, but she held her ground, looking over at Mohammed and telling them that "We're going to leave the country as soon as we can, so I'm not staying at the house."

That night she and Mohammed slept together again, for the first time since before she fled Bangladesh nearly a year earlier. "It was hard, real hard," she recalls, biting her lip. "But it was necessary." She knew if she couldn't convince him that she still loved him, he would panic and probably disappear, so she had returned to Bangladesh committed to having sexual relations with him as part of the ruse to get him to drop his guard.

The next day, Don and Judy returned to Dacca and checked in at the Sheraton. "The second time we arrived in Bangladesh was no different than the first," says Judy, "except that I was more prepared." Once ensconced at the hotel, Judy's first priority was "to eyeball Terry and make sure she was okay." She found a comfortable sofa in the lobby area, ordered a cup of tea, and opened a book. "I didn't actually see Terry until seven or seven-thirty that evening," she remembers. "I spent nearly eight hours in that lobby drinking tea. I got very, very tired of drinking tea."

They had instructed Terry to pretend they were strangers if they passed in the lobby or the hallways, or ran into each other in the dining room. Because they didn't trust anyone at the hotel, and knew that Mohammed had several relatives working on the staff, they discarded the idea of even meeting late at night in one of their rooms. Instead, all communications were to be written; Judy and Terry arranged to pass notes to each other via the ladies room off the hotel lobby. They would never go to the ladies room at the same time, but instead leave the notes taped underneath the lip of the third sink.

Some days, nevertheless, it was difficult for Terry even to get to the ladies room, because Mohammed, still uncertain of her motives, watched her like a hawk. On several occasions, she and Mohammed spent the whole day in their hotel room watching television and ordering meals from room service. If she tried to slip out of the room for a few minutes, he would challenge her, saying, "You don't need to go running around the hotel. It looks bad if I'm not with you."

## INVESTMENT CONSULTANT

As his cover, Don purported to be a New York investment consultant interested in Bangladesh's cheap labor and native silk. He let everyone know that he was exploring the possibility of opening a textile factory in the country, a wholly plausible story, and began to arrange meetings with government economic development officials and local suppliers. He continued to assess the various exfiltration routes under the guise of looking for an appropriate plant site. Don carried the role off so convincingly that within days word of his enterprise had gotten around, and he started to receive unsolicited offers of assistance and résumés from people looking for jobs.

He also made surreptitious contact with the Professor, who recommended two other Bangladeshis who might be of some help. One was a man named Basil who, for a fee, could fix or expedite many things at the airport. The other was a high-ranking government official by the name of Dr. A. K. Ahmed (not his real name). Dr. Ahmed was something of a local "godfather," who regularly fixed problems with the government for a handsome price. Without giving all of the details, Don described Brittney's abduction and solicited Dr. Ahmed's intervention with the Bangladeshi government to secure the little girl's return to her mother. Explaining his interest in the case, Don identified himself as one of Keli's cousins.

Dr. Ahmed indicated his sympathy for Keli and suggested that the Bangladeshi government was embarrassed by such incidents. He was particularly troubled by Mohammed's failure to take advantage of the opportunity to get an education in the United States, saying that people like him made it so much more difficult for other Bangladeshis to obtain visas to study abroad. He told Don not to judge all Bangladeshis by Mohammed. "We're poor but we're good people," he offered. "We're honest people who are trying very hard to build our country." However, as to the question of whether he would be willing to help, Dr. Ahmed was noncommittal; he recommended, instead, that they retain the services of a particular local attorney. Nevertheless, Don felt that the meeting was successful, and that they had won the sympathy of an important man for their cause.

Mohammed, meanwhile, virtually moved into the hotel and was taking advantage of everything it had to offer—especially room service and the hotel restaurant. After several days with Mohammed, Terry cautiously brought up the subject of Brittney, but he quickly shrugged it off, saying that she was fine. By this time, he had noticed Don and Judy, and wondered aloud, on several occasions, what had brought them to Dacca.

One day he turned to Terry and, with a flick of his head toward Judy, who was sitting on a sofa across the lobby, said: "That woman. Wonder what she's doing?"

"She's probably taking a vacation," responded Terry, trying to sound detached and uninterested. "She's reading a book. What's with you? Are you more interested in her than me?"

"No, no, baby. Nothing like that," Mohammed replied. "I'm just interested in what she's all about."

On another occasion, while dining in the hotel restaurant, he motioned in Don's direction and told her, "That guy's watching me." Terry laughed and indicated that she thought he was paranoid, but he insisted that people were spying on him and that Don might be one of them.

Each passing day was a struggle for Terry. She absolutely loathed Mohammed and found it disgusting to have him crawl all over her at night in bed. It was work to keep her emotions in check, and at times she nearly lost control. One night she got up to turn the light switch off and, as she stood in the darkness summoning up the courage to slip into bed, she heard Mohammed ask in a plaintive voice: "Terry, where are you? Terry? What are you doing?"

"I'm going to kill you," she responded, the words tumbling out of her mouth before she knew it.

"Terry, d-don't do this to me." There was a note of disbelief in Mohammed's voice, tinged with apprehension. "Terry?"

Terry pulled herself together and tried to laugh it off. "Oh, Mohammed, don't be such a baby. I'm just teasing."

"But I wasn't teasing," Terry says today.

After Terry had been in Bangladesh for a week, they were no closer to their objective than the day she'd arrived. They still didn't know whether Brittney was dead or alive, and Don and Judy were worried about how long their funds would hold out. Mohammed appeared content just to stay in the air-conditioned comfort of the hotel and consume as much food and television as possible. Something had to be done. But what?

Then fate intervened.

## A REMARKABLE STROKE OF LUCK

Mohammed had grown used to seeing Don and Judy around the hotel, and heard about Don's interest in opening a textile plant through the grapevine. He soon forgot his earlier concerns, and began edging closer and closer to Don whenever he was sitting in the lobby in order to eavesdrop on his conversations.

Saturday is the beginning of the Moslem work week in most Islamic countries, especially those too poor to observe an extra day off following Friday, the Moslem sabbath. It is the equivalent of Monday in the West, and characterized by the same beginning-of-the-week blues. August 11 was no different than any other Saturday that August in Dacca: the weather was unbearably hot and humid, there was no breeze, and during the midday hours anyone who could either retreated to a patch of shade or stayed indoors.

Don and Judy were holding a very visible meeting in the lobby of the hotel with some locals when Mohammed and Terry walked through and spotted them. Mohammed decided to sit down on a sofa across the lobby and observe them, much to Terry's chagrin. She was worried about the new interest Mohammed had taken in her confederates, and tried to distract him with some chitchat about her eventual need to return home; but he ignored her. After the meeting broke up, Judy excused herself, saying she had to type something, and went to an office off the lobby that the hotel had made available to her.

When Don was alone, Mohammed suddenly turned to Terry and said, "I'm going to go talk to that guy."

"What?" Terry gasped, caught off guard.

"I'll be right back," he told her, rising to his feet.

Terry immediately panicked and tried to think of some way to stop him, but he was gone before she could react.

Don was looking over a stack of papers about his bogus textile factory when Mohammed sidled up to him and introduced himself.

Absorbed in thought, Don too was taken off guard and reacted with a start when Mohammed began speaking. He told Don that he had heard about his business venture and that he was an American-educated Bangladeshi, married to an American woman, with important friends and contacts in Dacca. "My wife is very rich," he continued. "And we, too, are interested in building a business in Dacca. Perhaps we could get together and discuss our common interests."

Don was stunned. In all of their contingency planning, they never dreamed that Mohammed might approach them. Speechless for several moments, Don quickly recovered and told Mohammed that he appreciated his interest but that he had to leave for another meeting in a few minutes. He decided to play a little hard to get and not seem too eager or receptive to Mohammed's overture.

Mohammed motioned for Terry to come join them, and he introduced her to Don, who of course acted like he had never met her before. Then they said goodbye and were starting to leave, when Judy reappeared from the hotel office. She stopped dead in her tracks when she saw Don talking with Mohammed and Terry.

Seeing the apprehension on her face, Don waved to her. "C'mon over here," he called. "I've got some folks for you to meet."

Judy shook hands with both Mohammed and Terry and they exchanged a few pleasantries, before Don got up and said he was sorry, but he was late for the other meeting. "I'm sure we'll run into each other again around the hotel," he said. "And we can make plans to get together at that time."

Once Don and Judy were in the elevator, she looked over at him and said, "What's going on? How on earth did that come about?"

Don quickly filled her in on what had happened, dismissing the possibility that Mohammed was onto them. They agreed that it was a fortunate development, even with the increased risks involved in face-to-face dealings with Mohammed, such as someone slipping up and inadvertently tipping their hand. Besides, now they could communicate directly with Terry since Mohammed had introduced her to them.

After talking it over, they decided not to delay, but to push the relationship ahead as quickly as possible, in view of their concern over Brittney's well-being and their rapidly depleting resources. Judy called Terry's room and learned that Mohammed had gone out for a while. Terry told them he had been extremely pleased with himself over the way he had handled Don and established his credentials. Judy suggested that the four of them have dinner that night in the hotel dining room, and Terry promised to get back to her as soon as she could ask Mohammed, but she was certain he would jump at the invitation.

When Mohammed returned to the room a short time later, Terry said: "They've asked us to dinner tonight."

"See," replied Mohammed. "Didn't I tell you? They know a winner when they see one."

The dinner was a cordial affair, with plenty of wine and lots of laughter. According to Judy, at the outset Mohammed was at his "most charming," but as they plied him with drink he started talking more and more about himself, including his first marriage and, much to their surprise, even his relationship with his daughter, Brittney. He described how he had taken Brittney and brought her to Bangladesh, and his ex-wife's attempts to get her back. "My wife has hired trained killers . . . CIA . . . to kill me," he said with an absolutely straight face. "They sent a CIA guy named David Chatellier to kill me."

At the mention of Dave's name, both Don and Judy nearly choked. There was little question but that Mohammed had really been spooked by Dave's call, and that he apparently had used his contacts at the hotel to do some checking. They both commiserated with Mohammed and agreed that his former wife certainly sounded like a terrible woman.

Their support only seemed to encourage Mohammed to talk all the more; ultimately Don was forced to conclude the evening by saying that he had to be up early for another round of meetings on the textile plant project. But before he and Judy left, Don praised Mohammed and his business acumen, and said that they would have to get together again soon to talk about the kind of managerial positions he needed to fill.

Mohammed was beaming from ear to ear as they said good night. He later told Terry that "Don is a very smart man, and very important. He would be a good man to do business with." After months of feeling impotent, Mohammed reveled in Don's apparent esteem for him.

### SHE'S ALIVE!

In the days that followed, Don met with Mohammed several times and raised the possibility of offering him a position in New York City as liaison with the textile plant in Bangladesh. It would mean "big bucks," said Don, and the deal even included a company apartment.

Now it became more important than ever for Terry to work on Mohammed for news of Brittney. When Terry first arrived, he had mentioned offhandedly that Brittney was with relatives in Saudi Arabia, but Terry knew that he wasn't telling the truth. War looked imminent in the Gulf, so it was hardly the place to send one's young daughter. Besides, Terry knew that while many Bangladeshis worked at menial jobs in Saudi Arabia, it was an extremely expensive place to live, and the Saudis granted very few visas to other family members. On several occasions she went with Mohammed to visit his family at their house in the Mirpur district, but saw no trace of Brittney. Gradually, however, she began to suspect that the little girl was being taken care of by one of his aunts.

Finally, she confronted Mohammed and demanded to know where Brittney was, and he once again told her that she was in Saudi Arabia.

"I think she's dead," Terry shot back. "And if she's dead, I need to know that because I loved her, too."

"My daughter's not dead," Mohammed protested. "I guarantee you she is not dead."

"Look, there's a war coming. We'll go to Saudi Arabia and get her."

"No, no, no," Mohammed said. "My dad will go to Saudi Arabia."

It was patently clear that Mohammed was lying because, as Terry put it, Mohammed's family didn't have "the kind of money to fly back and forth to Saudi Arabia." So she decided to force the issue.

"No, we can do it," she told Mohammed.

"No, my father will do it," he argued.

They argued back and forth in front of his family for some time, before Terry backed off and let the matter drop. But she had made her point, and Mohammed was clearly on notice that he had to produce Brittney if he wanted to stay in Terry's good graces. With the prospect of securing a dream position in New York, Mohammed didn't want to do anything to set Terry off again, for fear that she would flee the country as she had done the previous year. He would need a visa to take advantage of the opportunity Don was talking about and, to that end, Terry's money was critical. With it, he could hire a new and better attorney and file an appeal to his deportation, based on his marriage to her.

On the night of August 16, they were at the hotel when they received a call from Mohammed's father, saying: "Brittney's here. She just got in from Saudi Arabia." The following morning, they took a pedicab over to his house and Terry finally was reunited with Brittney. She was a vastly different little girl from the one Terry had left behind. The good news was that Brittney appeared to be in better physical health than they had expected. On the other hand, her skin was dark from the sun and she was filthy. The only clothing she had on was a pair of torn and dirty panties. She had forgotten how to speak English, and regarded Terry with suspicion and distrust, shrinking from her touch or embrace.

"She was just like some kind of little wild animal," says Terry. "A totally changed child. Instead of looking into the face of Brittney, I was looking into the face of a child from the streets of Bangladesh."

Terry subsequently bought her some clothes and toys, and Brittney tore them from her hand and ran to the back bedroom without so much as a word of acknowledgment. Only later was Terry able to coax the little girl to her side with a piece of candy.

"Well, why don't we get Brittney dressed and we can take her to the hotel?" Terry suggested.

But Mohammed wouldn't hear of it; he didn't want her to leave Mirpur. "I love you, but I don't trust you," he told her. "You've run away from me once; you might do it again."

"She's alive!" Terry cried to Don and Judy, when she returned to the hotel late that afternoon. "I've seen her."

They all embraced at the news that the object of their mission was well and, at least temporarily, back at Mohammed's family home. But Mohammed had indicated to Terry that she wouldn't be staying there long, so it was vital that they move quickly. Find some way to draw him out of Mirpur with the girl, Don told Terry. Agree to go anywhere with him so long as he brings Brittney along.

That night Terry spoke with Mohammed about their future, especially as it related to leaving Bangladesh. Mohammed was excited about the prospect of going to New York or, if Don's position didn't come through, trying to get a visa to Italy or someplace in Western Europe. However, he firmly rejected any thought of taking Brittney with them out of the country. Maybe later, he said, they could send for her.

Terry went back to Mohammed's house the following day, and they took Brittney to a birthday party at the home of a family friend. In the middle of the party, the electricity went off, plunging the house into gloom. Mohammed immediately leaped to his feet and ran to Brittney, who was sitting with Terry, and pulled her away.

"What do you think? That I'm gonna steal Brittney?" laughed Terry. "How would I even get her out of here with all of these people around?"

Realizing that he looked foolish, Mohammed relented and let Brittney return to Terry's side. "Well, I guess it's okay," he mumbled.

Despite her effort to make light of the situation, Terry was deeply troubled. Mohammed's distrust of her clearly was deep-seated, and it was very unlikely that he would permit Brittney to leave the security of the Mirpur district any time soon.

Don, meanwhile, was meeting regularly with the Professor to devise a plan of action. According to the Professor, he could buy a judge and an attorney who would cooperate in an elaborate court charade to grant Keli, if she was in the country, custody of Brittney, enabling her to leave Bangladesh legally with the child. Don was intrigued.

"How much will it cost?" he wanted to know.

"Three hundred dollars for the judge and three thousand for the attorney."

"Let's do it," Don instructed the Professor. "What else?"

"You've got to make sure Mohammed is not able to challenge the court's decision. He cannot be physically present in the court-room."

"Okay, he won't be there," Don promised, although he really didn't know how they were going to remove Mohammed from the scene. They could always kidnap Mohammed and lock him up someplace, but Bangladesh was a hostile environment, and it would be impossible to hold him against his will for very long since everything they did attracted far too much attention. A much safer and more feasible plan would be to lure Mohammed out of the country; but to do that he would need a visa somewhere.

That night Judy called Keli, back in Tulsa, and told her that her daughter was alive and well. They would need her to come to Bangladesh as soon as possible. She was instructed to travel with Dave to Bangkok. He would handle the arrangements, Judy explained, and then see that she was booked on a plane to Dacca.

## VISA PROBLEMS

Terry and Mohammed made the rounds of various embassies the following day to see if anyone would give him a visa, but the prospects were not encouraging. That afternoon, while Mohammed was back at home in Mirpur, Terry got a call from a man at the Italian Consulate whom they had met with earlier.

"I need to speak with you, Mrs. Chowdhury," he explained to her in hushed tones. "Alone."

A short time later he came to the hotel. He described how he had almost granted Mohammed a visa, but then decided to do some more checking. What he discovered, he said, was very disturbing. "Now, I don't know if you know all this," he told her, "or if you're involved in some way, Mrs. Chowdhury, but your husband has done some bad things here in Bangladesh." He implied that they were criminal offenses.

"No, I-I don't know anything about it. Please tell me."

"He's tried to obtain a visa through fraudulent means and by buying one, and done other things that I'm not at liberty to discuss. I'm not trying to break up a marriage here, but there are possibly things about Mohammed that you don't know."

Terry assured him that she wasn't involved in any of Mohammed's illegal activities. "I didn't know any of this," she told him.
"I've just come to get my husband."

The man from the Italian Consulate then left, but Terry was
shaken by the visit. Not only did she wonder what kind of illegal
things Mohammed had been involved in, but it was evident that he
was well known to most of the Western embassies and unlikely to
get a visa any time soon, if ever. After she described the meeting
to Don and Judy, and in view of Mohammed's general paranoia,
they all agreed that the only option left was the one they dreaded
most: they would have to go into the cloistered confines of Mirpur
itself and snatch the girl.

As they were breaking up, sobered by the knowledge of what
lay ahead, Don asked Terry, almost as an afterthought, "For
Christ's sake, isn't there any place a Bangladeshi can get a visa to?"

Terry shrugged. "Probably India. Maybe Thailand. But I don't
think he needs one to go to Thailand."

Don stopped and wheeled around.

"Are you sure?"

"Y-yes."

A distant look drifted into Don's eyes and he stroked his chin.
"I've got an idea," he said at last, "and it just might work." Perhaps
attesting to their many years of marriage, Judy was seized with
exactly the same idea and nodded knowingly at her husband.

## BANGKOK VACATION

On August 19, the Professor contacted Don and told him that
everything was ready; a court date had been set for Wednesday,
August 22. There wasn't much time, so they would have to move
quickly.

Don met with Mohammed, offered him the job in New York,
and asked him about his visa problems. Mohammed indicated that
he wanted to accept the position but admitted that he hadn't been
able yet to secure a visa. However, he told Don not to worry, that
he had things under control.

But Don casually dropped the suggestion that he could help
him get a visa. "I have some . . . shall we say . . . 'dirty' contacts

in Bangkok that may be able to help, for a price," he explained to Mohammed, whose eyes lit up at the suggestion.

"Really?"

"Yeah. But if you've already got things under control . . ."

"Well, if you know somebody . . ."

"Let me look into it."

Later that day, Don informed Mohammed that it was all arranged. He would have to fly to Bangkok, where Don had set up a meeting for him on the 22nd with a man who would provide him with a legitimate visa to the United States.

"Listen," Don told him, "why don't you take Terry with you? Have a little vacation? It's all on me. I've got a great hotel already booked for you."

Mohammed agreed, but later that evening his joy began to subside. He started to have second thoughts. It was all too good to be true, he told Terry. There was probably someone waiting in Bangkok to kill him.

Terry once again laughed off his concerns and told him that he was being ridiculous. Things were finally breaking their way, she argued, and he was going to screw everything up because he was paranoid. "Pull yourself together," she snapped at him. Appropriately chastised, he dutifully applied for the visa and began making preparations for their departure to Bangkok.

Keli flew into Dacca late on the night of the 19th, so as to avoid Mohammed's uncle and cousins, who worked at the airport on earlier shifts. Don met her and took her straight to another hotel, where they had booked a room for her. He was tense and all business, and kept a sharp eye for any sign of trouble. Mohammed had threatened to kill Keli if she ever came to Bangladesh. "We'll cut off your head and roll it through the streets," he had repeatedly warned her, and Don took him at his word.

The next day, Don took Keli to the Professor, who explained what would happen in court and introduced Keli to her lawyer. After covering all of the details, they agreed on a time to meet the following morning. With that, Don dropped Keli off at her hotel and then returned to the Sheraton, where he called Dave, who was in Bangkok, to make certain that there were no hitches on his end.

When he finally fell into bed late on the 21st, Don was exhausted. But if everything went well tomorrow, he told himself, it would all be worth it: "We will have reunited a little girl with her mother and be on our way back to the United States. Then I can sleep for a week."

## "THAT'S MY BABY!"

On the morning of the 22nd, Judy and Keli went to court with the attorney and secured an order from the judge requiring Mohammed to produce Brittney. The judge then designated several court officers to serve the papers on the family, with the help of the local police in the Mirpur district. During the weeks they had been in the country, they had come to realize that nothing in Bangladesh happened on schedule or without a host of delays and other problems. Thus, Judy was nonplussed when they finished up at the court more than an hour ahead of schedule. It was too early to go get Brittney; Mohammed and Terry's flight wasn't supposed to leave until 2:00 P.M. Even if they had already left for the airport by the time Judy and the court officers got to the house in Mirpur, there was probably still time for Mohammed's family to contact someone at the airport and alert him as to what was going on.

It was critical that Mohammed and Terry be airborne before the papers were served on Mohammed's family and Brittney was taken to the courthouse. Judy realized that she would have to stall for time, so she insisted to the court officers that they drive by, accompanied by the attorney and his men, and pick up Don at the hotel before retrieving Brittney.

Don was at the hotel working on contingency plans in case something went wrong. There was no time to telephone ahead. When they reached the hotel, Judy jumped out and ran inside to call him on one of the house phones.

"Get downstairs," Judy told Don. "Now!"

"You must hurry! You must hurry!" the attorney was screaming at her through the open window of one of the cars parked in front of the hotel entrance.

Thinking Judy was in some kind of trouble in the lobby, Don arrived with his shirt unbuttoned and his telescoping police baton in his hand, ready for anything.

Judy quickly explained what had happened at the courthouse, as the attorney gestured wildly at them from the car.

As Don buttoned up his shirt and stuffed the tail into his pants, he and Judy piled into one of three vehicles waiting in front of the hotel. In their little convoy were the Professor, the Professor's son, Dr. Ahmed and his daughter, the attorney, several burly men who worked for him, and the court officers. It was 1:50 P.M. when they finally reached a police station in the Mirpur district, near Mohammed's house, to pick up a contingent of police officers in case there was any trouble. They also were supposed to be met by an officer who knew the location of the Chowdhury home. But, as usual, there had been a communication problem between the court and the police officials. The police hadn't been briefed on what they were supposed to do, and weren't ready in any event. The Professor, Dr. Ahmed, the attorney, and the court officials got into a protracted discussion with the police, accompanied by a great deal of arm-waving and shouting. Now, instead of being early, they were beginning to run late. They had to get Brittney back to the court before the close of business, otherwise the case would be extended to the following day, possibly necessitating a new order for production of the child. Someone at the police station was sure to tip off Mohammed's family as to what was up, and his father would certainly call Bangkok that night to tell his son what was happening.

In an effort to break the deadlock, Don stepped out of the car and began passing out cash to the police, and the situation quickly began to turn around. A half dozen policemen piled into a truck, and four vehicles set off in search of the Chowdhury house.

Although Don and his contingent had been promised someone who knew the exact location of the house, the police had only a vague idea of where it was, since there are few street signs or numbers on the houses in Mirpur. As they drove through the neighborhood, the little convoy began to draw a crowd. People spilled from their miserable dwellings to see what all the commotion was about. This, Don knew, could jeopardize their whole mission. "If you don't get there and get there quick," Terry had insisted, "and they know there's cars and there's Americans, they're gonna hide Brittney and you'll never find her in that neighborhood."

Suddenly, Judy spied a house with chicken coops on the roof that fit Terry's description, and they pulled up in front of it in a swirl of dust. Mohammed's mother peered out at them from behind the rusty iron gates leading to the house. Recognizing her from photographs, Keli yelled: "That's her! That's the grandmother!"

Mohammed's mother ran into the house, sounding the alarm, with Don and the police close on her heels. She slammed the front door and bolted it, and while the police began battering the door down, Don ran around back to prevent any family members from escaping through the rear door. He arrived just in time to see the door open, but when they spotted him, they fled back into the house.

With the police hammering the door in the background, Judy and Keli began running from window to window looking for Brittney. All they could see was chaos inside, with dark shapes racing through the dim light from room to room.

"That's my baby!" screamed Keli, as she peered into the house and spotted her bewildered little daughter standing momentarily alone in one of the bedrooms. Then an arm reached out for her, through a doorway, from another room. "That's my baby!" Keli screamed again. "Brittney!"

The arm was pulling Brittney through the doorway, but the child turned, just for a split second, and made eye contact with her mother. "Everything just stopped for a moment," recalls Keli. "It had been so long and she was so little. I don't think she knows what made her stop and look at me, but it must have been some kind of flash of recognition because she jerked away from the arm tugging on her and started walking toward the window. Something clicked."

Brittney had a dazed look on her face. "She had on a filthy pair of underwear and nothing else," says Keli. "And the only thing I could think about was how she looked so little and frail. I just kept screaming her name and then someone grabbed her and started shoving her under a bed."

"Get your goddamned hands off of her!" shouted Don through the window at Mohammed's mother. She released her grip on Brittney, who was instantly scooped up by one of the attorney's men as he burst into the room at that very moment, pushing

Molutie out of the way. He carried Brittney outside to where Keli was standing. Whatever recognition had flashed through the little girl's mind moments before was gone. She was shaking and looked up at Keli with fear in her eyes. They later learned that Mohammed's family had filled Brittney's head with lurid stories about "bad white people who would one day come and chop her arms and legs off."

"I wanted to take her but I didn't want to scare her," says Keli, who had brought along a photo album of pictures of the two of them and began to flip through the pages, speaking softly to Brittney amid the tumult around them.

"This is you and this is me," Keli said, pointing at the pictures. "Remember this? This is your room back home. And this is Minnow. Remember Minnow?" she asked, indicating a photo of a cat.

"Y-your name's Keli," Brittney said, in heavily accented English. "You're my . . . momma."

"Yes, baby," cried Keli, bursting into tears. "I'm your momma."

Brittney, who was still being held by one of the attorney's men, reached out to Keli, who enveloped her in her arms and held her tight. Keli says that she had lived in fear of that moment for months, terrified that when she finally was reunited with Brittney, her daughter "might reject me or have forgotten me." But all her fears vanished as the little girl looked up at her mother and hugged her.

"C'mon, guys, we gotta get outta here," barked Don, indicating the large, angry crowd beginning to form in front of the house. He led them to one of the cars and Judy and Keli, with Brittney in her arms, climbed into the back seat. "There were so many people," Keli remembers. "I don't know where they all came from. They were everywhere!"

Keli didn't want Brittney to withdraw back into her shell, so despite the clamor around them, she started singing to the little girl to soothe her and make her forget the trauma she was experiencing, and Judy quickly joined in. They sang "Mary Had a Little Lamb," "Twinkle, Twinkle, Little Star," "The Wheels on the Bus Go Round and Round," and other nursery songs, one after another, just to try to keep Brittney's mind occupied.

The crowd outside was becoming more and more unruly and people were pressing against the car, faces to the glass, staring

inside. The car began to rock back and forth between the crush of
bodies. Don, who was trying to round up the others and get them
back to the vehicles so they could leave, saw the crowd surge
forward. He pulled out his telescoping police baton, ran back to the
car, and began circling it, swinging the baton menacingly, pushing
people backwards. "Don's not that big in stature," observes Judy,
"but he sure looked big that day. He puffed out his chest. His shirt
was open and his T-shirt was exposed, and he looked like a big man
that day." They later learned from the Professor that not everyone
in the Mirpur neighborhood regarded them as interlopers. It
turned out that many of the Chowdhurys' neighbors knew that
Brittney was not being properly taken care of and were cheering
the intervention of the police and the Americans.

When everyone had returned to the vehicles, they pulled
quickly away from the house, scattering the people in front of
them. However, instead of returning directly to the courthouse,
they stopped at the Mirpur police substation to take care of some
bureaucratic formalities. The local police chief also wanted them to
share a drink with him and toast their success. But the crowd
quickly caught up with them and began, once again, encircling the
cars. Suddenly, Mohammed's father materialized from the mob
and, reaching through one of the car windows, grabbed at Brittney.
The terrified child shrank back and clutched at her mother, who
tried to pull her away from the grasping hand. Don heard Keli
scream. When he saw what was happening, he ran back to the car
and forcibly pulled Mohammed's father away.

Realizing that the situation was getting out of hand, Don
shouted to Judy to stay put and went back inside to find out what
the delay was all about. The attorney began a long-winded explanation, but Don cut him short, handed the senior police official
some money, and told him that they were leaving. Moments later,
Don and the rest of the convoy were speeding toward the courthouse.

Judy, meanwhile, returned to the hotel to await a call from
Dave, which she received within moments of her arrival.

"Is it a go?" he asked.

"Yes, it is," she responded.

"Well, they're here and I'm gonna proceed."

"Good."

"I'll let you know what happens."

"Okay," answered Judy. She replaced the phone in the cradle. A shudder of excitement went down her spine. There was no turning back now.

## COURTHOUSE DRAMA

Keli was shocked by the decrepit old courthouse. They were immediately ushered into the judge's chambers, where they were verbally assaulted by Mohammed's relatives. "She's not the mother!"they screeched at her in Bengali. "She's not the mother!" They shook their fists and spat at her, while court bailiffs tried in vain to bring some order out of the chaos.

"You'll have to give up the child until I make my ruling," the judge told Keli. A female bailiff stepped forward to take Brittney, who was holding on to Keli for dear life. The little girl started to squeal and Keli drew back, wrapping her protectively in her arms.

"No! Nobody's going to take her from me," cried Keli.

The Professor attempted to reason with her, but Keli wouldn't listen. "Why don't you just let me have her? She's my daughter," she pleaded with the judge.

Don tried to convince the judge to let Keli keep Brittney with her during the court proceedings, but the judge was running out of patience and declared Don "out of order," even though the actual hearing hadn't yet begun.

With that, the whole room erupted into a shouting match between the various parties. The judge lost his judicial demeanor and bearing and began yelling, his face red with anger, that everyone was "out of order." At that moment, Keli stood up, with Brittney still clinging to her, and called—with outstretched arms— for the judge to "let us go home. Please let us go home."

The entire room suddenly became quiet.

"Look, I'm not holding her," continued Keli. "I'm not making her stay with me. If I'm not her mother, why's she clinging to me? If these people . . ." she indicated Mohammed's family with a sweep of her hand ". . . hadn't abused her, wouldn't she go to them?" She continued to stand with her arms dramatically outstretched for several seconds after she finished speaking.

The judge cleared his throat and, once again in control of his own emotions, looked around the room; then he began speaking in a soft but authoritative voice. He instructed Keli to give Brittney to the female bailiff for the duration of the court hearing, promising that she would remain in his chambers throughout the proceeding and that nothing would happen to her.

"We're gonna have to do what he says," Don grudgingly informed Keli. "It's the only way we're gonna be able to sort this thing out."

"Okay," Keli finally said, choking back tears, "but if Brittney can't be with me, then he . . ." she whirled around and pointed a shaky finger at Mohammed's father ". . . doesn't get to stay here with her. I won't leave her alone with him."

The judge ruled that Mohammed's father would have to leave the room as well, and Keli, tears streaming down her cheeks, handed Brittney over to the bailiff. Sobbing loudly, the little girl protested that she didn't want to leave her mother, but Keli told her it would be for just a few minutes and that she'd be right back.

As they left the room, Mohammed's father attempted to slip into the judge's chambers through the open door behind them, but Don saw what he was up to and slammed the door on the older man's fingers, with a bone-crunching sound. Then Don took up a position in front of the door and Mohammed's father slunk away in the direction of the court room, nursing his hand.

Instead of the carefully choreographed morning session, things were now completely different. The deal worked out by the Professor and the attorney apparently had come unraveled and the judge refused to recognize the attorney's motion for the court to recognize Keli's rightful custody of Brittney. He would not make a final ruling, said the judge, until the father could be located and had the opportunity to present his claim for custody. In the meantime, he declared, Brittney could remain with her mother at the Sheraton, but only if they turned their passports over to the court, to ensure that they would not flee the country. He also directed that armed guards be stationed at the hotel to keep an eye on them. And, in a final affront, the judge granted liberal visiting rights to Mohammed's family until the issue of custody was permanently resolved.

Keli couldn't believe it. She broke down in the courtroom and had to be helped out by Don. They returned immediately to the hotel.

## "HI, MOHAMMED"

While the courtroom drama was under way in Dacca, Mohammed and Terry were en route to Bangkok, after a late departure. Mohammed's doubts about the trip had resurfaced and he was feeling sick to his stomach. Nerves, he told Terry. A short time later, he began to pray.

"What are you doing?" Terry asked.

He stopped praying, grabbed her hand, and looked into her eyes. "Terry, I love you so much," he said to her.

"I love you, too."

"Well, I feel like . . . something's going to happen to me. Something bad."

Terry laughed and said, "C'mon, Mohammed. What's gonna happen to you?"

"I think someone's going to hurt me."

"No, no, now calm down," she reassured him. "Relax, honey. We've got money and we're going to Thailand to have a good time and spend some of it, and you're gonna get a visa. What could happen?"

After they arrived at the airport, Terry and Mohammed took a taxi into the city. Mohammed was extremely nervous and sweating profusely. Since she was unsure of exactly when or where Dave would appear, when they reached their hotel Terry went in first to check on the reservation.

Mohammed was going to accompany her inside, but she told him to watch the bags as they were being unloaded from the taxi.

"No, they'll do it," he said, indicating the various bellmen. "I'll go with you."

"Just because it's a nice hotel doesn't mean someone won't take off with one of our bags. You stay here," she ordered.

While Mohammed remained with the bags, she approached the check-in counter. "I believe there's a room for Terry Chowdhury," she announced.

The clerk pulled out her reservation. "Oh, yes. Mr. Chatellier has taken care of everything for you."

Terry leaned forward across the counter and told the clerk in a hushed voice: "Don't ever mention the name Chatellier again. Got it?"

"Ah, yes, ma'am. Certainly," responded the baffled desk clerk. "Anything you say."

As the clerk handed Terry the key, Mohammed stepped up behind her, followed by a bellman with the luggage. When she turned to greet Mohammed, she suddenly spotted Dave sitting nonchalantly on one of the couches across the lobby. While Mohammed knew Dave's name and had spoken with him on the telephone, he had never seen him before, so there was no fear that he would recognize the CTU man.

They went up to their room, which was spacious and well appointed, and Mohammed began to relax in the luxurious surroundings. However, his stomach was still giving him trouble and, despite the heat outside, he complained of having a case of the chills. He was supposed to call his father as soon as they arrived, but all he wanted to do was rest for a few minutes.

"You just lie down," Terry reassured him. "I'll go downstairs and get you something for your stomach. When I get back, I'll call your dad, okay?"

"Okay," he replied feebly.

When she got down to the lobby, Dave was nowhere to be seen. Unbeknown to Terry, however, Dave had gone up to the room and confronted Mohammed.

He knocked on the door and when Mohammed answered, Dave stuck out his hand and said, "Hi, Mohammed."

Without thinking, Mohammed extended his hand, which Dave grasped in his powerful grip, jerking Mohammed out of the room, literally off his feet. With his left hand, Dave grabbed Mohammed's elbow and sank his thumb into the radial nerve, numbing the hand and "putting him right up on his tippy-toes so that he couldn't do anything. I locked his wrist in the down position so that it really put excruciating pain up his arm." Mohammed tried to cry out but was in so much pain that all he could do was open his mouth in a soundless scream. "His lips were pulled so far back from his teeth," says Dave, "that he looked like a mule eating briars." Then Dave jammed him up against the wall.

"Mohammed," continued Dave menacingly. "I'm Dave Chatellier and I've got a message for you from Don Feeney. I'm gonna give you a ten-minute head start and then I'm gonna come after you. And if you ever mess with Keli or Terry again . . . I'll pinch your head off like a bug's." When Dave dropped him, Mohammed fled for his life.

Terry called Dave's room from the lobby but no one answered. After hunting around the shops and restaurants for him, she gave up and decided to return to her room. But when the elevator doors opened, she found Dave standing in the middle of the little landing in front of the bank of elevators.

"Dave!" she exclaimed with relief. "Where have you been? I was so worried."

"I just had a little talk with Mohammed." He grinned. "And when I got finished, I've never seen Reeboks smoke so much."

"You mean . . . he's gone?"

"Yep. Now let's go back to your room and get your suitcase. We're moving."

Terry quickly gathered up her things, but as she and Dave were leaving the room, Mohammed reappeared with a man from the hotel staff in tow.

His eyes were red and he was crying. When he spotted Dave, he stopped in his tracks and looked over at Terry.

"Terry," he choked. "What's going on? What are you doing?"

Dave stepped in front of Terry and growled at Mohammed, "Look. I'm her uncle. I don't want you messing with her. I told you what would happen if I ever saw you again."

Mohammed drew back in fear, clutching Terry's hand. She pulled it away from him and reached into her purse and withdrew his passport. "Here," she said, shoving it into his chest.

"But why, Terry?" he asked plaintively. "Why?"

"I'm going back to America," she said with finality, and brushed past him down the hall without further discussion. He leaped backward as Dave passed, scrunching up flat against the wall like a human tapestry.

Dave stopped in front of Mohammed and looked at his watch.

"Hey, bud, you're wasting time. You've already lost three minutes."

A look of panic crossed Mohammed's face and he broke and ran, squeezing by Terry and nearly running over the top of the man from the hotel staff, who had remained a spectator and hadn't said a word.

"That was the last I ever saw Mohammed," says Terry. "At that moment he didn't even know that our real goal was to get Brittney."

Dave and Terry stayed in the same hotel after changing rooms, since it was too late to fly back to the United States that night. Mohammed disappeared. Friendless and without money, it was later learned that he spent the next six or seven days on the streets of Bangkok, fearing some kind of retribution from Dave and Don.

Late that night, Terry received a call from Mohammed's father.

"Where's my son?" he demanded to know.

"Gee, I don't know," she responded innocently. "I don't believe what happened. We got to the hotel and some men grabbed him, and now I don't know where he is."

"You've done something with my son. Tell me what you've done with him. I need my son."

"I don't know where he is and I don't know what to do. You know, I think it's because of the credit cards," she offered, referring to the money he owed in the States. "I bet they took him to jail."

## BREAKOUT

Back at the hotel, the phone rang and Judy snatched up the receiver.

"Yes?"

It was Dave, and he had good news to report. He described all that had happened. When he got to the part about his threat to Mohammed, Judy doubled up with laughter. But a short time later, Don reappeared with Keli and Brittney, and Judy could tell by the looks on their faces that all had not gone well.

Reunited with her daughter at last, Keli's joy was mixed with concern over her daughter's alarming physical condition. Brittney had head lice and bug bites all over her body. Her hair had been dyed black, and whole clumps were missing because of impetigo-like eruptions all over her scalp. Her teeth were yellow with visible decay, and her gums bled when she ate, which was constantly. The little girl was absolutely ravenous and gobbled up nearly everything in sight, greedily scooping the food into her mouth with her hands. Her teeth were so bad that when she later got back to Tulsa, she had to have four teeth pulled, as well as getting several filled and one capped.

Brittney also was dirtier than Keli thought possible. She probably hadn't been bathed in weeks. Her hair was "ratty, filthy, and her panties were supposed to have been cream-colored, but they were brown. Her ears were packed with dirt, and there was unbelievable crud behind her ears as well; it was like it was growing." According to Keli, "when we finished bathing her, the bathwater was brown."

What most amazed Keli and Judy was how wild and physical Brittney was, almost uncontrollable at times. Her eyes would go flat, and she would scream and cry and kick, lashing out with all her strength for no apparent reason at all. Other times, she would hold on to her mother with such fervor that Keli says "she hurt me." Back in Tulsa, the doctors told Keli that Brittney was reacting to bad memories intruding on her consciousness, which they compared to the flashbacks suffered by some Vietnam veterans. "The reason for the emptiness in her eyes was that she wasn't here with me during those fits," explains Keli.

Keli and Judy went to work on Brittney, and after several hours of effort had her looking almost normal, except for the fact that she was "skin and bones." With the exception of the fits, she reverted almost immediately to being a little girl, and her English rapidly began to return, although she had a distinctive accent. Before her kidnapping, Brittney had been "extremely feminine, almost prissy," and now she asked her mother for something nice to wear and for some makeup, "so that she could play dress-up."

At 5:00 P.M. the following afternoon, Mohammed's mother and two of his sisters arrived at the hotel for a visit with Brittney, as mandated by the court. Far from an opportunity to see their "beloved little Brittney," it was a way of exerting their rights to a piece of property, and they weren't about to give an inch on the subject. The session was strained, almost unbearable to Keli, since she now realized how much they had neglected her daughter and how little love there was between Brittney and Mohammed's family. Brittney started screaming the moment she saw them, and clung to Keli's and Judy's legs with all her might. "It seems to me," says Judy, "that if she had been in a healthy environment, with healthy relationships, she would have bonded with some of these people, or at least had some kind of allegiance to them, but she didn't."

When Brittney calmed down, she ran over behind Don, grabbed him by the legs, and looked up at him. "Make them go 'way," she pleaded with him. "Make them leave now."

Don looked down at her and shook his head. "I'm sorry, but you have to visit with them now," he told her.

The next day, Mohammed's father also was present, and the third day the visitors consisted of Mohammed's father, mother, one of his sisters, and a male cousin. The routine varied little. They would simply sit in stony silence and stare at Keli, Brittney, Don, and Judy. Occasionally they would speak to Brittney in Bengali and warn her that Don and Judy were going to poison her, or that Keli was going to give her to Don, who would beat her. Fortunately, Don had taken the precaution of having one of the Professor's sons present to listen in on the conversations, so that they could reassure Brittney later that Mohammed's family was lying to her.

The meetings were held in a lounge on the same floor as their rooms, and after the second encounter, the Bangladeshi bartender approached Judy and said, "I don't know what's going on, but these are very bad people. The things they are telling that child [Brittney] are not right. They were scaring her."

After the third meeting, Don had had enough and cornered Mohammed's father privately for a little talk. He described Mohammed's kidnapping of Brittney, credit card fraud, and his deportation from the United States, concluding that "those were not things to be proud of." Mohammed's father said that he was unaware of his son's transgressions, but while he seemed genuinely uncomfortable to be reminded of Mohammed's shortcomings, he did not offer to be of any help resolving the situation.

As each day passed without resolution of Brittney's status,

Don became more and more concerned that the efforts by the Professor and the others to clear the way for their departure were not bearing fruit. He was worried, moreover, that Mohammed would eventually make his way back to Bangladesh and challenge Keli's custody of Brittney in court. Don knew that if the judge granted even partial custody of Brittney to Mohammed, they probably would never see the girl again.

Drastic action was called for, and he resolved to take it. The most immediate problem was the presence of three young men from Mohammed's neighborhood who had staked out the hotel, watching Don and Judy's comings and goings. "I knew they were there," says Don, "and I knew that as long as they were there, I wasn't going to be able to sneak out of the hotel with the kid. So I grabbed them and told them, 'If I see you near the hotel, they're gonna find your body in the dump.' Right there in broad daylight, right there in front of the hotel. I said, 'If you're standing out here this evening, then you're gonna be missing.' " His threats had the desired effect. One of the men left immediately, and the other two stayed for about an hour and then disappeared. "I never seen them again," Don laughs.

Although there were armed guards stationed outside the hotel to prevent them from leaving the country, Don had observed them for some time and concluded that they were very lax. Anticipating that they might need to slip out of the hotel without the guards' knowing it, Don instructed Keli, Judy, and Brittney to take a leisurely walk around the hotel grounds each evening, until the guards became accustomed to watching them come and go.

On August 25, after their usual meeting with Mohammed's family, they took their regular walk around the grounds, only this time Don accompanied Keli and Brittney. There were bushes alongside the path, and when they reached a break in the foliage, out of sight of the guards, Don hustled Keli and Brittney through the gap and into a cab idling, by prearrangement, near the curb. The cabdriver transported them to the Professor's, where they waited an hour before going on to the airport. Keli put her hair up and changed into different clothes, so as to alter her appearance.

Back at the hotel, no one noticed that Keli and Brittney hadn't returned from their walk. In a charade for the many preying eyes in the hotel, Judy made a great show of knocking on the door to

Keli and Brittney's room and saying good night. Then she received a call from the States, which someone at the office in Fayetteville had been instructed to place, and pretended that she had been informed of a family emergency and would have to leave immediately. "The others are staying," she told the hotel staff. All of their luggage had been consolidated into two bags, which Judy took with her when she checked out.

They rendezvoused at the airport just in time for their 10:00 P.M. flight to London. Don was not going to come with them, since it was up to him to maintain the pretense that they were all still in Bangladesh. He wasn't planning to go directly to the United States anyway, as he was scheduled to begin another mission immediately in Saudi Arabia. Judy took Brittney with her, and Keli followed along close behind as though she was traveling by herself. Don had managed to secure temporary new passports for Keli and Brittney, since their passports were being held by the court. Normally their new passports and the fact that they had no entry stamps would have meant trouble at passport control; but Basil, the man with connections at the airport, was supposed to take care of everything. However, when they reached passport control, there was some confusion and they nearly found themselves in the wrong line. Fortunately, Basil quickly sorted things out and their passports were stamped, allowing them to proceed on to the departure gate. "It was so scary," Keli recalls, "because if anything screwed up, we would have gone to jail and Brittney would have gone back to that hellhole."

Don, who had been shadowing them up to this point, couldn't accompany them any further. Once on the other side of passport control, Judy stopped and threw Don a kiss, and he threw one back at her. "It was not a good feeling leaving him behind," she remembers.

"It seemed like forever before we finally got on the flight," recalls Keli. "We had to walk so far to board the plane outside, and we kept thinking, 'They know what's going on and are going to be waiting for us at the plane.'" When they boarded the plane, they took seats in different rows, and there was another long delay; by the time they taxied out to the runway, Keli's nerves were nearly shot. Finally, the plane lumbered down the runway and lifted into the dark sky. "When the wheels came off the ground, Judy looked back at me—she was up a couple of rows—and I looked at her, and we both started to cry."

They flew to London, and then caught a flight on to the United States. The three of them were seated together and listening to the country western selections on the headphones when they heard Lee Greenwood's rendition of "God Bless the USA." Without any cue or prompting, Judy and Keli started to sing the words out loud, with Brittney joining in.

Tears were running down Judy's cheeks; as she says, "the faucet just came on." Simultaneously laughing and crying, Keli and Judy leaned forward and put their arms around each other and cradled Brittney, who was sitting in the middle, letting out all the pent-up emotion of the past months. People in the surrounding rows looked on uncomprehendingly.

In early September 1990, Mohammed finally reappeared in Dacca and called a press conference at the city's National Press Club. He told the assembled reporters that he had divorced Keli because of her "infidelity, cruelty and alcoholic problem," and accused her of having "kidnapped" their daughter, with the help of foreign mercenaries, and taken her to the United States. He called on the United States to return his daughter or, if not, he wanted permission to go to America to fight in court for his daughter's custody.

Based on Mohammed's announcement, there were a number of lurid and sensational accounts of the rescue operation in the Bangladeshi press, including one entitled "Commando-Style Child Lifting." According to the report, Keli had earlier kidnapped Brittney from Mohammed at gunpoint, and Mohammed was forced to kidnap the little girl and flee the United States. He had been lured to Bangkok, he said, where a man "fell upon [him], pressing a pistol against his chest and saying, 'I am Chatellier whom you avoided meeting in Bangladesh. Now you have nowhere to go.' The stranger informed him that his people were out to hijack Brittney and [Mohammed] would be held as a hostage. If they failed to lift Brittney, [Mohammed] would be killed." Mohammed, the article went on, fled from Chatellier and sought help in Malaysia from the Bangladeshi ambassador. Since returning home, Mohammed "has been running like mad trying to get a U.S. visa, which has been denied."

The U.S. Embassy in Dacca ignored Mohammed's charges and demands, and the State Department subsequently passed on to Keli a report that he had been apprehended in Eastern Europe with a forged passport, presumably en route to the United States, and deported back to Bangladesh. Nevertheless, Keli lives in fear that he will one day show up in Tulsa and try to kidnap Brittney again.

"I'm so scared," she says. "Every day I'm scared. At night I'm scared of noises. I'm scared of strangers. I'm scared to be open with people. I don't know who I can trust." She vows that she will kill him if he ever tries to take her daughter away from her again, and wants Mohammed to know that she has a gun. "I'm not afraid of him," she maintains.

Like so many other mothers in the same situation, Keli finds that her fear of what her ex-husband might do circumscribes both her life and that of her daughter. They live in a cocoon of concern and security precautions. "Brittney does not play in the front yard," she explains. "She doesn't sit on the front porch. She's not allowed to ride the school bus."

Keli dismisses her own role in the recovery of her daughter, saying only that "I did what I had to do for my child. If I had to, I would have spent the rest of my life trying to get her back." Keli is particularly grateful to Terry for the sacrifices she made in returning to Bangladesh, and to Don, Dave, and Judy for the risks they took: "I thank God for them and their families, and I ask Him every day to keep them safe." But she saves some of her deepest gratitude for Amelia Smith, whom she calls "a godsend. I didn't believe there were people like that in this day and age."

# FOUR
# Operation
# Amy and
# Jeremy

# 10
# One of
# Their
# Own

## KIM'S STORY

■   Kim had a rule against dating military men. Around Savannah,
Georgia, where she was raised, they had a bad reputation. They
were too loud and too macho, and many of them drank too much
and didn't treat their women very well. And God forbid, if you fell
in love with one of them, he'd either break your heart or you'd
marry him and be dragged around from one crummy base to the
next, raising three or four kids by yourself since he was usually
away. At least that was Kim's impression.

In 1982, however, she met a quiet young Army Ranger by the
name of Charlie Hefner. He didn't have a date for a military ball,
and so some mutual friends called her and she reluctantly agreed
to go with him. Of medium height and build, Charlie had sandy-
colored hair and blue eyes, and Kim immediately fell for him. "He
was never a romantic or anything like that," says Kim, but he was
"always real considerate" and possessed a down-to-earth charm.
She also liked his self-confidence and take-charge attitude; in this
regard, he was so much more mature than many of the other young
men she had dated. Since she had blue eyes and sandy hair, and
almost identical features, people often mistook them for brother
and sister.

During the following six months, Kim and Charlie saw a good
deal of each other; then he left for Special Forces training in Mis-

souri. When he finished, Charlie came back to Savannah and asked Kim to marry him. She accepted, and a short time later they were married in a quiet ceremony. They had barely begun to set up house together when Charlie was shipped off to Honduras, the first of several assignments in Latin America due to the fact that he spoke fluent Spanish.

A Texas native, Charlie had spent many of his formative years in Mexico, Paraguay, and Bolivia, where his father worked as an agricultural consultant. Because they often lived in remote rural areas, Charlie didn't complete more than the first six or seven grades in school, but instead was taught at home and ultimately received his GED and even attended several semesters of college before joining the Army.

Although he was only about 5 feet 9 and weighed 150 pounds, he was all muscle, and had the reputation for being "as tough as cactus and touchy as a teased snake." Charlie was a demolitions engineer, and when he returned from Central America, he and Kim moved to Fort Bragg, North Carolina, where they were to spend the next five years.

The first few years of marriage, reflects Kim, were very happy years, and on May 31, 1985, Kim gave birth to a son they named Jeremy. It had been a troubled pregnancy and an even more difficult delivery. She spent twenty-three hours in labor, and lost a great deal of blood during the ordeal. Afterwards, it took her several months to fully recover and her doctor warned her that she might not be able to carry another baby to full term.

By the end of 1986, she and Charlie were beginning to have problems. "It wasn't anything major," she says. "Just the closeness wasn't there anymore." Nevertheless, that fall she discovered she was pregnant again and vowed, despite the doctor's concern, to have the baby if she could.

There were other problems as well. Charlie was being court-martialed for having misappropriated some explosives, and while he beat the main charge on a technicality, his career in the military was over. He escaped a jail term, but was reduced in rank and barred from reenlistment, even though many of his superior officers spoke up for him. This was a devastating blow to Charlie. He loved the military and had always presumed that he would make a career of it.

Their daughter, Amy, was born in July 1987, and until Charlie's discharge in April 1988, they bided their time in Fayetteville and tried to make plans for the future. After his discharge, Charlie tried to get a mule-packing contract with the Army, but that didn't work out, and he was forced to take a job mucking out a local stable to make ends meet.

Some months earlier, Charlie had stopped by CTU and dropped off his résumé. Bob Senseney, a Special Forces veteran working for the company, liked Charlie's attitude, youth, and his fluency in Spanish. When CTU got a security contract in Peru, Bob called Charlie to offer him a job, and he readily accepted. The contract, however, was on a month-to-month basis, and there was no assurance how long it would last. Initially, he returned to the States to visit Kim and the family every two months, and generally would stay two weeks each time. "At first we did real good," observes Kim. "He was good about sending me flowers and cards, and he would call. But the longer he was there, the less he did; the harder it got to write, to send flowers, to send cards." His absences were particularly difficult for the children, especially his son, Jeremy, who Kim describes as "very close to his daddy. Every other sentence was, Daddy this and Daddy that. God was on the right hand of Daddy."

Although Charlie faithfully sent Kim $2,000 each month, she began to have growing concerns about the marriage, especially in view of the amount of time he was spending away from home. "I always felt like he was putting his career before us," she reflects. "It became more and more hard on the kids because they didn't know him anymore."

In August 1989, Charlie convinced Kim to come to Peru with the kids, and he rented a comfortable apartment in a high-rise building. Kim had a hard time adjusting to life in Peru, and describes it as "the nastiest place I have ever been. It was a big culture shock." She hated the poverty, the beggars, and the fact that she didn't know anyone. She missed her friends back in Fayetteville and her large extended family in Savannah. Because she couldn't speak Spanish, she was practically confined to the apartment when Charlie was away, which was most of the time. "I cried just about every day because it was so horrible to me," Kim says. The marriage was foundering and she just didn't have the patience or energy to regard Peru as an adventure. She claims, moreover, that she never agreed to go to Peru on a permanent basis, but rather that Charlie had promised her he would eventually get a job back in the States so that she could finish college and obtain her elementary education teaching accreditation.

Kim returned to the States in November 1989, and rented a place near her folks' home in Savannah, so she could enroll again at Savannah State College. The CTU contract Charlie was working on ended shortly after she left; although he found other work training the security detail of a wealthy gold mine owner, it didn't pay as well and it was a struggle each month to send Kim and the kids $2,000. Hoping to get a fat new contract in Peru, he put off a visit back home until the middle of February 1990.

Kim never suspected that there might be another woman. According to Kim, "Charlie wasn't the type of person that would ever do something like that. I always thought of him as being a Christian man, and I guess I thought that was against his morals."

Those who worked with Charlie, however, knew of his philandering because he was very open about it. Judy first learned that Charlie had a mistress when she arrived with Don in Rio de Janeiro in the summer of 1990 to complete a training contract. Don had offered Charlie a job on the contract and directed him to fly, along with two other CTU contract employees, to Brazil. Their flights, it turned out, arrived within minutes of each other. Gus, one of the other CTU contract men, pulled Judy aside and tipped her off to the fact that Charlie had brought his Peruvian mistress, Iliana, along on the trip.

A few minutes later, Charlie approached Judy and told her, "Look, I know how you feel about these things, but I've brought my girlfriend with me. I guess I've been living in Latin America too long and have adopted some of their ways of thinking and living."

Although Judy questioned Charlie's professionalism for traveling with his mistress, she tried to leave her personal feelings about marital fidelity out of the discussion. "Hey," she responded, "you do your job, I can't complain."

Nevertheless, Judy was very upset. "I don't believe in adultery," she explains. "I believe if a man and a woman stand before God and make a vow of love and honor and devotion, that's the way it should be. But that's my personal feeling, and I don't put other people down who don't agree. The fact is, I live and work in a man's world, and I understand that there's some things I have to accept to get along."

But it made her "blood boil" when Charlie and Iliana remained in Rio after the course was completed to "enjoy the beach and relax. We were all fully aware that Kim had no idea of Charlie's infidelity and was struggling financially at home while he was enjoying the beach."

Charlie's bad judgment in bringing Iliana to Brazil was one of the factors that soured his relationship with CTU. The Brazilian client was critical of Iliana's presence, and Charlie had the chutzpah to try to get CTU to pay for Iliana's plane ticket and expenses. The last time Charlie worked for CTU was in July 1990. After that, he went out on his own.

When Charlie finally showed up in Savannah, the exuberant homecoming reunions that had once characterized their marriage were a thing of the past. They argued from the moment he walked in the door, and Kim gave him an ultimatum: Either come home permanently or I'm going to get a divorce. "I was tired of living the way we were living," she says. "He had told me, in the beginning, 'Give me one year. Just give me a year to get things going, to make contacts, get some experience, and then I can come back.' Well, it was going on two years, and I was tired of living alone. I was tired of raising the kids all by myself."

Charlie, for his part, blamed Kim for interrupting his work in Peru and for his loss of a lucrative contract, although in reality he had lost it for other reasons. Nevertheless, he agreed to remain in Savannah to see if they could work things out. He applied for a number of jobs, as a pizza deliveryman and as a security guard, but only got one offer as a guard, which he turned down. Then he received a call from a friend who offered him a job in Ecuador. Despite Kim's protests, Charlie accepted the position, saying, "We don't have any money, so we don't have any choice." In early September, he left for Guayaquil, a port city of approximately 1.3 million people in western Ecuador. Before he left, he promised Kim that he would return home not less than every two months.

But when two months rolled around, he begged off, telling Kim that "we're just really getting started here and I can't leave right now." One excuse followed another, and it wasn't until Christmas that he reappeared. By this time, Kim had had enough. The day after Charlie arrived, she sat him down and explained that "there are certain things that I've got to have. I don't have a husband every day, and I don't have his love every day, and I need it." He was noncommittal, and blamed her for nagging him every time he came home and for not sharing his life in Latin America, where he could make a decent living doing the things he was trained to do. Their love life was cold and perfunctory during his visit; as Kim puts it, they had sex but they didn't make love. What Kim didn't know was that Iliana had moved with Charlie to Guayaquil.

Before Charlie left for Ecuador after Christmas, Kim demanded that he call frequently, write at least once a week, and come home every two months. He responded that she was being unreasonable, and challenged her, if she really loved him, to follow him to Ecuador. He told her that "the wife was the one that was supposed to be submissive to the husband. That the husband was the head of the household and the boss." She refused. The kids were enrolled in school, Kim told him, and she was in the middle of the quarter at Savannah State, and had only one more quarter left before she received her degree. Then she had second thoughts: was it really worth the collapse of their marriage? Perhaps she should move to Ecuador? But as she began to weaken, he suddenly flipflopped and talked her out of it, saying that "things aren't real good there right now."

By the time they said goodbye, it was clear to Kim that the marriage was in serious trouble and that they were just marking time. In the weeks that followed, every phone conversation seemed to deteriorate into an argument. In March 1991, she called him about the taxes. There was the usual friction and tension, and suddenly the words just rolled out of her mouth: "There's somebody else, isn't there?"

Her directness took Charlie off guard: "T-there's somebody who is supportive. Who believes in me."

"Does she support you in your bed?"

There was silence on the other end of the line for what seemed like the longest time. "What am I supposed to say to that?" he finally asked.

"Well," responded Kim, "I'd like for you to say no, but I think honesty would do a lotta good here."

Another pause. "Yes," Charlie answered.

"The only way we can fix this is for you to come back to the United States and get a job here . . . where you're not gone as much from home."

"No, I can't do that. I plan on settling down here or in Colombia eventually. It's where I want to stay for the rest of my life."

"I'm sorry. Is this girl worth your marriage and your children?"

"No."

"Well, Charlie, I'm gonna file for a divorce as soon as I get through school. I can't handle a divorce right now, what with the kids and my student teaching."

"That's fine," Charlie told her without emotion. "Do whatever you have to do. I'll keep on sending money, like before, but I'd like the children to come see me this summer."

"No, you come here and see them. It'd be better that way." Kim didn't know why, but something told her if she ever permitted the children to leave the States, they might never return.

## "I'VE TAKEN THE CHILDREN"

A week later, Charlie called Kim, and by contrast to the strained tone of their previous conversation, he was "all baby this, and honey that, and I want to come home and talk this thing over. I think we can work this out."

Kim was totally confused; it was the last thing she had expected. "I can't handle this right now," she told him. "Leave me alone for a little while. Let me get my thoughts together. You just tore my whole world apart and I don't think I can deal with this."

"Well," responded Charlie, "I think I'll come home anyway."

"No," she pleaded with him. "Please don't do that to me. The kids don't know what's going on, and frankly I don't either. Leave us alone just for a little while and then you come home and we'll talk to the kids together."

"Look, I'll be home next week," he said, and then hung up.

Something was wrong, she told herself. Charlie was being too nice, too reasonable, too accommodating. What was his game?

More than a week passed with no sign of Charlie. Kim was relieved. But a few days later he appeared unexpectedly, late in the afternoon, on their doorstep. Normally he called her from the airport to pick him up, but this time he informed her that he had taken a taxi so as not to bother her.

They neither kissed nor embraced. He simply walked in and threw his gear down on the floor. Kim had been ironing when he arrived, but needed some time to pull herself together for what she knew would surely be an unpleasant confrontation over their marital status. She did not want to face him without time to organize her thoughts and to rehearse the little speech she was preparing to deliver. He had not sent her the monthly payment for maintaining the household on time, and instead gave her some cash when he arrived. As a result, "I had been living the first two weeks [of the month] with no money. So I went and did my errands, grocery shopping, and all that, and he said he'd look after the kids." After she finished shopping, she went over to her parents' house "to be by myself for a little while."

When she returned home, the children were ready for bed. Amy wanted to sleep with her as she had done when she was younger, but Kim felt the child should get used to sleeping by herself, and said no. Later, her refusal to let Amy sleep with her that night was to be one of her greatest regrets. Jeremy slept with his dad on the couch.

The following day was Friday, April 5, but Jeremy didn't have to attend school because of Easter break. Charlie and the kids were up early. He bathed and dressed them, then made breakfast. Afterwards, he told Kim they were going to the movies and would then stop by their storage locker on the other side of town. Jeremy was dying to see *Teenage Mutant Ninja Turtles*, so Kim thought, "Well, that's fine. Have a good time." He sent the children into her room to tell her goodbye, but when he came to do the same, she slammed the door in his face.

After they left, she came out of the bedroom and began tidying up the house. Then it hit her: "His stuff had been in the middle of the living room and I was thinking it looked so good without that junk there." But if his gear was gone, where was it? She looked around the house but couldn't locate it. Instinctively, she went to her jewelry box where she kept their passports and discovered that the passports were gone.

A sense of dread began to set in. She phoned her mother.

"Momma, I know that I'm panicking," she said, trying hard not to cry, "and I know this is crazy, but I think Charlie's taken my children."

"Taken?"

"Kidnapped!"

"No, he wouldn't do that to you."

"I know, Momma, but something's wrong. He's taken the passports."

Since Charlie was using the family car, her father came over and picked her up. She drove her parents' car over to the storage locker and was informed that she had missed Charlie and the kids by just ten minutes. So she went to the movie theater where *Teenage Mutant Ninja Turtles* was playing and tried, unsuccessfully, to locate her car in the parking lot. Although it was a long shot, she also went to the other theaters in town just in case they had decided, at the last minute, to see a different movie. But still no luck.

Denial started to set in. The longer she drove around, the more she wanted everything to be all right, to be normal, so she convinced herself that all would be fine if she just didn't panic and went about her usual routine: when she finished up, she would return home, and Charlie and the kids would be there, waiting for her. She had a previously scheduled hair appointment and decided to show up for it. Afterwards she returned home, still hoping against hope that she was the victim of an overactive imagination.

But as she pulled up, her car wasn't in front of the house or in the driveway. The front door was locked and there were no sounds from inside. As she entered, it was clear that the house was exactly as she had left it that morning. She ran over to see if there was a message on the answering machine, punching the "playback" button.

It was Charlie's voice: "I'm sorry to have to do this, but I've taken the children, and we're going to Ecuador. We have a three o'clock flight. I'll call you when we get there, but it will take a week."

Kim was stunned. Hearing the words from Charlie's mouth was like a blow to the solar plexus; suddenly she couldn't breathe and she slumped to the floor, trying to catch her breath, tears streaming down her cheeks. "I couldn't believe he had done it to me," she reflects sadly. "I thought he loved me a little bit. I mean, we'd been married close to eight years then."

But she quickly shook off her anguish. Slowly, shakily, she stood up and stumbled toward the phone. She called the police, she called her parents, she called her lawyer, she called "everybody I could think of. All they could say was, 'He's their father. He has the right. We're terribly sorry, but there's nothing we can do.'"

In the weeks that followed, Kim, hearing nothing from Charlie, alternated between periods of despair and anger. She continued to place phone calls, trying to find anyone, anywhere, who might help her. While the State Department and her congressman offered her little encouragement, she finally found a sympathetic ally in the Georgia office of Senator Sam Nunn. The staffer, a young woman named Jennifer, drove down from Atlanta to Savannah to meet with Kim and hear her story in person. Outraged by the injustice done to Kim, Jennifer pledged to do anything she could to assist her, and a day later called back to confirm that the senator's office was working on the case. "We don't know what we can do yet," Jennifer told her, "but we want to do something."

Kim also talked to the security firm Charlie was working for, and executives of the company expressed their sympathy and deep concern about Charlie's actions. There was little, however, they could do. As one executive told her, "We're sorry this has happened, and we'll try to assist in any way we can; but we can't help you get your children back. We can fire him, but then you may lose contact with him."

"No, don't fire him," Kim concluded, conceding that it was better to know where he was and what he was doing.

Employees of the company checked up regularly on Charlie and the children in Ecuador and reported back to her, which was a source of great comfort. The worst thing, she observes, would have been not to know anything.

## "I'M GOING TO GET YOUR CHILDREN BACK FOR YOU"

About a month after Charlie took Jeremy and Amy, Kim returned home one evening and found a message on her answering machine. "This is Tommy from Fayetteville," said the voice. "Call me."

At first, she couldn't figure out who Tommy was. She didn't know a Tommy in Fayetteville. The voice was familiar, but it took her several minutes to realize that it belonged to Tommy Carter, an ex-Delta Force operator and friend of her husband's whom she had known in Lima. At 5 feet 11 and 175 pounds, with long hair and a scraggly beard, and "more guts than you could hang on a fence," Tommy often intimidated people; but underneath the rough facade, says Judy, "is a real caring individual." Tommy had gone to work for CTU on June 25, 1988, one day after leaving Delta in the same scandal that prompted Don to resign. He had spent sixteen years and seven months in the military, the last six years in Delta.

Tommy and Charlie had worked on the same CTU contract in Peru. Kim had become friends with the ex-Delta man during one of Charlie's frequent "absences" from Lima. In reality, says Tommy, he wasn't out of town at all but was "shacked up with his mistress five or six blocks away."

Peru at the time had been in the throes of a presidential election, which was accompanied by civil disturbances and violence. Troops were deployed throughout the city and Kim didn't know what was happening. "I was terrified," she recalls, "and didn't want to be alone." On top of everything else, Amy became very sick. Tommy came over and sat up with Kim while she nursed Amy, and he bought medicine and ran errands for her. After Amy was better, Tommy continued to drop by once Kim had put the children to bed, and they would sit and talk or watch television. On two occasions, Tommy took care of one child so that Kim could take the other one to the doctor or to school. Tommy seemed to enjoy the kids, says Kim, and even took them on walks and to buy ice cream. Tommy knew that Charlie was two-timing Kim, but he didn't say anything; he just tried to be a friend to her.

Despite her friendship with Tommy during the time they

were in Lima, he was one of the few people Kim had not turned to for help after April 5. She regarded Tommy as Charlie's friend, and did not realize that Tommy had little respect or affection for her husband. Indeed, Tommy regarded him as "a lazy bastard," adding that "most of the folks I ran with in Peru hated him."

Only with a certain amount of trepidation did Kim even return Tommy's call. After exchanging a few pleasantries, he told her that Charlie had called him from Ecuador. According to Tommy, he had heard the sound of children's voices in the background and had said to Charlie, "Hey, you've got your family down there with you. That's great."

"Yeah," responded Charlie.

"How'd you get Kim to let you take the kids down there?"

"She . . . didn't exactly know."

"What? You kidnapped your kids?" Tommy was incredulous. He regarded Charlie as a "low life," but that was even more low down than he could have imagined. While he was shocked by what Charlie had done, he didn't let on.

"Do you have Iliana there?" Tommy asked casually.

"Yeah."

Tommy told Kim that "all he could think of was that I can't let him know how angry I am that he did this, because I've got to help Kim." She was a fine mother, Tommy said to Kim, and deserved to have her kids back. Then he made a pledge that touched her deeply.

"I'm going to get your children back for you," he vowed.

"Tommy," she responded gratefully, "I have no money. I don't have a job. I can't pay you."

"Look, we'll raise it. Somehow, we're gonna get those children back. If I have to do it myself, I'm gonna get those children back."

Tommy indicated that he would stay in touch with Charlie because it could prove helpful in the future, and that Kim should view him as a friend who was on her side and wanted to help her. After hanging up, Kim was heartened but not fully convinced of Tommy's sincerity. On the one hand, she wanted to believe Tommy; but on the other hand, she regarded his vow to her as more rhetoric than a genuine commitment to action.

She spoke regularly to Tommy by phone in the weeks that

followed, often calling him at one or two in the morning. The news, however, was not particularly encouraging. Tommy explained that he had gone to see his boss, Don Feeney, to tell him what Charlie had done. Kim had met Don and Judy a few times, but didn't really know them, and had heard only vague details about CTU's various rescues of women and children involved in custody and marital disputes. As far as she knew, CTU was simply a security firm that performed fairly traditional services like executive protection and guarding high-risk facilities. Tommy indicated that Don sympathized with her but had cautioned him against any effort to rescue her children. "You're not going to do it by yourself," he told Tommy. "It's too dangerous." Don also was concerned by the fact that Charlie was a professional, like themselves, and wouldn't take kindly to any effort to return his kids to their mother. He was a trained killer and knew where they lived. If they intervened on Kim's behalf, they were putting themselves and their own families at risk.

There was another reason Don was hesitant to get involved: he wasn't certain of Tommy's real agenda. "Charlie had been one of the reasons Tommy Carter had been divorced," explains Don. "Because Charlie had gotten drunk one time and spouted off in front of Tommy Carter's wife about all the girls in Lima and all that shit. And Tommy's wife took it real serious, even though Tommy wasn't screwing around." Don wanted to make certain that Tommy's only motive was a genuine desire to help Kim; he didn't want to be part of an effort to retrieve the kids as a way of getting even with Charlie for his loose talk.

Tommy, meanwhile, went to work on Judy.

"We've got to do something," he'd say.

"Tommy, we can't get involved in this one," Judy would respond.

"But it's just not right," he'd shoot back. "In fact, it's so totally wrong, it's pathetic. He's got some whore raising his kids."

Initially, Judy was adamant about not getting involved. They were just too busy, she told him. Besides, whatever his faults, Charlie had worked for them and they owed him some loyalty. But Tommy kept up his lobbying effort, and Judy slowly began to relent. Finally, Judy received a call from Tommy's ex-wife, who was also a friend of Kim's.

"Judy, somebody needs to help Kim," Patty Carter urged. "She doesn't have anybody else to turn to. Nobody can help her but you guys."

Judy was trying to explain, for the hundredth time, all of the reasons they couldn't get involved, when Patty interrupted her: "Would you just please talk to her?"

Tired of going round and round on the subject, Judy reluctantly gave in. "Okay," she agreed, "have Kim call me."

The next day Kim called and described her ordeal to Judy, whose hard veneer began to crack. "All I had to do was listen to her agony. Here was a woman who was devastated. She was lost. Her children had been ripped away from her and there was nothing she could do."

Judy spoke to Kim a number of times in the days that followed, and soon became an advocate for taking on the case.

"Tommy kept hounding at me, kept coming in," says Don. "Then him and Judy. 'We got to get this done for Kim,' they'd say."

But Don remained unconvinced.

### "I WOULD HAVE DONE ANYTHING . . ."

About a month later, Charlie finally called Kim and demanded that she give him legal custody of the children, threatening to cut her off permanently from contact with the kids if she didn't do so. The thought of never again seeing her children terrified Kim, and she pleaded with Charlie to give their marriage another try, saying that she still loved him and wanted to get back together with him. She told him that she was to blame for their problems, and promised that she would move to Ecuador if only he would try once more to work things out. "I would have done anything to get my children back," she says. But Charlie refused, arguing that she wasn't sincere, something Kim today admits. "He knew I wouldn't stay with him," she observes. "He knew all I wanted was to get the children."

On several occasions he put Amy and Jeremy on the phone to let her know that they were well. Amy wouldn't speak to her, says Kim, but would cry every time she heard her mother's voice. Jeremy, who was six, was reserved, almost distant on the phone. It was only later that Kim learned that Charlie was listening in on the conversation on another extension.

"Jeremy," she asked him at one point, "are you happy living there with your daddy?"

Defying his father, Jeremy said, "No."

"Do you want to come home?"

"Yes."

Up until that point, Kim had been wracked with self-doubts: perhaps she hadn't been a good wife or a good mother. Maybe the kids would be better off with their father. Was it right to traumatize them again by somehow retrieving them and bringing them back to the States? But when Jeremy told her what was in his heart, without hesitation, she vowed to get her children back.

Kim filed for divorce in Savannah and subsequently was granted, in view of the circumstances of the case, "emergency" custody of the children by the judge.

Judy, meanwhile, kept working on Don. He protested that they owed some loyalty to Charlie and shouldn't get mixed up in the personal affairs of their employees. Judy retorted that "it's not that we were stabbing Charlie in the back. Charlie wasn't loyal. First of all, he wasn't loyal to his wife, nor his children, and he certainly wasn't loyal to CTU."

At long last, Don gave in and agreed that if the opportunity presented itself, they'd help Kim get her kids back. "Play him," Don instructed Tommy.

Judy informed Kim of their decision and said they would need some expense money. Meanwhile, relying on his contacts in the region and his occasional phone conversations with Charlie, Tommy began to look for the right opportunity to carry out a rescue mission. The best time, everyone agreed, would be when Charlie was out of the country, since he was a formidable adversary and no one wanted to see anybody get hurt.

A contract to provide security for a Japanese film crew in Peru arose unexpectedly, and it coincided with a report that Charlie was going to be in Chile on business. This could be the opportunity they were looking for, since Don's and Tommy's airfares would be paid by the Japanese clients and there was nothing to prevent them from taking a short detour to Ecuador on the way back.

This threw Kim into a real dilemma. She mentioned to Jennifer, in Senator Nunn's office, that she was contemplating a rescue operation, and Jennifer—who was so personally involved by this time that she had offered Kim money out of her own pocket for legal and other expenses—was not enthusiastic and counseled Kim not to go forward with it. "It's against the law," she told Kim. "You're going to have a big gunfight and your kids might get hurt. At the very least, it will be too traumatic for them."

"But that's not the way it's going to be," retorted Kim, who explained how the CTU operators envisioned conducting the mission. But Jennifer remained unconvinced. She urged Kim to go to Ecuador and fight Charlie in the local courts. Kim rejected the advice, arguing that "I don't speak Spanish. I would go there, but I don't know how long it'll take. I'm alone and don't have anybody to turn to, but he's got his friends, he has a place to live, he has a job, and he speaks Spanish. I wouldn't have a chance."

Kim explained to Jennifer that Charlie wasn't going to fight on the level. "He's hit me way below the belt. He's gotten dirty, and I'm gonna have to get dirty, too. I've got these people who are willing to go in for me, and fight for me, and I'm gonna do it."

"All right," responded Jennifer. "We can't support you in this, you know that. But . . . if you need help, just holler."

Kim called Judy back and told her that as far as she was concerned, they should proceed with the rescue operation, and the sooner the better. As to the expense money, she said her parents—an elementary school teacher and a salaried employee of a bag-manufacturing company—had been able to come up with $5,000 in cash.

"Okay," responded Judy. "We'll worry about the rest later." She told Kim to stand by with a bag packed and her passport ready. Their window of opportunity was very narrow, she explained, and wouldn't stay open for long.


### "WHERE ARE YOU?"

"Kim?"

"Yes."

"It's Judy. It's a go. I want you to get your things and meet me tomorrow at Miami International Airport. Are you ready?"

Kim's heart was in her throat. She gulped and responded, "Yes," in a voice so strong and firm that she surprised even herself.

After all of the despair and heartache, something finally was happening. If everything went well, Judy explained, she'd have her children back within a week. Judy told Kim which flight to take and how she was to proceed directly to the baggage claim area, where they would rendezvous.

Kim did exactly as she had been directed. She flew to Miami on the afternoon of August 11, using a ticket obtained by a friend with her frequent-flyer miles. She could not remember what Judy looked like, but when she reached the baggage area, Judy walked directly up to her and reintroduced herself.

She was shocked by Kim's anorexic appearance. "She'd always been thin," says Judy, "but she had lost an extreme amount of weight since the children were taken. She looked so fragile; just a bundle of nerves and very shaky. I felt like I was going to have to hold her up."

The news from Judy wasn't good.

"I haven't heard from Don or Tommy," she told Kim. "I don't know what to do. I don't want to leave until I know that everything's okay and the kids are there."

It was nearly 4:00 P.M., and they were scheduled to depart for Guayaquil at 6:05 P.M. They located a bank of pay phones, and Judy called the office in Fayetteville to see if there was a message from Ecuador. But there hadn't been any calls. Confident that Don would contact the office at any moment, Judy said she would stay by the pay phone so that the CTU secretary could reach her the moment she heard from Don.

But Miami International was extremely busy, and a long line of people had formed, waiting for the chance to use a telephone. "So I had to stand there," says Judy, "acting like I was on the phone, with one arm up under the other holding down the receiver, for an hour." When she got tired of standing, they located the American Airlines Admiral's Club lounge and Judy called her secretary to let her know they'd moved. They waited another hour, but as it came time for their plane to leave, Judy decided that they would find a hotel and stay overnight. At this point, she wasn't particularly concerned. In their line of work, things rarely went according to plan; in fact, when everything went too smoothly, it had a tendency to unnerve everyone.

The next day, the wait began all over again. But as the afternoon wore on, Judy and Kim became more and more concerned. When the time of their flight approached, they checked out of the hotel and went back to the airport. Judy spoke at length to Dave, who was in Fayetteville; he advised her to wait. "Don said he would get in contact with you when he knew something," he told her. "I think you oughta stay there."

"Well, I guess we'll spend one more night," Judy agreed.

Kim froze as the words came out of Judy's mouth. Not another day? She was ready to leave for Guayaquil, and she didn't think she could bear to wait another day. She shook her head violently. Judy cupped her hand over the receiver and looked at her.

"No, I want to go," Kim told Judy firmly. "I don't care if Charlie's there. I don't care if the kids aren't there. They'll get there eventually. Maybe it'll take longer, but I want my children, and I can't take the waiting."

Although Judy sympathized with her, operational rules were operational rules; Don had told her to stay in Miami until she heard from him and she realized it would be foolhardy to do otherwise.

"I'm sorry," she explained to Kim. "But we've got to stay."

That night they went to another hotel and Judy insisted that, instead of snacking, they go to the restaurant for dinner. Although Kim rarely drank, Judy ordered two glasses of wine. She could tell that Kim was coming apart physically and emotionally; she needed to relax and, later, to get a good night's sleep. "I knew she couldn't go on in her state of mind," says Judy. "She was ready to collapse."

Early the following morning, Judy was jarred out of a sound sleep by the telephone.

"Where are you?" growled Don. "What's keeping you?"

"I've been waiting to hear from you."

It turned out that Don and Tommy had been delayed in reaching Guayaquil. Moreover, the phone number of their hotel, which they had left with CTU's secretary, had been transposed, so it had been impossible to link up with them. Once Don and Judy sorted things out on the phone, it was agreed that they would be on the 6:05 P.M. flight that evening, which was due to arrive in Guayaquil at 11:20 P.M.

## "WE'RE GONNA PLAY THIS ONE BY EAR"

When Don and Tommy reached Guayaquil, they had immediately set off in search of Charlie's house, which was located in a comfortable suburb in the hills above the city. They had a map, but it was not very detailed or accurate, and the streets and houses were marked and numbered in haphazard fashion. "We covered more ground that day than an F-4 Phantom," says Tommy. Finally, "we were at a stop sign and getting real frustrated when I looked up and, lo and behold, there was the street we were looking for. I think the Big Ranger in the sky had a hand in it."

Don eased the Jeep around the corner and stopped. If their calculations were correct, the house lay at the bottom of a long hill directly before them. Don cut the engine and they coasted down the hill until they spotted the house, which was a modern, two-story, white stucco design with a high wall around it. Next door, not more than a yard away, a new house was going up. It was just a skeleton of bamboo scaffolding and forms, with no walls yet. Don pulled over to the curb and Tommy jumped out, almost forgetting—in the excitement of the moment—that they were trying to avoid making any noise. He pushed the car door to close it and had to lunge after it in order to stop it from slamming.

It was growing dark. While Don waited in the Jeep, Tommy went to get a better look at what they believed was Charlie's house. He carefully climbed up the scaffolding in the house under construction next door and waited in the shadows to see if he could spot Iliana or the kids through the windows. As he peered through one of the windows into the kitchen, he was suddenly confronted by the lower half of a nude woman's torso, "at crotch level," just inches from his face. He was so startled that he lost his footing and fell backward, grasping at two bamboo poles that broke off in his hands, and landing on his back with a loud thump. "There's no chapter in the Ranger handbook that tells you what to do in situations like that," says Tommy.

The woman on the other side of the glass apparently was oblivious to the noise and simply went on doing her chores. As the floors of the two houses did not mesh exactly, he could not see the upper half of her body, so he continued to lie on his back, hoping that she would move back from the window so that he could catch a glimpse of her face. Finally, the woman did so, and Tommy confirmed that it was Iliana; what she was doing walking around the house stark naked he couldn't figure out.

Since it was getting late, Tommy made his way back down to the car and told Don that he had seen Iliana, but not the kids. They decided to return to the hotel, grab some sleep, and be back at the house early the next morning.

They returned shortly after daybreak and parked their Jeep in the middle of a construction site about two blocks away, from where they could watch Charlie's house. "Every now and then," says Don, "we'd get out and walk around and kick some dirt and throw some sand in the air, or take the maps out and look them over on the hood of the car." The construction workers on the site apparently regarded them as supervisors and left them alone. Around 7:30 A.M., they watched as the children, dressed in school uniforms, got into a sedan with an unidentified woman and drove away. They presumed the woman was taking them to school, and Don felt it was vital for them to discover its location. They jumped into the Jeep and tried to follow the sedan, but soon lost it in heavy traffic.

They returned to the construction site and continued their masquerade as construction supervisors. In mid-afternoon, they saw the car with the unidentified woman return with Amy and Jeremy. It was unlikely that the children would leave the house again, so Don and Tommy went back to the hotel to await Judy and Kim's arrival. Sometime after ten, they drove to the airport, and it was nearly 1:00 A.M. when they finally reached the hotel with the women. Everyone was exhausted, so they turned in immediately. Charlie was due back in two or three days, so no one had to be reminded that they would have to act with dispatch if they were going to rescue the kids.

They got up at dawn, made their way out to the parking lot, and climbed into the Jeep; Don drove, Tommy rode shotgun, and Judy and Kim sat in the rear. Kim, says Tommy, was so tense and excited that "she was hovering at the ten-foot level." They drove up into the hills and cruised slowly by Charlie's house. There was no evidence of any activity inside.

Don parked a short distance past the house and they waited for the children to appear. There was a residential parking lot across the street, patrolled by a large guard with a sawed-off stainless-steel 20-gauge shotgun. He kept eyeing them with suspicion. If he approached the car, Don was going to tell him that they "were waiting for somebody to come show us a house that was for rent."

Everyone looked at Don as if to say, "Now what?" He laid out the game plan—or more precisely, the fact that there wasn't a game plan. "Okay, here's what we're gonna do," he told them. "We're gonna play this one by ear. We're gonna make it up as we go. We're gonna follow the kids today and find out where they go to school. Then we'll decide what to do."

Since no one had a counterproposal, everyone nodded and settled in for what could prove to be a long wait. As the minutes ticked by, Kim became increasingly tense and worried. "I was terrified that one of the kids was sick and wasn't going to school," she relates, "or that she [Iliana] was just keeping them home that day."

Seven-thirty came and went without any sign of Amy and Jeremy. The guard across the street was growing more suspicious by the minute, but still hadn't made any effort to cross the street and check them out. As eight o'clock approached, most of the other kids on the street had already left for school. Finally, a small sedan pulled up in front of the gate leading to the house and Iliana appeared with the two children in their school uniforms.

"Her hair is shorter than yours," Tommy told Kim. He was observing the scene through a pair of binoculars. Apparently, Charlie had off Amy's long hair and Tommy could barely recognize her.

As Kim strained for a glimpse of her children, Don ordered her to "get down so they don't spot you."

Iliana opened the rear door of the sedan, Amy and Jeremy climbed into the back seat, and the car pulled away, leaving Iliana standing by the curb.

Don flicked on the ignition and engaged the gears in the Jeep, and they were off in pursuit. By contrast to the day before when they had hung back, Don closed up on the sedan aggressively, until they were right on its tail. He wasn't going to take a chance on losing it again.

"I don't know what we're gonna do right now," Don said,

cocking his head back toward Kim, who was huddled on the floor-boards, "but whatever I tell you to do, just do it." Then he turned to Tommy: "Whaddya think, Tommy?"

"I don't know."

"Well, I'm gonna follow her to school, and as soon as the kids get out, maybe we'll just grab 'em and go," he said, thinking out loud.

"Sounds good to me," Tommy answered.

It was apparent that the woman behind the wheel of the sedan was totally unaware that she was being followed. Don scanned the street: there was little activity of any kind. They might never get a better chance, he concluded, to grab the kids.

"Look, if I can find an isolated spot, forget about the school: we're going for it," he announced. "We'll just ad-lib it."

"Does that mean we're gonna do it?" said Tommy, his eyes lighting up with the excitement of the chase.

"You got it!"

Tommy opened his door just a crack, poised to jump out when the Jeep rolled to a stop.

The sedan turned onto a narrow two-lane street. There was no other traffic in either direction. "This is it, guys," Don said, gunning the engine of the Jeep and whipping it out into the other lane. They passed the sedan on the left and pulled around in front of it, then Don jammed on the brakes, blocking the street.

The sedan screeched to a halt behind them, and Tommy bounded out of the Jeep, followed closely by Don. Another car appeared behind the sedan and Don waved it on.

"Do you speak English?" inquired Don. As the young woman behind the wheel rolled down her window so she could hear what he was saying, Tommy tried to open the doors on the other side of the car, but they were locked.

"Do you speak English?" Don demanded a second time.

"Y-yes, I speak . . . a little," she responded, perhaps thinking he needed directions.

In the meantime, Judy was pushing Kim out of the Jeep, telling her to "Go, go, go!" Kim stumbled back to the sedan and began screaming, "Amy! Jeremy!"

Kim pulled at the doors and, like Tommy, found out that they were locked. The children were frozen in their seats, as though in shock from the disturbance outside.

"Jeremy!" cried Kim, pounding on the window. "Open the door! Please, open the door. It's your mother!"

He just stared at Kim, as though her identity didn't register in his mind.

"Please open the door!" she continued to plead.

The woman in the car was becoming hysterical, screaming at Don in Spanish. Don, however, tried to reason with her, never raising his voice. "Wait a minute," he pleaded. "Wait a minute. I know you speak English. I need to talk to you."

She began to calm down. Don told her that "I'm a friend of Charlie's," and as he did so, he reached inside and turned the car's ignition off. Then he pulled the keys out and dropped them on the floor.

Stunned by his actions, the woman was paralyzed by indecision and fear, and didn't notice as Don reached around behind her and unlocked the rear door.

Tommy quickly ran around the car, lifted Jeremy out of the car, and passed him to Kim, who clutched her son to her breast and then looked around for Amy. Amy, it turned out, was still sitting in the back seat, looking very alone and confused. At that moment she began to cry. Kim handed Jeremy back to Tommy, and, jumping over the car seat, grabbed Amy, and pulled her out of the car.

"Please don't be scared," she told Amy. "It's your mommy."

"Are you taking us home to America?" asked Jeremy.

Kim squatted down on her haunches and put her arm around Jeremy. "Yes," she told him. "We're going home."

There was no time for hugs and kisses, so Judy immediately began ushering Kim and the children back toward the Jeep.

"This is the mother of these kids," Don explained to the baffled woman in the car. "And we're taking these babies home. You tell the father we have a court order from the United States giving custody to the mother. And if he wants to fight it, he can come back to the States and fight it."

The woman broke into tears and whimpered, "No, no, no," and then leaned on the car horn, which blared out raucously. Don grabbed her hands and tore them off the wheel.

"Look," he said firmly. "There's not going to be anything happening here. I haven't hurt you. Just go home and tell him what we said."

Don turned and sprinted back to the Jeep, jumped behind the wheel, and jammed his foot against the accelerator. As they took off down the street, Judy began to sing to the Hefner children, trying to take their minds off what was happening, as she had done for Brittney in Bangladesh.

Don hadn't gone more than a block when he glanced in his rear-view mirror and spotted two motorcycle riders pursuing them.

"Trouble," he barked.

Tommy swung around and quickly spotted the problem. "I can clothesline 'em," he offered.

"Nah, let's see if we can't shake 'em first."

Don floored the accelerator, but the motorcyclists hung with them. Okay, he told himself, if Method A doesn't work, let's try Method B.

"Get ready, Tommy."

He hit the brakes, and the Jeep skidded to a stop. Don and Tommy jumped out as the motorcyclists bore down on them. One of the riders pulled up quickly, turned around, and "hauled ass in the other direction." The other, however, wasn't intimidated. He stopped a short distance away and just stared at them, without coming any closer. Don pointed his finger at him and warned him to back off, then he and Tommy returned to the Jeep and continued on their way.

The motorcyclist was still behind them, so Don increased his speed and began weaving in and out of traffic. Finally, they lost their pursuer and headed for the hotel, which was all the way on the other side of the city.

### "I HAVE MY CHILDREN"

When they arrived at the hotel, Don parked the Jeep and the rescue team reconvened in one of the rooms.

"We've got two choices," explained Don. "We go to the U.S. Consulate and try to get passports and stamps to get the kids out,

or we go on to Quito and try there." They needed new passports for
Amy and Jeremy, along with entry stamps, before they could leave
the country. In Don's mind, Quito was the better choice because
Ecuador was not very efficient administratively, and if they left
immediately they could probably get to the Ecuadoran capital before anyone there received word what had happened. The one
thing he knew for certain was that they had to leave the country as
quickly as possible, otherwise Charlie could tie them up forever in
the court system or perhaps even have them arrested for kidnapping. Charlie had a number of friends and associates in the government he might be able to call upon for help.

After discussing the alternatives for a few minutes with Tommy
and Judy, Don gave the order: "Pack up! We're goin' to Quito."

Judy went to Kim's room to tell her to get her things together.
Kim was smothering the children with hugs and kisses and talking
animatedly to them. She was a little distressed to learn that they
had forgotten so much of their English. Every other sentence that
Amy or Jeremy uttered was in Spanish. Judy explained that they
were far from safe and that there was no time for a reunion; that
would have to wait.

A few minutes later they left the hotel in two vehicles: Don,
Judy, Kim, and the children rode in a taxi, followed by Tommy, in
the rented Jeep, who kept an eye on them from a safe distance.
They also wanted Tommy alone in the Jeep just in case an alarm
had gone out for the vehicle and it was stopped.

There are frequent flights between Guayaquil and Quito, and
they boarded the first one they could get on, arriving in the capital
around midday. They rented a car, then went directly to a hotel
and checked in. At Judy's urging, Kim called Jennifer in Senator
Nunn's office to explain what had happened and to take her up on
her offer to help.

The receptionist asked if Kim would "please hold," but Kim
cried out: "This is an emergency! Put me through, now!"

Perhaps sensing the desperation in her voice, the receptionist
complied and the call was transferred to Jennifer, who fortunately
was in her office.

"Hello?"

"This is Kim Hefner."

"Yes, Kim, how are you?"

"I'm in Ecuador and guess what," Kim told her, not bothering with pleasantries, "I have my children."

"You're kidding?"

"No, I'm not kidding. I wouldn't kid about this."

"I can't believe it," gushed Jennifer. "That's great. That's really great. That's—"

"Wait, wait," interrupted Kim. "I need that help you promised. I really need it. I'm in a hotel a block away from the U.S. Embassy. I need passports for the kids and entry stamps so they can leave the country."

"You've got it," responded Jennifer, her voice cracking with emotion. "Give me thirty minutes and then call me back and I'll have it set up."

Kim waited the half hour and then placed the call to Senator Nunn's office.

"It's all set up," Jennifer told her. "They're not to ask any questions. They know what's going on and they'll have the passports for you." Then she told Kim who to see at the embassy.

"I can't thank you enough," said Kim, her eyes filling with tears. "You don't know what this means to me."

Judy and Kim, with the children in tow, made a beeline for the American Embassy. When they arrived, much to their surprise they were hustled into the consular offices, ahead of two waiting rooms full of people.

They were greeted by the vice-consul, who made it clear at once that he was skeptical about what they were doing.

"Why didn't you call us this morning if you knew that you needed passports?" he snapped.

"Why?" retorted Kim. "What would you have done? Alerted my husband? Tried to stop me?" Kim's nerves were frayed almost to the breaking point, and Judy could tell that she was close to losing it.

"Lookit," Judy interjected. "Her husband kidnapped those kids in the States."

"I see," replied the official haughtily, "so you rekidnapped them."

His attitude now made Judy's blood boil. "We didn't kidnap

them," she shot back. "These are her children. She has custody papers."

Judy knew they didn't have time to waste arguing with a consular official. Besides, according to Jennifer, the embassy wasn't supposed to give them any trouble. So Judy demanded to see the consul, and the vice-consul reluctantly ushered them into her office.

The consul was an elegant middle-aged woman who was far more sympathetic than her deputy. She explained that there was a countrywide all-points bulletin out for them, since Iliana had apparently gone directly to the local authorities as well as the U.S. Consulate in Guayaquil to describe the "kidnapping" of Amy and Jeremy. She also confirmed that she had received instructions to assist them in leaving the country.

"I understand that you hired a company from North Carolina to help you recover your children?" she continued.

"No," replied Judy. "She didn't hire us. We're her friends, and we're here to support her and that's all there is to it."

The consul studied Judy for a moment and then moved on.

"Do you know where the father is at this moment?"

Kim shrugged.

"I know, Mommy. I know," volunteered Jeremy.

"Shhh, shhh. Hush," Kim whispered to him. "Do you want Daddy to come get you?"

"N-no."

"Then be quiet," Kim told him.

"He's out of the country," Judy explained. "He left the children with his whore girlfriend," she told the consul, not mincing words.

"There's nothing legal I can do to stop you," the consul explained. "But I'm telling you one thing right now: get out of this country as fast as you can. If the father returns and gets any kind of local court order, we'll have to honor it. Now, I want to do anything I can to help you, but I have to be impartial."

Judy and Kim nodded as they listened to the consul going through her "for-the-record" speech.

"I can't deny you passports for your children," she concluded, "because you have custody papers."

She left the room and returned a few minutes later with new passports for the children, using photos that Judy supplied. She explained that they would have to take them to the Ecuadoran Immigration Office to get the entry stamps, but that there shouldn't be any problem.

As they departed, the consul dropped her detached and businesslike demeanor and wished them well. "I would gladly take you to the airport myself and put you on the plane, but as I'm sure you realize, I can't do it. But the least I can do is to see you out the back door so that no one will see you leave." With that, she escorted them to a rear door. Judy and Kim expressed their gratitude, but she waved them off, adding one more time for emphasis: "My suggestion to you is get out of Ecuador. *Now!*"

The hour was getting late and they still needed the entry stamps before they could leave, so Tommy and Judy rushed the passports over to the Ecuadoran Immigration Office. They were shown into an office right out of *Casablanca*, with thick whitewashed walls, whirring fans, and potted plants, and, in Tommy's words, introduced to "a bald-headed guy dressed in a neo-Nazi uniform, sitting behind a large mahogany desk. The only thing he didn't have was a monocle." He wore the rank of major on his epaulets. The major's vixenlike girlfriend, with pouty lips and long dark hair, sat next to him, her skirt so short that her garters and the tops of her stockings were visibly protruding beneath the hemline. The major was rubbing her silky inner thigh absentmindedly as he conducted the interview with Tommy and Judy and examined the passports. Contrary to what they had been told at the U.S. Embassy, the major said they'd have to go back through the files and confirm the information he had been provided with before he could stamp the passports.

It was a shakedown; but when Tommy became adamant, the major backed down and decided that he would take their word for the fact that the children had entered the country legally. He stamped the passports and pushed them across the immense desk at Tommy and Judy, then turned his attention back to his girlfriend.

## "IS THERE A PROBLEM?"

All of the flights leaving for the United States that evening were completely booked; in fact, they were oversold. They could not get on any flight leaving the country that night in any direction. "The whole time they were down at the embassy trying to get passports, I spent going from travel agent to travel agent, airline to airline, begging for seats," recalls Don. "Everything was booked solid, six, seven days in advance, since it was vacation time." Finally, he was able to purchase tickets on an Air France flight to Bogotá, Colombia, where they could connect to another flight to Barranquilla and then on to Miami. They returned to the hotel for the night, and the next morning left for Bogotá without incident.

Given Colombia's violent reputation, many people might have wanted to go anywhere but there, but it was Don's first choice if the United States was out of the question. "Now, most people don't think of going to Bogotá as a place of safety," explains Don. "But, being as I know Bogotá like the back of my hand, and have a lot of friends there if I need help, it was the first place I wanted to go."

Everyone was relieved when the plane landed in the Colombian capital. They later learned that they were nearly apprehended in Quito. "If we'd been delayed in Ecuador one more day, we'd all be in prison today," concludes Tommy. Charlie returned to Ecuador as soon as he learned what had happened and apparently filed criminal warrants against them, and an all-points bulletin went out to detain them if they tried to board a plane or any other conveyance. "It's one time where bureaucratic red tape and inefficiency worked in our favor," continues Tommy. "It took them too long to get their shit together."

Once in Bogotá, Judy and Kim were devastated to learn that their flight to Barranquilla and Miami had been canceled. They would have to wait yet another day.

"When are we going home?" Jeremy kept asking his mother. "Please take me home."

"Soon, honey. Soon," Kim reassured him.

They passed the night in Bogotá, and the following morning Judy, Kim, and the children left for Barranquilla, where they were to transfer to an American Airlines flight to Miami. Don and Tommy remained behind because they had to get back to Peru.

In Barranquilla, Judy checked in for the American Airlines flight, and then was directed to another line where she, Kim, and the children had to pass through a rigorous security screening. But when Judy asked for their passports back before going through the security check, the counter agent told her not to worry, that they would be returned shortly. Judy found this strange, since no one else's passports had been retained by the counter agent.

By contrast to most of the other passengers, their luggage was searched and X-rayed with extraordinary care. So thorough was the search that every one of Judy's Tampaxes was removed from the box and scrutinized to see if they had been tampered with. Something was up, but Judy couldn't figure out if local officials thought they were drug smugglers or if there was some kind of warrant or alert out for them in connection with the recovery of the children.

They were flying first class in order to expedite their transfers and get extra consideration if they needed it, so Judy demanded to see the airport manager.

"Is there a problem?" she insisted.

"Oh, no," he responded. "No problem."

"Then why weren't our passports returned? No one else's were kept."

The airport manager apologized and lied, saying that it was "just routine. There's nothing to worry about."

Contrary to what she was hearing, it was quite apparent to Judy that there was plenty to worry about. Kim had watched the encounter with growing anxiety and was nearly in tears when Judy walked over to try and comfort her.

"They're gonna do something to us, aren't they?" she asked with a trembling voice. "They're gonna do something to us."

Judy put up a brave front, despite her own growing anxiety: "Hey, we're out of Ecuador, aren't we? We're in Colombia. There's nothing to worry about. It's just some kind of mix-up."

As the time of departure neared, Judy, Kim, and the children still hadn't cleared passport control. Judy confronted the airport manager and the Immigration authorities again and insisted that they be permitted to board the plane.

When they demurred, she stood her ground.

"What's the problem?" Judy again demanded.

"Well," said one of the officials, studying Amy's photo, "this passport photo doesn't look right."

"Listen, if you have a problem with the passports, call the American Embassy in Quito. Ask them. I'll give you the name of someone to talk to."

Finally, at the urging of some local airline security officials who knew the Feeneys, one of the Immigration officers called the consular office in Quito and was told that "Kim Hefner is a mother traveling with her children and she is the legal custodian of those children."

That took the Colombian Immigration officials off the hook. At last all the passports were returned with the appropriate stamps, and Judy, Kim, and the children were allowed to proceed to the boarding area. But when they reached the gate, they were approached by two other security agents. One of them, a woman, took their passports again and began to scrutinize them. She kept staring at Amy and then at her passport photo, then at Amy again. Because her hair had been cut off, Amy bore little resemblance to the old photo Kim had brought from the States to use in her passport.

"All she did was have her hair cut," Judy explained.

"Look at her face," pleaded Kim. "It's the same child."

"No, it's not the same child," responded the woman.

Thinking quickly, Kim told the woman, "She got real, real dirty and we thought there was the possibility she had head lice, so we cut her hair."

But the woman continued to examine the passport photo.

"Is there a problem?" Judy wanted to know for the umpteenth time.

The woman finally shook her head, tossed the passports back into Judy's lap, and walked away.

To their great relief, they were allowed to board the aircraft, which took off a short time later for Miami. They had made it!

What they didn't know was just how close they came to being detained. An American Airlines security official later told them that even as their flight lifted off, the Colombian police were on their way to the airport to arrest them. The reason they had been held up during the check-in process and searched so thoroughly was that the Ecuadoran all-points bulletin had gone out to neighboring countries, and they had been recognized. If it hadn't been for their friends working in security at the airport, it is doubtful that Judy, Kim, and the children would have been allowed to leave before the police arrived.

Once they were airborne, Jeremy looked over at his mother and asked, "Mom, when we get to America, will I have to speak Spanish anymore?"

"No, honey." Kim smiled. "You won't have to speak Spanish anymore. You'll speak English just like you used to."

"That's good. I want to speak English."

## UPDATE

In the months since Kim returned from Ecuador, she has received a final divorce from Charlie and permanent custody of the children. He chose not to appear in court to contest the divorce or to request visitation rights. Kim regrets that he was not granted visitation rights. "I feel like I've done something wrong in cutting the children off from their father, but I don't have a choice," she says. "It's either that or take the chance of losing my children again."

Kim lives in permanent fear that Charlie will try again to kidnap the children and flee to some country south of the border. She even thinks that he might attempt to harm her. Nevertheless, she is more saddened than bitter about his efforts to rob her of her children. "I really believe what he did he did out of a strange kind of love," Kim reflects. "As far as I'm concerned, though, the man I married and the man I loved is dead. He doesn't exist anymore. The man I loved would never have done these things to me or to the kids."

Presently in hiding, Kim and her children have taken extensive security precautions. The sheriff's and police department in the city where she resides have been made aware of all of the details of the case, and are providing her with some protection, including increased patrols in her area and circulating Charlie's photo to all local law enforcement agencies.

Shortly after arriving back in the United States with her children, Kim received an unsigned letter, which was sent to her at her parents' address:

> You're probably the most supremely selfish person I have ever met. Did you actually think that you could manipulate me still with my kids? I'll never rest until I get them back, I just hope that I don't have to take them because I won't leave you in very good conditions [sic]. I know your fears and weaknesses but you don't know me. I will destroy you and everything you hold dear. Think of me every time you leave the kids anywhere, even for a few minutes. Wonder if it's me every time you hear a sound in the night. Every time someone looks at you, wonder if they work for me. I'll never leave you alone until I have them back. I won't take it to court because they have no right over me and my family. I'll hurt you like you've never dreamed of hurting. . . .

A second threatening letter, also unsigned, was addressed to Kim's mother.

Based on the threats contained in the letters, Kim pressed charges and a warrant was issued for Charlie's arrest.

Kim's plight struck a sympathetic chord among many of the rough-spoken, hard-living former special operators now plying their trade in Latin America, who knew both Kim and Charlie. Surprisingly, most came down on Kim's side. One ex-operator working in Peru, who knows of the threats against her, told Tommy Carter that he was on the lookout for Charlie, in the event he showed up again in Peru. Then he added, "We'll send you a photo of Charlie. You put the place on the picture where you want him shot." Needless to say, no one is contemplating such action, but the man's offer is clear evidence of the depth of emotion the case has generated.

Asked to reflect on her role in the rescue of her children, Kim says, "Mothers will do so much for their children. I'd do anything for my children." She still is a little amazed by the events of the past two years, and the rescue she and the CTU commandos were able to pull off in Ecuador. "I thought this was movie stuff . . . that doesn't happen in real life," she observes. "Stuff that doesn't happen to me. I thought I was the girl next door that nothing ever happens to."

Nevertheless, Kim plays down her own part in the drama: "I can't believe I got through it. My friends said, you must have had so much strength to do it. No, I had so much desperation."

# Afterword

WE LIVE in an age in the thrall of celebrity rather than real heroes. This is a great tragedy. Too often actors are extolled over people who do extraordinary things in real life, who take real risks and accomplish remarkable—and often selfless—deeds, and yet manage at the same time to raise decent families and live honest lives. One does not need to examine the tabloid press to be persuaded of this fact. Any magazine rack, the evening's television offerings or, for that matter, even the best-seller list will confirm the public fixation with those who only pretend to do, as opposed to those who really do.

Neither the creation of highly paid publicists nor the product of a screenwriter's hyperbole, the men and women of CTU are real, honest-to-goodness contemporary heroes, who—in the words of the poet Stephen Spender—wear "at their hearts the fire's center." Yet there is an ordinariness about them, like the people they help. They are blue-collar folks, with a dash of grit and more than a measure of good old-fashioned American can-do, and stick-it-in-your-ear guts and ingenuity. Perhaps their business cards should sport the Jolly Roger, since they also are part pirate, with that kind of roughneck irreverence and disdain of authority that is at the core of the American character.

All of their rescues have involved a "lot of low crawling over broken glass," says Don, and they're not unmindful of the risks they take. For most of CTU's existence, Don, Dave, and Judy lacked adequate life and medical insurance in case something went wrong. And when queried about the possibility that they might one day be arrested and thrown into a dark hole in some Third World country, they tend to be fatalistic. "If it happens, it happens," says Don, "and we'll deal with it then. But I guess I don't have a real fear of one of 'em [rescue missions] going wrong because I know I'm being guided on which ones to take. I know that sounds kinda over-spiritual, but it's the truth. I don't think these cases come to me because I'm Don Feeney; it's because I do what I do and I know if the Big Ranger in the sky don't want it done, it's not gonna get done."

Dave Chatellier's chief worry is that they will be labeled "terrorists." To guard against that possibility, he says, "we've never tied anyone up. We've never assaulted anyone. We've never pulled a weapon on anyone." If they develop a reputation for being terrorists, says Dave, their corporate clients—who are the backbone of their business—"just would not touch us."

According to Dave, "we don't break any laws. We don't even take the kids. We don't go into some country and snatch the kids. What we do is we set up a situation where the mother or father takes their own kids back again. It's their hands that touch the child, not ours. We create the conditions and put everything in play, and let the parents get their kids."

They worry about anti-mercenary legislation at the United Nations and possibly even efforts by the U.S. government to shut them down, if the State Department ever decides that they are too disruptive to the conduct of foreign policy.

What they don't fear is retribution from one of the fathers, believing that they would have to be "real ignorant" to try something in the United States against veterans of America's most elite special warfare units.

The CTU people have never been warned or contacted by any government agency and told to curtail their activities. The only really negative aspect of their rescue-for-hire business, says Dave, is the fact that they've never made a profit or, for that matter, even come out whole on a rescue operation. It also places some restrictions on any future travel or business plans in countries like Jordan,

Tunisia, and Bangladesh. "Yeah, but we still got a hundred 'n' sixty countries to go," says Don, smiling.

They are critical of the U.S. government, particularly the State Department, and maintain that if the government did its job, there wouldn't be any need for their services. "Talk about people who should back up to the pay window," observes Tommy Carter of the State Department. This is seconded by all of the mothers, who are extremely critical of the lack of help provided to Americans whose children have been abducted in custody disputes. "When this happens," says Keli Walker Chowdhury, "our children's rights are taken away. They cease to exist once they're out of the country."

There is some bitterness that the State Department apologized for CTU actions in Jordan and Tunisia. As Don explains, referring to the rescue of Lauren Bayan, "I can't understand why they did that. All we did was stop and talk to a bus driver. I mean, he wasn't hurt. He wasn't scratched. We pulled his keys out of his bus and threw them in the bushes. That's all we did. We didn't take the kid. The mother took the kid."

Asked to reflect on which rescue gave him the most satisfaction, Don is hard put to select one over the others: "It's a little like having kids. You don't have any one kid you favor more, you just kinda love them all the same. At certain times, however, you feel more for one than another. I sometimes think the rescue that appeals most to me is Bangladesh. I mean, the little girl recognized me as the one that helped her. Then I can turn around two days later and think about driving down the road with Laurie in the car and change my mind and say, no, that was the best one. And, then, taking those two kids out of Ecuador. You know, they're all so gratifying. It's what you do. You bring kids back—kids that might have had no chance if you hadn't rescued them. They might have suffered for the rest of their lives."

"I'm not sure what has kept us going," adds Judy. "Perhaps it was sheer determination to succeed or refusing to say 'uncle' to those who said we'd never make it. I believe in CTU. I feel good about who we are and what we have done. The fact that we've come this far and lasted this long is a success by itself. But I also believe there's still a lot to be done. A lot of children to save."

# Sources
# and
# Acknowledgments

■  I am indebted to the following people who generously agreed to sit for interviews or to discuss the issues and events contained in this book: Don Feeney, Dave Chatellier, Judy Feeney, Bill Swint, Barbara Swint, Laurie Swint-Ghidaoui, Valerie Swint Holley, Jerry Holley, J.D. Roberts, Jim Hatfield, Frank Baker, Everett Alvarez, Jr., Keli Walker Chowdhury, Terry Smith Chowdhury, Tommy Carter, Amelia Smith, and Kim Hefner. Several other sources, who wish to remain anonymous, also cooperated. I owe additional thanks to many of those above for providing me with maps, photographs, drawings, tapes, notes, receipts, diaries, and other materials used in or referred to in the book.

I am especially grateful to David Halevy for his collaboration with me on "Operation Lauren," which appeared in *The Washingtonian* (September 1988) and *Reader's Digest*. He generously gave me permission to use the research materials he had collected in connection with the article.

In addition, I have used some of Laurie Swint's quotes which appeared in an article by Antoinette Martin entitled "Mission Incredible" in the *Detroit Free Press*, May 14, 1989. I also referred to Frank Grieve's "Daring Commando-Style Raid Unites Family," in the *Charlotte Observer*, January 29, 1989, and Gary Moss's "CTU Team Succeeds in Tunisian Rescue," in the *Fayetteville*

*Observer-Times*, February 5, 1989. Upon her return from Tunisia, Laurie gave a number of local television interviews which were of assistance.

Cathy Mahone's December 28, 1990, "700 Club" interview was particularly helpful in terms of understanding the background of her case and her personal motivations, as were articles that appeared in *People*, *Star*, the *Washington Post*, and Knight-Ridder newspapers, and on the Associated Press wire.

I made use of various public, as well as internal, documents and letters from the U.S. State Department and the U.S. Congress on the subject of parental abduction and the Hague Convention.

I want to extend my deep appreciation to Susan Lightfoot and her colleagues at Private Secretary, who so meticulously assisted in the preparation of more than five hundred pages of transcribed interviews. Finally, I am deeply indebted to Bob Bender of Simon & Schuster and my literary agent, Audrey Adler Wolf, for making this book possible.